A CLIMBING GUIDE TO

COLORADO'S FOURTEENERS

Third Edition

Walter R. Borneman and Lyndon J. Lampert

PRUETT PUBLISHING COMPANY
BOULDER, COLORADO

Printed in the United States
10 9 8 7 6 5 4 3 2 1

Cover and book design by Jody Chapel, Cover to Cover Design

Photographs not otherwise credited are by Walter R. Borneman.

Library of Congress Cataloging-in-Publication Data

Borneman, Walter R., 1952-
    A climbing guide to Colorado's fourteeners / Walter R. Borneman and Lyndon J. Lampert. — 3rd ed.
        p.   cm.
    Includes bibliographical references (p.) and index.
    ISBN 0-87108-850-9 (acid-free paper)
    1. Mountaineering—Colorado—Guidebooks. 2. Mountains—Colorado—Guidebooks. 3. Colorado—Guidebooks. I. Lampert, Lyndon J., 1956-   . II. Title.
    GV199.42.C6B67   1994
    796.5'22'09788—dc20   93-47980
                                                                CIP

Warning: Mountain climbing is a high-risk activity. This guide is not a substitute for the user's judgment and personal responsibility. The route descriptions in this guide have been carefully prepared from first-hand experience. Please remember that some access routes are subject to change by private or government action. You alone are responsible for coming prepared with proper equipment, experience, and common sense.

A Climbing Guide to Colorado's Fourteeners

This time, for Rusty

Contents

Red, Rugged, and Rotten: The Elk Range

Sentinels of a Spanish Legacy: The Sangre de Cristo Range

A Land of Endless Mountains: The San Juan Range

Preface to the Third Edition

The third edition of this guide is published in cooperation with the U.S. Forest Service in an attempt to encourage the use of one or two minimum-impact trails or clearly established routes to each Fourteener.

After almost thirty years of climbing these mountains, and more than fifteen years of revising this guide, I deeply miss "the good old days." During the summer of 1972, Omar Richardson and I climbed seventeen Fourteeners—and encountered only two other people the entire summer. Then, meeting someone on a summit was a special event: We still climb with Tim Duffy, whom we met on Mount Elbert on Labor Day that summer. In the summer of 1992—on a weekday—I shared Elbert's slopes with at least fifty others.

If the good old days are so recent for me, what must it have been like in the days when Carl Blaurock, Steve and Jerry Hart, Eleanor Davis, Mel Griffiths, Bob Ormes, Virginia Nolan, and a few others had Colorado's mountains largely to themselves? Regardless of the answer, the fact remains that in the 1990s we are using these special mountains to death. Their wilderness character is rapidly disappearing.

As the time for this third edition approached, Lyn Lampert and I had serious misgivings about keeping this book in print. To be sure, we did not invent or even promote "the Fourteener craze." We have always encouraged climbers to use our natural resources in a caring and respectful manner, but deteriorating conditions on the Fourteeners make us cringe with no small measure of guilt by association.

We decided that in a guidebook to such heavily used peaks as the Fourteeners, the most environmentally responsible approach is to recommend strongly that climbers and hikers stay on established trails or routes. The days of wandering over mountainsides and descending any scree slope are over. Too many have done that for too long, and the resulting damage on Mount Yale, La Plata Peak, Uncompahgre Peak, and many others will take generations to heal.

Fortunately, we found that the U.S. Forest Service had similar concerns. In particular, Mary Beth Hennessy and the staff of the Leadville Ranger District, San Isabel National Forest, in cooperation with an American Mountain Foundation project, have taken a leadership role in mitigating the visitor impacts occurring on Sawatch Range Fourteeners. Consequently, the third edition of this guide is published in cooperation with the U.S. Forest Service in an attempt to encourage the use of one or two minimum-impact trails or clearly established routes to each Fourteener. In many cases, even these routes are heavily eroded and in need of trail construction or maintenance. The Forest Service and volunteer organizations such as the Colorado Mountain Club and Volunteers for Outdoor Colorado are hard at work stabilizing these areas. Visitors to these peaks have a responsibility to assist these efforts by following the recommended routes.

A word of caution to old and new climbers alike! Know your mountain and know the limits of your experience and physical condition. Although most Colorado Fourteeners require little more technical ability than strong legs and hardy lungs, knowledge of mountain safety is a must. Increasingly, in the rush to climb all of the Fourteeners, too many people have raced up the slopes of the Sawatch and Front ranges and then met with tragedy on the Crestones, Little Bear, El Diente, or other more difficult summits. Frequently, this has happened because they have underestimated the complexities of the climb or been poorly equipped to deal with Colorado's fickle weather.

It is impossible to overstate the importance of watching and respecting mountain weather. The only thing predictable about Colorado weather is that it is apt to change dramatically within the hour. Come prepared with adequate clothing and gear. Use extra caution on loose rock slopes and snowfields; ice axes may be necessary for some routes well into the summer. A careless step on even the easiest Fourteener or an unheeded thunderstorm can spell disaster; *above all, climb with care and common sense.*

The mountain you set out to climb—whether Crestone Peak or Mount Sherman—has been there for millions of years. Chances are that it will still be there long after you are gone. Experienced climbers have tales by the dozens of aborting climbs, sometimes within feet of the desired summit, because of weather, avalanche danger, a party member's fatigue, or any conceivable situation that threatened the safety of the climbing team. The mountain will wait for another day. Do not push yourself beyond the limits of common sense and your experience.

The route descriptions in this guide assume summer climbs from late spring until early fall unless specifically noted otherwise. Climbing earlier in the spring or later in the fall may help you avoid some of the summer hordes, and spring snowfields may offer a fun approach or descent without making an environmental impact on the tundra below. Here again, however, "experience" is the key word. Above all, respect the avalanche conditions and come prepared for any extreme in weather.

Finally, with the third edition of this book, we continue to state our personal philosophy of walking in harmony with the land and minimizing —to whatever extent is possible—our impact on the mountains and waters we visit. We encourage each of you to do the same. Such an attitude will not turn back the clock, but it may help slow the change and preserve a wilderness legacy for our children.

Wilderness Ethics

With the passage of the 1993 Colorado Wilderness Bill, thirty-three of Colorado's fifty-four Fourteeners are located within or on the boundary of wilderness areas. Preserving the wilderness experience in these special areas and throughout the national forest system is a key part of the minimum-impact ethic this guide encourages. Although each wilderness area and national forest has its own set of use regulations, the following general guidelines apply to all areas. You are strongly encouraged to know and follow the regulations in the particular area you visit.

BACKCOUNTRY TRAVEL

- Travel quietly and in small groups. Avoid disturbing others.
- Spread out impact by exploring less heavily visited areas.
- Leave your pets at home to keep from bothering wildlife and other visitors.
- Stay on maintained trails whenever possible. Do not cut switchbacks.
- Minimize horse use when trails are wet.

CAMPSITE SELECTION AND USE

- In heavily visited areas, use existing campsites to confine impact to a small area.
- In less-visited areas, choose a site well away from streams and lakes and out of sight of other users. Eliminate all traces of your camp.
- Carry out all trash. DO NOT bury it, because animals will quickly dig it up.
- Clean up with soapless hot water. If you must use soap for washing or bathing, do so at least 150 feet from any water sources, and pour the water into absorbent ground.

STOVES AND FIRES

- Use a gas stove for all cooking. Wood is scarce in the high country and an essential part of the ecosystem. Gas is quicker, cleaner, and won't leave a scar of charred and sterilized soil.
- If you absolutely must build a fire, use only dead and down wood. Use existing fire rings and keep the fire very small. Use only as much wood as will burn completely.
- Never leave fires unattended, even for a moment. When you leave, make certain that the fire is dead and cold. Clean out fire rings so they will be ready for the next visitor.

SANITATION

- Bury human waste in a small cathole about six inches deep and dug in organic soil away from heavy-use areas and at least 150 feet from any water.
- Soiled toilet paper, diapers, and sanitary napkins should be carried out.

Acknowledgments

Part of the joy of mountaineering is in the companionship of those special friends who travel the trail with you. We extend a grateful thanks to our many friends—old and new—who have shared at least one summit with us, as well as to the many people who have provided assistance and photographs for one or more of the three editions of this book: Omar, Anne, Naomi, and Nathaniel Richardson; Gary and Dolora Koontz; Craig and Debbie Koontz; Tim Duffy; Duane Vandenbusche; Ron Pierce; Dave Hunter; Dave Huntley; Bob Hooper; Adam Csoeke-Poechk; David Younger; Brian Baird; Steve Richardson; Bill Salisbury; Jody Like; Richard, Sadie, and Steve Taylor; Ken and Lois Lampert; Jasper Welch; John Chesley; Jay Fell; Don Holmes; Mel Johnson; Steve Iwanicki; Rob Iwanicki; Eleanor Gehres and the staff of the Western History Department of the Denver Public Library; Maxine Benson and the staff of the Colorado Historical Society; Jim Pruett, Jerry Keenan, and the staff of Pruett Publishing Company; John L. Jerome Hart; Stephen H. Hart; Carl Blaurock; William M. Bueler; Robert F. Rosebrough; Joseph D. Kramarsic; Dan Roberts; Phil Schmuck; Glen Gebhardt; Robert Ormes; and "Skipper."

In this third edition, we are particularly grateful to David Duffy and Mark Hesse of the American Mountain Foundation, and to Mary Beth Hennessy and the many members of the Fourteener Management Committee of the U.S. Forest Service for their leadership in seeking to minimize environmental impact on these peaks.

We continue to offer special thanks and recognition to Jim Gehres, who has climbed all of the Fourteeners at least ten times. Jim's input into the first edition of this guide and his assistance with subsequent updates have been invaluable.

As always, warm thanks go to our companion of so many miles and summits, R. Omar Richardson.

WYOMING

CRAIG ○   ○   *Never Summer Mtns.*   *Rough Range*   *Mummy Range*   ○ FT. COLLINS

STEAMBOAT SPRINGS   Rocky Mtn. ○   ESTES PARK ○   ○ GREELEY

N.P.   LOVELAND

▲LONGS PK.

○ LONGMONT

MEEKER ○   *Gore Range*   ○ BOULDER

▲   ARAPAHO PK.

MT. POWELL▲   *Front Range*   ○ **DENVER**

GLENWOOD SPRINGS ○   **MT. OF THE HOLY CROSS**   ▲ ▲MT. EVANS GRAYS PK.

▲

LEADVILLE ▲MT.

GRAND JUNCTION ○   **MT. SOPRIS**   ▲ ASPEN ○LINCOLN   *Sawatch Range*   *Mosquito Range*   *Rampart Range*

▲MT. ELBERT

CASTLE PK. ▲   ▲MT. HARVARD   PIKES PK.▲   ○ **COLORADO SPRINGS**

○ DELTA   ○ BUENA VISTA

▲MT. ANTERO

○ SALIDA

○ MONTROSE   ○ GUNNISON   ○ CAÑON CITY

Sangre De Cristo Range

WEST-CLIFF ○

○ **PUEBLO**

OURAY ○   ▲ **UNCOMPAHGRE PK.**

MT. SNEFFELS ▲○

TELLURIDE ○   **CRESTONE**▲ **PK.**

MT. WILSON ▲   ○ SILVERTON

San Juan Mtns

○ WALSENBURG

La Plata Range   **WINDOM PK.** ▲   **BLANCA PK.** ▲

○ ALAMOSA

DURANGO ○   ○ PAGOSA SPRINGS   ○ TRINIDAD

N E W   M E X I C O

▲   **PEAK**

·········   **RIDGE**

○   **TOWN**

So Bold, So Beautiful a Land

The General Geography and Geology of Colorado

Like the spiny backbone of an ancient dinosaur, the Colorado Rockies wind their jagged course along three hundred miles of the roof of the continent, from the range country of Wyoming to the Spanish haciendas of New Mexico. Few geographic formations can boast the majestic beauty and rugged splendor of these mountains, and equally few have had such a profound influence on the peoples of the surrounding regions.

The magnificent Rocky Mountains are legendary—the mere mention of "the Rockies" conjures up vivid pictures of towering peaks, verdant forests, torrential rivers, and unspoiled wilderness. Also connected with the Rockies are less dramatic images of peaceful herds of grazing elk, trembling golden aspen leaves, and the lone prospector and his burro. Undoubtedly, it is a combination of all of these factors that add up to what may be called the "mystique of the Rockies." Whatever the specific reasons, the Rockies well deserve their legendary status and undoubtedly will hold a special place in the hearts of North Americans for countless generations to come.

A good portion of the Rockies' prominence and allure is due to their geographic dimensions. From the forbidding barrenness of the Brooks Range of northern Alaska, the Rockies sweep southward for more than three thousand miles, terminating in the arid American Southwest in the vicinity of Santa Fe, New Mexico. Between these two points, the Rockies are mountains of incredible variety, but they are always impressive and frequently an imposing barrier to those desiring to cross them.

Indeed, the histories of both Canada and the United States have been significantly affected by the presence of the dominating Rockies. Besides being impressive as a very lengthy mountain chain, the Rockies have

1

equally imposing vertical dimensions. Most Rocky Mountain summits average 8,000 to 12,000 feet above sea level, and it is understandable how the early traveler, accustomed to the rolling Appalachians, would be awed by the sight of snowy peaks rising up to 10,000 feet above the high plains. To be sure, it remains an impressive sight today.

The apex of the Rocky Mountain chain, the concentration of its highest summits, lies in the state of Colorado near the southern terminus of the Rockies. More than 1,500 Colorado points rise above 12,000 feet, and 637 separate summits reach over 13,000 feet. The elite of Colorado's mountains are the fifty-four peaks that surpass 14,000 feet—the Fourteeners. Colorado holds almost eighty percent of the sixty-eight Fourteeners in the contiguous United States. California boasts thirteen, while Washington claims Mount Rainier. Truly, with such statistics considered, no state more deserves to be called "the crest of the continent" than does Colorado. Even with its many Fourteeners, however, it is an unfortunate assumption made by some that Colorado's only great peaks are its Fourteeners. In truth, many of the state's most spectacular and interesting peaks do not reach the 14,000-foot level and deserve more attention than is usually given them.

That Colorado is a state of multitudinous high peaks and vast expanses of rock and tundra is of no question, but to think of it solely as this would be a grave mistake. In reality, the Rockies cover only about the middle two-fifths of the state. To the east extends the immensity of the Great Plains, stretching for 150 miles to the Kansas border and then beyond. The importance of the plains to Colorado is often overlooked, but they have provided a historically solid agricultural base for the state as well as the best transportation routes for those seeking to travel into Colorado's mountains. The plains gradually slope upward from about 3,500 to 5,000 feet, meeting the Rockies along a line of approximately 105° west longitude, roughly from Fort Collins to Trinidad. The contrast formed by the interface of the gentle plains meeting the sharply rising Rockies is significant, for other than proximity, the mountains and plains have little in common. Geography has led to contrasting histories, cultures, and atmospheres between the two areas.

Likewise, to the west of the Colorado Rockies lies a vast land quite unlike the mountains. This area may be termed the plateau and canyon region and roughly occupies the western fifth of Colorado. Geographically, it is a part of the Colorado Plateau and is akin to the character of the great Southwest, complete with massive red cliffs towering above muddy rivers and high, cool mesas, some reaching over 11,000 feet.

Like the plains, the plateau and canyon region has developed in a unique way that is quite unlike the mountains. Here, population is sparse, the local economy revolves around ranching and agriculture, and the culture has a decided Spanish flavor. Truly, Colorado is much more than "just mountains," and realizing this can be very enriching, even to those who are primarily attracted to its peaks.

Colorado's mountains, then, are only a part of the varied geography of the state, but it will probably always be the Rockies that first come to mind when one thinks of Colorado—and what mountains they are! Range upon majestic range line the central part of the state, each shimmering in the intense mountain sunlight. Most of Colorado's ranges are aligned north to south, paralleling one another, but the San Juans bulge extensively into the southwestern part of the state, providing the major exception to this north-south trend.

West of the impressive Front Range rise the Park and Gore ranges; neither contains any Fourteeners, but they are nonetheless every bit as rugged as Colorado's higher ranges. These two ranges are separated from the Front Range by North and Middle parks—large, relatively level basins that are ringed with peaks. South Park is the largest and most striking of Colorado's parks; it separates the Front Range from the Tenmile and Mosquito ranges, which are small ranges, but they contain five Fourteeners and are rich in mining history. The valley of the upper Arkansas River divides the Mosquito Range from Colorado's highest range, the Sawatch.

The Elk Range is somewhat of a northwest spur of the Sawatch, but it is quite unlike any other Colorado range in terms of geology and the unique layered character of its peaks. The Sangre de Cristo Range is long and narrow, stretching from the vicinity of Salida well into New Mexico. Last, but by no means least, the San Juans round out the roster of Colorado's major ranges, occupying a sizeable chunk of the southwestern part of the state. No two of Colorado's ranges are alike, and this variety offers everchanging joys for the casual tourist, the photographer, the backpacker, and the climber.

It is impossible to discuss the geography of Colorado without mentioning the important element of water. The great "divider of the waters," the Continental Divide, winds through the heart of Colorado's mountains, making a great western bend as it travels through the San Juans. Most of Colorado's high peaks cluster near the Continental Divide, but the Divide itself does not necessarily follow the highest ridges. Of fifty-four Fourteeners, only Grays and Torreys sit squarely on the Continental Divide.

Three of North America's great rivers originate deep within the Colorado Rockies—the Rio Grande, the Arkansas, and the Colorado. The importance of these rivers and the Colorado snowpack from which they are born is impossible to overestimate. The availability of water from these rivers is vital to the survival of large numbers of communities, farms, and ranches. Colorado is a semi-arid land, and although the mountains receive greater precipitation than the rest of the state, it is far less than in such ranges as the Cascades. Therefore, the Colorado Rockies are mountains of unique character, void of dense vegetation and large glaciers but abounding with clear blue sky, and in winter, world-renowned dry-powder snow.

The individual ranges of the Colorado Rockies are of almost infinite variety—combinations of massive peaks, ragged ridges, flower-sprinkled meadows, sheltered valleys, serene lakes, and cascading streams. The mountains are much more than mere masses of rock; they are inseparably bound to their flora, fauna, weather, and water. Given this, any written description is bound to be inadequate, for only when one has actually climbed the peaks, traveled the valleys, breathed the mountain air, and personally experienced Colorado's mountains does their full character come alive.

To fully grasp the character of the Colorado Rockies, something of the processes and forces that went into forming them must be understood. The geologic story of Colorado's mountains is a long and ancient one, beginning in the first era of geologic time, the Precambrian. During this era, most of the earth's "basement rocks" were formed in one of three ways. *Igneous* rocks were formed by the solidifying of molten rock from deep within the earth. *Sedimentary* rocks were formed by the accumulation and cementing together of eroded particles of other rocks and were distributed by wind, streams, or oceans. *Metamorphic* rocks were formed when either igneous or sedimentary rocks were subjected to tremendous heat and pressure.

Much of Colorado was part of an ocean bed for at least a portion of the four-billion-year Precambrian Era. Underwater sedimentary deposits, eroded from the neighboring land, piled to depths of up to forty thousand feet, and the resultant pressure changed much of the sedimentary rock into metamorphic rock: the two most common types in Colorado are gneiss and schist. Later, forces from within the earth caused the bedrock to rise and the sea to retreat. This uplifting was accompanied by molten rock rising from within the earth and filling the cracks in the gneiss and schist. When this molten rock solidified, it formed granite, the igneous rock that is the third major type of Precambrian rock found in Colorado. The end of the Precambrian Era was a time of great erosion: The upland of gneiss, schist, and granite in the Colorado region was eroded to a nearly level plain at sea level, and the area became highly susceptible to encroachments by the everchanging seas. Indeed, during the next two eras of geologic history, the Paleozoic and Mesozoic, a combined span of 500 million years, the area was alternately invaded by the sea and then uplifted. Each time the sea encroached upon the land, a layer of sediment was deposited. These sediments became cemented together and formed many of the sandstones and shales found in Colorado.

About 70 million years ago, the sea retreated from Colorado for the last time. Causing this retreat was a great uplift of the entire Rocky Mountain chain, called the Laramide Orogeny. This event ushered in the last geologic era, the Cenozoic, which is divided into two periods: the Tertiary, lasting from 70 million years ago to 3 million years ago; and the Quaternary, lasting from the end of the Tertiary to the present.

The Laramide Orogeny occupied the first half of the Tertiary period, and it was during this time that most of Colorado's ranges were formed. Mountain ranges of the Laramide Orogeny were formed in several different manners, but the most common in Colorado is the *faulted anticline*. The Front, Sawatch, Park, Gore, Tenmile, and Mosquito ranges are all examples of basically faulted anticline ranges. Anticlines are formed when forces within the earth cause flexible sedimentary layers of the earth's crust to be bent in a series of upward-arching corrugations, or anticlines. In Colorado, the lower layer of Precambrian gneiss, schist, and granite, being less flexible, was often lifted as a block below the sedimentary layers and broken rather than bent by these forces. When the Precambrian layer was broken, or faulted, along the edges of the uplift, a faulted anticline was produced.

The bent sedimentary layers, now considerably higher than the surrounding land, were immediately attacked by erosion. These soft layers were eroded away relatively quickly, leaving only the hard Precambrian core exposed. Therefore, many of Colorado's faulted anticline ranges are composed of a hard Precambrian core or "spine" of peaks that are flanked by upturned sedimentary layers, as is so vividly seen along the Front Range in such areas as the Flatirons near Boulder. While most of Colorado's ranges are faulted anticlines, there are some exceptions: the Elk, the northern Sangre de Cristo, and the San Juan ranges are the major ones. The geology of each of these ranges is discussed in the individual range introductions.

The uplifting and faulting of the Laramide Orogeny in Colorado was accompanied by flows of igneous rock from deep within the earth. Flows that cooled and solidified before reaching the surface are called *intrusions;* these are of two major types, *batholiths* and *stocks.* A batholith is a massive blister-type formation that never quite reached the surface but that may have become exposed later due to the erosion of overlying layers of rock. Stocks are similar in formation to batholiths but are smaller. Igneous flows that reached the surface and then solidified are known as *extrusives* or *volcanics.* Tertiary volcanism was most prevalent in the vicinity of the San Juans, and thus most San Juan peaks are composed of layers of volcanic rock.

One important consequence of the Laramide Orogeny and associated Tertiary intrusions was the deposition of minerals in Colorado. The uplifting and intrusions caused mineral-rich solutions to seep into the many cracks in the rocks. These minerals, among them silver and gold, crystallized into veins and eventually led to the development of Colorado as one of the important mineral producers of the West.

The Quaternary period in Colorado, due to general climatic cooling, was characterized by the formation of immense mountain glaciers reaching down the valleys as far as elevations of 8,000 feet. Because they were far south of the great continental ice sheets of this period, Colorado glaciers formed only in areas where the elevation and snowfall were great enough for the winter snow accumulation to exceed summer melting. These glaciers began near the crest of the ranges and slowly ground down into valleys previously occupied by streams.

The glaciers had a dramatic effect on the landscape. They deepened valleys, steepened slopes, carved cirques, and deposited great masses of rock debris at their terminuses and along their edges; these debris accumulations are known as *moraines.* The effects of glaciation in Colorado are probably most strikingly seen in the great glacier-carved cirques of the Sawatch Range, the spectacularly polished east face of Longs Peak, and the ubiquitous alpine lakes that were frequently formed by glacial scouring of the bedrock.

Today, climatic conditions are too mild for the presence of large glaciers in Colorado. The Front Range contains a number of very small glaciers found in the most sheltered cirques, but these are leading only a marginal existence. Although there are a number of permanent snowfields and ice bodies in the other Colorado ranges, they cannot technically be called glaciers unless they move and show signs of that movement, such as crevasses.

It remains for future generations to know whether or not climatic conditions will cause great mountain glaciers to form once again in Colorado. In the meantime, the geologic story continues in the Colorado Rockies. Wind, water, and frost are at work in the mountains, slowly but constantly changing the physical nature of the peaks. The fact remains, too, that although the mountains appear to be permanent and unchanging, their geologic history bears out that they are, in reality, a very dynamic part of the landscape.

Early Ventures Into a Beckoning Land

Colorado's History to 1860

Humans first ventured into the labyrinth of the North American continent somewhere between fifteen and twenty thousand years ago. Nomadic bands crossed the land bridge linking Siberia and Alaska and slowly made their way across North America. Archaeological evidence suggests that descendants of these early inhabitants may have roamed the San Luis Valley as early as 8000 B.C. Yet, it was not until roughly the time of Christ that a people arrived in Colorado who would leave a definite legacy.

Gradually forsaking the nomadic wanderings of their ancestors, an Indian people settled on the mesas of southwestern Colorado and slowly adopted an agrarian lifestyle. Referred to as Basket Makers or as the Anasazi, a Navajo word meaning "ancient ones," these people subsisted on small game and a variety of crops grown on the mesa tops. Their civilization culminated in the Classic Pueblo Period of A.D. 1100 to 1300, when the architectural masterpieces of Mesa Verde were constructed.

Venturing from their homes in Cliff Palace or Spruce Tree House, these cliff dwellers could stand on Mesa Verde's crest and gaze north into the heart of the San Juans. From the main settlements on Mesa Verde, hunters and traders ventured into the foothills of the range. Is it possible that an ultimate Anasazi manhood rite may have included a climb to the mountains now called the Wilsons and El Diente? If so, the bold adventurers' names have been lost to history.

By 1300, years of sustained drought and crop failures caused the Anasazi to abandon Mesa Verde and gradually migrate southward to be assimilated by the Pueblo tribes of the Southwest. Two centuries after the abandonment of Mesa Verde, an Italian seaman under the auspices of the Spanish flag sailed west from Europe and, rather than falling off the edge of the earth as some notables of his day had predicted, explored a new world. Columbus's voyage sparked an age of exploration by the great powers of Europe, which by the early 1600s saw permanent colonies planted on three of the four corners of what would one day be the United States.

American history has frequently heralded the accomplishments of the French frontier of the St. Lawrence River Valley and the English frontier of the Atlantic Seaboard while paying little or no attention to the third great power battling for empire in the New World. To be sure, Spain established the provincial capital of Santa Fe, New Mexico, in 1609, two years after the founding of Jamestown and a full eleven years before the Pilgrims' arrival at Plymouth Rock. Indeed, Santa Fe was but the northern fringe of a huge Spanish empire that stretched from Cape Horn to the Colorado and Rio Grande rivers and that dated from Cortes's conquest of the Aztecs in 1520.

While French and English fur traders pushed westward across the Appalachian Mountains and through the Great Lakes region, Spanish adventurers made repeated excursions into the lands north of Santa Fe. In 1706, Juan de Ulibarri reached the Arkansas River in southeastern Colorado and claimed its drainage for the Spanish king Philip V. Ulibarri confined his activities to the eastern plains and did not venture westward to explore the lands at the river's headwaters.

A dozen major Spanish expeditions traveled the eastern Colorado plains in the first half of the 1700s, searching for precious minerals, spreading Christianity, pursuing runaway slaves, and countering French fur-trader advances, but all stayed clear of the towering mountain ranges of central Colorado. However, although no documented report of Spanish exploration into Colorado's mountains prior to 1776 remains, there is evidence of mineral explorations to the La Plata Mountains and also abundant tales of lost mines and buried treasure in the Sangre de Cristo Range. Indeed, when Franciscan priests Francisco Dominguez and Silvestre Escalante led their small band of adventurers through southwestern Colorado in 1776, they were following a well-established trail of prior Spanish exploration.

In 1776, as English colonists wrestled with the tyranny of George III, Dominguez and Escalante left Santa Fe to blaze an overland supply route to Spanish missions in California. Their desire to contact Ute Indians and the uncertainty of the trail westward took them on a swing around the San Juans, over the Uncompahgre Plateau, across Grand Mesa, and finally to the Green River in northeastern Utah. Although a series of problems kept the expedition from reaching California, Father Escalante's well-kept diary of the trek provided a valuable description of Colorado's western mountains. Dominguez and Escalante were the first European explorers to travel the length of Colorado's Western Slope and document their achievement.

While the Utes inhabited the high mountains of Colorado, the plains were roamed by tribes of Arapaho, Kiowa, Cheyenne, and Comanche Indians. In 1779, Comanche raids on New Mexican settlements became so intense that an outraged Spanish governor of New Mexico, Juan Bautista De Anza, marched north from Santa Fe with six hundred men to give battle. Although previous Spanish explorations had simply crossed Raton Pass and marched across the eastern plains, military strategy dictated that De Anza advance on his enemies by a less conspicuous route.

With the element of surprise in mind, De Anza marched his force up the Rio Grande Valley, through the San Luis Valley, and over Poncha Pass to the headwaters of the Arkansas River. In doing so, he made the first documented penetration of the inner Rockies. Passing under the summits of the Fourteeners of the Sawatch Range, the Governor turned east over Trout Creek Pass, crossed South Park, and descended onto the plains just south of Pikes Peak. If only these adventurers, out for gold and glory as well as God and king, had known they were riding over what would become the richest gold camp in the world, Cripple Creek!

Once on the plains, De Anza rode south and surprised his adversary, a Comanche chieftain named Cuerno Verde. Cuerno Verde wore a buffalo headdress that boasted two great horns colored with green dye— thus his Spanish name, meaning "Greenhorn." In a pitched battle just east of Greenhorn Mountain in the Wet Mountains, Cuerno Verde was killed and the Comanche power checked. De Anza returned to New Mexico by crossing Sangre de Cristo Pass just north of the present-day U.S. 160 route across North La Veta Pass, and in so doing he became the first to circle Colorado's Sangre de Cristo Range.

By 1800, Spanish power in the Southwest was rapidly declining, and the stage was set for the fledgling United States to flex its muscles of Manifest Destiny and discover what lay west of the Mississippi River. In July of 1806, Lieutenant Zebulon Pike, then twenty-seven, led an expedition west from St. Louis to explore the southern part of the newly acquired Louisiana Territory and to search for the Red River.

Pike moved up the Arkansas River Valley, and in late November of 1806 he constructed a breastwork of logs at the present site of Pueblo. To the northwest, a great peak towered above the plains. In the first recorded attempt to climb a Colorado Fourteener, Pike and his companions set out for its summit. After two and one-half days the summit still loomed far away. The explorer abandoned the attempt and promptly noted in his journal that the peak was well over 18,000 feet in elevation and unclimbable in the existing winter conditions. Pike proceeded to entangle himself in the labyrinth of Colorado geography, as well as the intrigue of Spanish politics, during his search for the illusive Red River, but Pikes Peak remains the young explorer's greatest claim to fame.

In the spring of 1820, an army expedition commanded by Major Stephen H. Long marched west from Council Bluffs to locate the source of another river, the Platte. Long's reports of the Great Plains left the region branded "the Great American Desert" until a later generation of hardy immigrant farmers proved otherwise.

By June of 1820, Long neared the headwaters of the South Platte and viewed what he first thought to be Pike's "great peak." Only as the expedition crossed the divide separating the Platte and Arkansas valleys, near present-day Sedalia, did another great peak loom to the south. Convinced that this second one was Pike's "great peak," Edwin James, the expedition's twenty-three-year-old botanist and physician, set out with a party to attempt its summit. After one and one-half days, James and two companions reached the summit; this was the first documented ascent of a Colorado Fourteener. Their claim must include the word "documented," because there is ample evidence to suggest that Indians and even possibly some wandering Spanish explorers reached the summits of at least several Fourteeners prior to 1820.

James was delighted by the view from the summit and went into great detail describing the climb in what later became the expedition's official report. Major Long chose to honor James's efforts, which must rank as a pioneering cornerstone in Colorado climbing, by naming the great mountain "James Peak." Trappers and traders, however, chose to refer to the mountain as "Pikes Peak," and in time James was left to lesser fame. The trappers and traders were kinder to Major Long. The great peak the expedition first sighted became known as Longs Peak.

Close on the heels of the explorers came the mountain men. These men were a hardy breed who trapped the high streams of the Rockies for beaver, fought Indians (and anyone else in their way), and once a year gathered for a great rendezvous to talk over the season and consume great quantities of "Taos Lightning." That was the name given to the favorite potent drink of the mountain men, one of whom summed up its kick by saying, "It was so strong that no one ever lived long enough to become an addict." The mountain men were so much the questing type that it is almost impossible to believe that at least one of them did not venture up some Colorado Fourteener just "to see what was there."

As the fur trade declined, the cry of "Gold!" was raised on the banks of the American River in California, and a tidal wave of prospectors spilled across the continent. The addition of California to the Union in 1850 led some farsighted individuals to dream of a railroad linking East and West. In 1853, four teams of government surveyors crossed the continent to explore possible routes. Captain John W. Gunnison was chosen to lead the exploration of the land between the 38th and 39th parallels.

Gunnison followed the well-established trail of trappers and traders over Sangre de Cristo Pass into the San Luis Valley. The expedition report made particular mention of the spectacular sight De Anza and Pike had undoubtedly viewed before—the Crestones. Gunnison's route took him past Fort Massachusetts (later Fort Garland), founded in 1852 at the foot of Blanca Peak. Crossing the San Luis Valley, the expedition hauled wagons over Cochetopa Pass, the Utes' "Pass of the Buffalo." By the time he reached the treacherous Black Canyon of the Gunnison River, Captain Gunnison had concluded that any railroad daring to battle Colorado's high mountains would require extensive tunneling.

Railroads were fine dreams, but the brewing cauldron of civil war in the East postponed any grand transcontinental schemes. Yet, on the very eve of the Civil War, news came from the Pikes Peak country that was destined to catapult the land of mountains into national prominence. To be sure, the first report was sketchy and the amount of mineral found was small, but the small whisper uttered in May of 1858 at the confluence of Cherry Creek and the South Platte River soon swelled to a hurricane roar of "GOLD!"

By 1859, a new tidal wave of prospectors, speculators, boomers, and get-rich-quick con artists poured across the Great Plains with signs of "Pikes Peak or Bust!" For a time, the Front Range dammed the flood of "fifty-niners" along the eastern Rockies, but within a few years the lure of new Eldorados in the mountains to the west caused the tidal wave to spill across the high mountain passes into the inner Rockies, thus inexorably entwining the stories of Colorado's people and its mountains.

Giants Above the Plains

The Front and Mosquito Ranges

To many, the Front Range is the opening scene of Colorado's mountain drama. The farthest east of Colorado's ranges, the Front Range has been the first range to greet many a miner, tourist, and mountaineer from across the endless miles of prairie, and what a fitting introduction it has provided. More than anything else, the Front Range peaks emphasize the awesome height of the Colorado Rockies—soaring up to 8,000 feet above the foothills at their base, a rise no other Colorado range can match.

In the broadest terms, the Front Range applies to the continuous line of mountains that border the Great Plains from the Wyoming border to Cañon City, a distance of 180 miles. The Continental Divide passes through the northern part of the range before making a swing westward across the Mosquitos. The South Platte River is the dominant drainage of the eastern slope of the Front Range; the mighty Colorado heads on its western slope north of Grand Lake. The western boundary of the range is not so clearly delineated as the obvious eastern boundary but is roughly defined by North, Middle, and South parks.

The western border of expansive South Park is formed by the Mosquito Range, which is about thirty-five miles long and has a northerly twelve-mile extension, the Tenmile Range. These two ranges contain five Fourteeners, which are of greater interest for their extensive mining history than for their mountaineering challenges.

In many ways, the Front Range is the classic example of Colorado's anticlinal ranges. The longest continuous uplift in the state, most of its peaks are composed of Precambrian granite, gneiss, and schist, the overlying Paleozoic sedimentary layers having long since been stripped away. The breaking of the once overlying sedimentary layers is well displayed

15

along the Front Range. Areas of up-sloping sedimentary layers, such as the Garden of the Gods and Boulder's Flatirons, make evident the great forces of the Laramide Orogeny.

After the uplift, intrusive and extrusive igneous activity occurred in many parts of the Front and Mosquito ranges. Many small intrusions were responsible for most of the gold and silver deposits in the Front Range. The largest center of extrusive volcanic activity was in the vicinity of Cripple Creek, now legendary for its mineral wealth.

The mining booms caused the Front and Mosquito ranges to be the first mountain regions of Colorado to be explored and climbed extensively. As prospectors moved west, they found Ute, Kenosha, Loveland, and Berthoud passes to be gateways through the range and the flat expanse of South Park to be a veritable speedway into the Mosquito Range. Many prospectors continued over Mosquito Pass into Oro City (soon to be overshadowed by Leadville), but some were attracted by the gold placers at the foot of the Mosquitos. As a result, headquarters town Fairplay was established in 1859, and the surrounding Alma Mining District was officially organized two years later.

As miners searched for the elusive yellow metal in the Front and Mosquito ranges, they also climbed and named many peaks. The naming of the Mosquito Range is attributed to Judge Wilbur F. Stone, who was painfully aware of the abundance of insect pests in the rarefied mountain air. Undecided on a name for his new mining company, Judge Stone left the space on the incorporation papers blank and was stumped until a passing mosquito obliged by landing directly on the blank space. Thus, Judge Stone gained the inspiration for the Mosquito Mining Company, and later the name was adopted for the entire range.

As the mining boom spread west, the easier passes through the Front Range were occupied by narrow-gauge rails. As the "baby railroads" began to prove that mountain railroading was indeed possible, the standard-gauge lines gave it a try. The Colorado Midland climbed Ute Pass in 1886, and the Denver, Northwestern, and Pacific completed its spectacular line over 11,670-foot Rollins Pass, the highest rail pass in North America, in 1907. The culmination of great railroad construction in the Front Range, however, was the completion of the Moffat Tunnel in 1927, which was bored under the Continental Divide beneath James Peak for more than six miles.

Tourism on a small scale was known in the Front Range as early as the 1860s, but it received real impetus from the extensive rail network and the growth of health spas such as Colorado Springs. As photographic techniques improved, the images of great Front Range sights such as Pikes Peak and Longs Peak were widely circulated throughout the United States as lures to the Centennial State. Consequently, thousands flocked to Colorado and provided revenue never dreamed of in struggling mining towns.

After World War II, Colorado's economy boomed, fed in part by government spending and the tourism potential of its mountains. Aside from the mountain range, the term "Front Range" came to be applied to the urban area spreading from Denver north to Fort Collins and south to Colorado Springs and Pueblo. In the mountains, pre-war ski areas such as Winter Park matured and others sprang up near the old mining towns of Breckenridge, Dillon, and Saints John. Interstate 70 replaced the windings of U.S. 6 and 40 leading into the Front Range west of Denver, and by the mid-seventies, the completion of the Eisenhower Tunnel sped development along the quiet western backside of the Front Range.

There were also events signaling a growing concern that the natural resources of Colorado's mountains be prudently managed and preserved. In 1972, Colorado voters passed a referendum that prohibited the expenditure of state funds for the 1976 Winter Olympics. The 1980s saw the construction of the Colorado Trail, a 470-mile wilderness link between Denver and Durango. Citizen groups such as Volunteers for Outdoor Colorado were formed to build and maintain trails and otherwise support local land management agencies. And, in August of 1993, after more than a decade of wrangling over water rights, Congress finally passed the Colorado Wilderness Bill, setting aside more than 600,000 acres as wilderness. In the Front and Mosquito ranges, the bill created the Byers Peak, Vasquez Peak, Ptarmigan Peak, Bowen Gulch, and Buffalo Peaks wilderness areas, and enlarged the Lost Creek Wilderness Area.

Tourism remains the biggest "cash crop" of the Front Range, but its continued success will in large measure depend on our ability to balance and manage the competing demands it places on our natural resources.

Longs Peak 14,255 feet (15th highest)

Longs Peak is undisputedly the monarch of the northern Front Range and one of the outstanding peaks of the entire North American continent. It has gained prominence in the eyes of explorers, settlers, writers, tourists, mountaineers, and technical climbers. Longs Peak offers something for virtually everyone either in its striking beauty or its climbing possibilities, but first and foremost, Longs is a climber's mountain. Even the easiest routes up Longs are classic climbs, and nothing in the Rocky Mountains quite compares with climbs on Longs's mark of individuality—the magnificent 1,675-foot east face, crowned with the sheerest part of all, the 1,000-foot Diamond.

The history of Longs Peak is so rich that any detailed account deserves an entire book. Two such books are Stephen Trimble's *Long's Peak: A Rocky Mountain Chronicle,* which was published in 1984 with some fine color photography, and Paul Nesbit's *Longs Peak—Its Story and a Climbing Guide,* which was the standard guide to the mountain for many years. Also, Bill Bueler's *Roof of the Rockies* devotes a chapter to Longs Peak and vicinity.

Stephen Long made the first recorded American sighting of the peak that bears his name in 1820. Longs and its companion, Mount Meeker, had previously been dubbed *Les Deux Orielles* (The Two Ears) by French fur traders who used the pair as a prominent landmark. Longs Peak was the name that stuck, however, and in the early years of settlement it was one of the foremost unconquered mountaineering challenges in the entire Rocky Mountain region. Its fame spread quickly, even to the extent of becoming the fictional site of a 280-foot telescope in Jules Verne's *From the Earth to the Moon* in 1866.

The upper east face of Longs Peak from the Boulderfield. The cable route once climbed the slope to the right of the east face. The Keyhole lies out of the photograph to the right (west).

Longs's physical dominance made it a natural goal for climbing, and its allure was intensified by the first documented ascent of the Matterhorn, in 1865. Colorado had its own Matterhorn in the form of Longs Peak, and reports from climbing parties that the peak could not be scaled only fueled the fire for an ascent. Finally, on August 23, 1868, a party led by the indomitable John Wesley Powell, which included newspaperman William Byers, reached the summit via the south side after a long approach from Grand Lake. This climb was widely acclaimed as the first ascent of Longs, but the testimony of an old Arapaho Indian in 1914 indicated that the peak had been climbed previously by one "Old Man Gun," who had trapped eagles on its summit. Although the Powell party did not notice an eagle trap on the summit, it may easily have been overlooked in the four-acre expanse, and there is little reason to doubt that the peak was indeed climbed by Indians prior to 1868.

After the first documented ascent, two prominent people emerged in the history of Longs Peak—Reverend Elkanah J. Lamb and Enos Mills. Lamb made his first climb of Longs in 1871 and then made the first descent of the east face via a couloir now known as Lambs Slide, appropriately named because the Reverend quite inadvertently made much of the descent on his seat instead of his feet. In 1878, Lamb became the first regular guide for climbs up Longs, operating out of his lodge to the east of the peak. He charged $5.00 to guide parties up the peak and once said, "If they would not pay for spiritual guidance, I compelled them to pay for material elevation." By his enthusiasm and his completion of the first trail to the Boulderfield, Lamb contributed immensely to the popularity of climbing Longs; his work was taken over by his son, Carlyle, in 1885. In 1902, the Lambs sold their lodge to Enos Mills, who carried on their tradition of expert guiding in excellent fashion.

Mills was a naturalist of some repute, and his knowledge of the flora and fauna of the area added greatly to a climb of Longs. He constructed the Timberline Cabin in 1908 and made a total of 297 climbs of the peak. Most important, Mills's great love for Longs Peak and the surrounding area spurred a drive to protect the region, which culminated in the creation of Rocky Mountain National Park in 1915.

In 1925, two sets of cables were installed on the north face of the peak to aid in climbing, and until 1973 the majority of climbers ascended by the "Cable Route." In 1927, the Boulderfield Shelter Cabin was erected at the foot of the north face. Many climbers rode on horseback to the cabin and then climbed the peak the next day. The cabin, however, lasted only until 1937. On July 20, 1973, the cables were removed from the north face and the circuitous Keyhole route became the easiest and most popular route. Climbing Longs has become increasingly popular in recent years, with as many as four thousand climbers reaching its summit in a single year.

Although mountaineering has often been thought of as a male sport, Longs was one of the first major peaks in the United States to be climbed frequently by women. In 1873, Addie Alexander became the first woman to climb the peak, and later that same year Miss Anna Dickinson made her much-heralded climb. Earlier, Miss Dickinson had ascended Pikes, Grays, and Lincoln, mostly by burro, but on Longs she demonstrated her real climbing skill. She accompanied members of the Hayden Survey, and along with them decided on the naming of nearby Mount Lady Washington and Mount Meeker (for Nathan Meeker, a friend of Anna's who later gained a place in history by being killed by the White River Utes in 1879). Incidentally, Nathan Meeker's son, Ralph, was along on the climb and was courting Miss Dickinson, but while they reached great heights together on the climb of Longs, they apparently never reached the pinnacle of marriage, much to Ralph's chagrin.

During the month following Miss Dickinson's climb, Miss Isabella Bird, a cultured English author, made the ascent and wrote of it. She was guided by the very uncultured mountain man Rocky Mountain Jim Nugent, "a man any woman could love, but no sane woman would marry," as Isabella put it. With plenty of "direct aid" from Jim, Miss Bird eventually did make the summit and then wrote of her experiences in *A Lady's Life in the Rocky Mountains,* which was great publicity for the Longs Peak area and is still entertaining reading.

Technical climbing on Longs did not come into vogue until the 1920s. While the great east face had been descended by Lamb in 1871 and by Mills in 1903, that side was not climbed until Werner Zimmerman did it in 1919. A more direct and now classic route was pioneered by James Alexander in 1922. After these ice-breaking ascents, climbs of Longs's east face read like a list of climbing all-stars. Carl Blaurock, the Stettner brothers, Tom Hornbein, and Layton Kor are just a few of the many climbers who have pioneered new routes on Longs.

Although many new routes were found on the east face of the peak, the ultimate technical climb, the ascent of the spectacular 1,000-foot sheer Diamond Face, was not accomplished until 1960, due in part to national park climbing restrictions before that year. In the summer of 1960 the restrictions were lifted, and California climbers David Rearick and Robert Kamps gained the right to begin an assault on the Diamond on August 1. After two days of difficult rock and aid climbing with obviously incredible exposure, the two reached the summit of Longs on the afternoon of August 3. Since this milestone in Longs Peak climbing history, a number of other climbs of the Diamond have been made, including the first winter ascent in 1967 by Layton Kor and Wayne Goss. The great east face of Longs will unquestionably continue to challenge climbers for generations to come, and, as Robert Ormes has stated, Longs Peak will continue to boast "the nation's greatest concentration of high country rock routes."

Due to the extreme popularity of Longs (it is estimated that nearly 100,000 have climbed it), it is inevitable that a number of fatalities have occurred. From 1884 to 1972, twenty-six fatalities were reported, the causes ranging from gunshot wounds to falls to lightning. The most publicized of these fatalities was the Agnes Vaille tragedy, which followed the first successful winter ascent of the east face by Miss Vaille and Walter Kreiner, in 1925. On the descent, Vaille collapsed due to exhaustion. Keiner went for help, but she froze to death in his absence. To add further to the loss, Herbert Sortland, a member of the rescue party, became lost on the mountain and died as well. Despite these fatalities, Longs has been

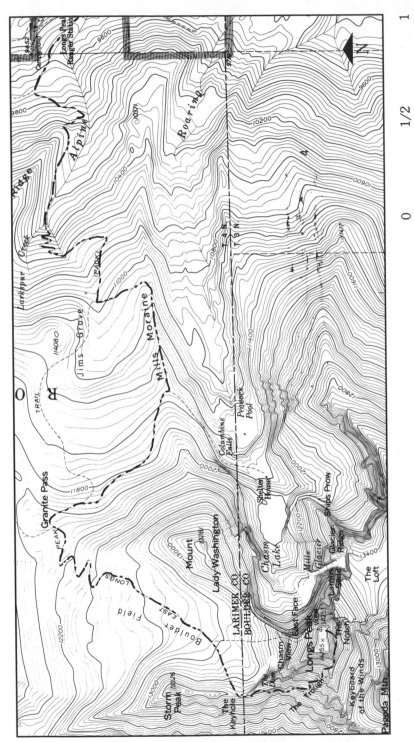

Longs Peak

safely climbed by five-year-olds, an eighty-five-year-old, people on crutches, and a six-piece band. It is not, however, a peak to be underestimated.

While Longs Peak is a worthy goal in itself, perhaps it achieved its greatest worth by providing training for four members of the 1963 American Everest Expedition. Allen Auten, Barry Bishop, Dick Pownall, and Thomas Hornbein all credited climbs of Longs as important to their climbing development. Of these, Bishop and Hornbein reached the summit of Everest, and thus Longs Peak gained the prestige of playing a part in the conquest of another great peak more than twice its height.

In 1974, Longs achieved literary fame as an important geographic landmark in James Michener's classic novel, *Centennial*. In *Centennial,* Michener referred to Longs as the peak upon which a huge stone beaver appears to be climbing upward. Indeed, if one looks closely, and with imagination, a beaver does appear etched against the skyline, just to the south of the Diamond Face—just one more unique feature of the incomparable personality of Longs Peak.

THE ROUTES

Keyhole Route

Since the removal of the cables, the standard route available to the nontechnical climber is the Keyhole route. Drive south from Estes Park ten miles on Colorado 7, and turn right, going for one mile west to the Longs Peak Campground and Ranger Station, at 9,400 feet. From here, an excellent trail leads six miles to the Boulderfield. Hop over the abundant boulders for one mile to the prominent Keyhole at the southwest corner of the Boulderfield. Just to the left of the Keyhole lies the Agnes Vaille Shelter Cabin, which shelters more snow than anything. Once the Keyhole (13,100 feet) has been passed through, the route is marked by red and yellow paint spots that lead over "the Ledges" and then descend into the broad couloir known as "the Trough." It is six hundred steep feet up the snow and/or talus of the Trough to a notch at the top of it.

At the notch, the still-marked route swings to the south side of the peak and immediately crosses the most spectacular part of the climb, "the Narrows" ledges. The Narrows are fairly exposed, but they are broad enough to be crossed easily if there is no snow. *If there is snow,* which is a possibility well into July, an ice axe is a necessity for a safe climb

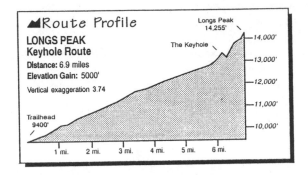

of the Ledges, the Trough, the Narrows, and the Homestretch. The Narrows lead to the bottom of the Homestretch, a short, shallow couloir leading directly to the summit. This section will be extremely slippery if the rock is wet. Descend via the same route.

Do not underestimate Longs. It is a long climb, and if it is snowy or icy, the Keyhole route requires an ice axe and the ability to use it correctly.

The National Park Service permits backcountry camping only in designated areas. Permits are required, and reservations well in advance are strongly recommended for the peak summer season. The backcountry office phone number is (303) 586-3565, extension 243.

▲ *Longs Peak Ranger Station to summit: 6.9 miles, 5,000 feet.*

Mount Evans 14,264 feet (14th highest)
Mount Bierstadt 14,060 feet (38th highest)

Dominating the Front Range skyline to the west of Denver is the sprawling massif of Mount Evans. Connected to Mount Evans with the forbidding Sawtooth Ridge is Mount Bierstadt, lying one and one-half miles west of Evans, and therefore not visible from Denver. The Evans massif figured as a prominent landmark early in Colorado history, and during the gold rush of the 1860s was known simply as the Chicago Mountains. As one might expect, it was named by a group of 1859 miners who hailed from the Windy City.

Evans and Bierstadt are the only two Colorado Fourteeners whose histories are tied closely to the life of a painter. Albert Bierstadt is perhaps the best known painter of great Western scenes from the 1860s and 1870s, and it is fitting that a Colorado Fourteener bears his name. Bierstadt made his first trip west in 1858, when he journeyed to famed South Pass in Wyoming. On that trip, he was inspired to paint *Morning in the Rocky Mountains* and *Rocky Mountains—Landers Peak*, which measures six feet by ten feet, a typical size for Bierstadt's work.

In 1863, Bierstadt began his second trip west and, with William Byers, visited the Chicago Mountains. Bierstadt climbed some of the peaks of this "range" and may well have made the first ascents of both Mount Evans and Mount Bierstadt, although there was some mining activity not far from Mount Bierstadt at that time. While camped at the Chicago Lakes, north of Mount Evans, Bierstadt was impressed by a large storm cloud playing about the summit of Mount Evans, which he had christened Mount Rosalie, for his wife. Afterward, in 1866, he painted *Storm in the Rocky Mountains*, which featured this scene. After the 1863 trip, Bierstadt made four additional trips west and continued producing huge

25

Mount Evans from the north across the Chicago Lakes Basin. Summit Lake lies beneath the snowfield beyond the headwall of the basin. *(Photograph courtesy Colorado Historical Society)*

sensational western paintings, including a classic one of Longs Peak that now hangs in the Denver Public Library's Western History Room.

Although Albert Bierstadt would have loved having "Mount Rosalie" retained as a name for the highest peak of the Chicago Mountains, it was not. In 1870, at a celebration in Greeley, it was suggested that Mount Rosalie be renamed "Mount Evans," in honor of Colorado's second territorial governor, who served from 1862 to 1865. John Evans had no spectacular achievements on the political front, but after his retirement from the political scene he promoted the building of the Denver Pacific Railroad and the Denver, South Park and Pacific. He also donated the property upon which the University of Denver was eventually built, and he was one of the original supporters of the Colorado State Historical Society. The name change was popularly supported, and Mount Rosalie was renamed Mount Evans by a Colorado legislature resolution on March 5, 1895, coinciding with Evans's eighty-first birthday. The name Rosalie was then applied to a 13,575-foot peak southeast of Mount Evans. Mount Bierstadt was officially named in 1914, as proposed by Ellsworth Bethel.

Mount Bierstadt (*right*) and the Sawtooth, with the tip of Mount Evans visible from Guanella Pass and the infamous willows in the foreground.

While not as accessible as Pikes Peak during the first two decades of the twentieth century, Evans and Bierstadt were relatively popular with climbers. One climber who frequented Mount Evans was Albert R. Ellingwood (see La Plata Peak), who climbed Mount Evans on snowshoes in March of 1916. Ellingwood also probably made the first ascent of Evans's 600-foot north face in 1922, just as safe technical climbing was being introduced in the United States. Mount Bierstadt also saw some climbing at this time, and while not offering the challenges of technical climbs, it may have been ski-climbed for the first time in 1934. The date of the first traverse of the ragged Sawtooth Ridge between Evans and Bierstadt is not known, but it is likely that it also occurred in the 1920s or 1930s.

In the 1930s, a crude road was constructed to the summit of Evans, and thus it became the second and last (we hope) Colorado Fourteener on which one could drive to the summit. In 1939, the road was improved and was widely hailed as the highest automobile road in the world. In 1941, the original summit house was constructed, and flocks of tourists began invading the mountain. In addition, scientists discovered the summit of Evans to be a convenient location for high-altitude studies, and the University of Denver built its Cosmic Ray Research Laboratory there in 1936. A wide variety of experiments has been conducted there, and in July of 1973, a four-ton, twenty-four-inch reflector telescope was installed, becoming the highest fixed astronomical telescope in the world. Mount Evans is an ideal site for an observatory because of its accessibility and the dryness of the Colorado air at 14,000 feet, which makes for ideal viewing conditions.

In the summer months, when the paved road is open to the summit, Mount Evans swarms with people desiring to avoid the heat and congestion of the city. As a result, climbing accidents have become more frequent on the peak. In late August and early September of 1976, two fatalities occurred on Evans within a two-week period. The first victim was Brian Driscoll, twenty-eight, who attempted to descend from the summit via the treacherous snow and ice couloirs of the north face. He slipped, slid out of control for six hundred feet, and was fatally injured on the rocks below. Then, in early September, Thomas R. Gibbons, eighteen, also lost his footing on the snow and fell about four hundred feet. Despite first aid given by fishermen, he died before a rescue helicopter could reach him. Even Colorado's most popular and easiest peaks can be deadly if one is ill equipped and inexperienced—know your abilities!

THE ROUTES

Mount Evans Road, Mount Evans

Quite frankly, the most environmentally sensitive approach to the summit of Mount Evans is via the Mount Evans Road. From Idaho Springs, follow Colorado 103 southwest and then south thirteen and one-half miles to Echo Lake. From Bergen Park, follow Colorado 103 west eighteen and one-half miles to Echo Lake. Colorado 103 is open year-round to Echo Lake. From Echo Lake it is nine miles to Summit Lake and a total of fourteen and one-half miles to the summit via the Mount Evans Road. There is an adequate parking area at Summit Lake—when the road is open that far.

Get challenged on this one and do the climb when the road is closed to vehicles, or arrive by some other means, such as by bicycle. Early in the season, if snow still covers the slopes, it is permissible to climb directly from the road just southeast of Summit Lake to the summit. These slopes have seen significant erosion in recent years, however, and should be avoided after the snow has melted.

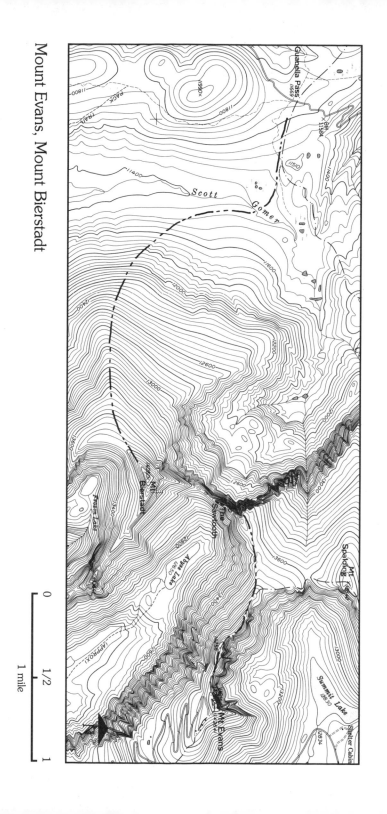

Mount Evans, Mount Bierstadt

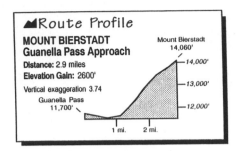

▲Route Profile

MOUNT BIERSTADT
Guanella Pass Approach

Distance: 2.9 miles
Elevation Gain: 2600'

Vertical exaggeration 3.74

Whatever you do, be certain to avoid the cliffs and the treacherous snow and ice couloirs immediately south of Summit Lake.

▲ *Echo Lake to Mount Evans: 14.5 miles, 3,600 feet.*
▲ *Summit Lake to Mount Evans: 5.5 miles, 1,400 feet.*

Guanella Pass, Mount Bierstadt

From Georgetown, drive south up the Guanella Pass road for ten miles to the immediate vicinity of the pass (11,669). The rounded summit of Bierstadt appears to the east along with the jagged Sawtooth, in impressive relief against the sky. Guanella Pass may also be approached from the south, ten miles from Grant on U.S. 285. From the pass, one of the classic Colorado climbing obstacles is confronted—the infamous Guanella Pass willows! Once there were only rumors of a trail through the three- to five-foot-high vegetation between the road and the base of the peak. Small children and climbers under five-ten often roped up here. In recent years, however, a trail has become increasingly clear, although it will still be a wet bog early in the season, not to mention the cold excitement of early morning dew on bare legs.

From the middle of the parking lot atop Guanella Pass, take a single-track trail that descends due east. (The double-track road leading southeast from the southern end of the parking lot only leads to more willow-bashing in the Scott Gomer Creek drainage.) The trail descends to the east and then loops south of Lake 11,510. After crossing Scott Gomer Creek on a series of well-placed boulders, the trail swings to the right (south) of a pyramid-shaped boulder and then climbs southeast up the grassy slopes of the broad west ridge. The boulder can be a landmark in helping you locate the stream crossing on the return. Follow the ridge east to the summit.

Although boggy spots have led to a number of detours in the willows,

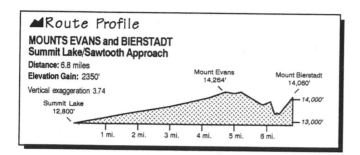

◢◢Route Profile

MOUNTS EVANS and BIERSTADT
Summit Lake/Sawtooth Approach
Distance: 6.8 miles
Elevation Gain: 2350'
Vertical exaggeration 3.74

Mount Evans
14,264'

Mount Bierstadt
14,060'

Summit Lake
12,800'

1 mi. 2 mi. 3 mi. 4 mi. 5 mi. 6 mi.

14,000'

13,000'

this is the classic case of the need to make a supreme effort to stay on one established path rather than trample a many-braided route across these wetlands. Bierstadt makes a great ski climb if the snow is well packed over the willows and the avalanche danger is low.

▲ *Guanella Pass to Mount Bierstadt: 2.9 miles, 2,600 feet.*

Evans and Bierstadt: The Sawtooth Ridge

One of Colorado's most impressive ridges is the Sawtooth, which connects Evans and Bierstadt. Despite its fearsome look, it is a relatively moderate scramble if it is free of ice and snow. From the summit of Evans, follow the west ridge northwest, then southwest one mile to the tip of the prominent Sawtooth. From this approach, the Sawtooth drops away abruptly. Just when you are certain a rappel is necessary, continue west across the high point and down about one hundred feet. A prominent series of welcome ledges leads down the west side of the tooth to the bottom of the cliff. From the Sawtooth's base a series of ups and downs with good handholds and some exposure on the west side leads south a half-mile to Bierstadt's summit. Obstacles are best skirted on the east side of the ridge. The route is a good warmup for other ridges, such as Wilson–El Diente and Little Bear–Blanca, but it is not the place for beginners.

▲ *Evans summit to Bierstadt summit: 2 miles, 900 feet.*

Grays Peak 14,270 feet (9th highest)
Torreys Peak 14,267 feet (11th highest)

During the 1870s and 1880s, when reference was made to Colorado's most famous mountains, it was not the peaks of Pike and Long that were mentioned but rather twin summits named after two of America's most noted botanists. Asa Gray and John Torrey first achieved fame in 1838 by publishing the first part of their monumental *Flora of North America*. Reference to "Torrey and Gray" in botanical circles soon became as widely accepted as reference to "Ormes" among Colorado climbers.

In 1861, Charles C. Parry, a student and coworker of Torrey and Gray who was destined to become an eminent botanist in his own right, climbed the higher peaks of the Front Range and took altitude readings. The prominent "Twin Peaks" or "Ant Hills," as Indians called them, Parry named after his colleagues, Torrey and Gray. A lesser peak, just to the north, he named after botanist George Engelmann.

Four years later, in the summer of 1865, three rip-roaring prospectors, Richard Irwin, John Baker, and Fletcher Kelso, stormed into the large valley north of the peaks to hunt the ever-elusive glimmer of gold and silver. Locally, Torreys Peak became known as Irwins Peak, while Baker gave his name to the little town of Bakerville, and Kelso replaced Engelmann's name with his own on Kelso Mountain. Always a promoter, Dick Irwin soon had a horse trail leading up Grays Peak, the easier of the twin peaks, and was encouraging tourists to take in the view.

The names of Torreys, Grays, and Irwins peaks changed back and forth until 1872, when visits by Parry, Gray, and Torrey to the peaks helped to establish Grays as the eastern summit and Torreys as the western summit. Gray made a climb of Grays Peak with Parry in July of 1872; Torrey visited Georgetown in August and was content his daughter reached its summit.

Grays Peak (*left*) and Torreys Peak (*right*) from the slopes of McClellan Mountain above the Stevens Mine.

Dick Irwin moved on to give his name to a boom-town silver camp in the Gunnison country in 1879, and for twenty-five years continued to follow the lure of the mining frontier, eventually finding his way to Nome, Alaska, in 1901. The tourist business he first encouraged on Grays and Torreys, however, reached boom proportions during the 1870s and 1880s. Tourists came from all over the country, and accounts of their climbs made national news. Published accounts appeared in such premier magazines of the day as *Atlantic Monthly, Overland Monthly, Appleton's Journal, Scribner's,* and the *Appalachia Journal.*

By 1884, when the Colorado Central Railroad had completed the famous Georgetown Loop and passengers could ride in comfort to Silver Plume, Grays and Torreys were musts for tourists bent on seeing Colorado. The ascents were described as "an easy day for a lady," providing, of course, that one rode horseback to the top, as most did!

Despite their reputations on the tourist circuit, Grays and Torreys were very much mining mountains. In the late 1800s, when Georgetown and the Clear Creek Valley were one of the key mining regions of the state, claims were staked and major properties developed in the high valleys surrounding Grays and Torreys. Of particular note were the Waldorf and

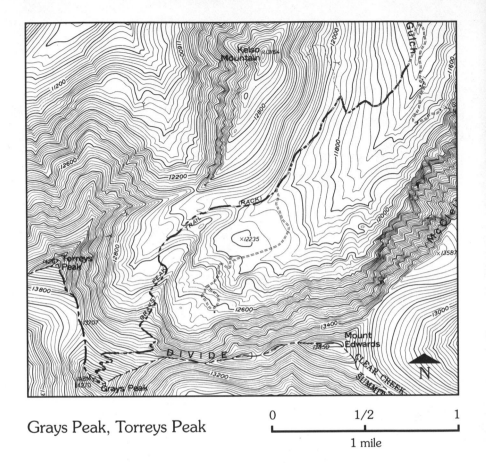

Grays Peak, Torreys Peak

0   1/2   1

1 mile

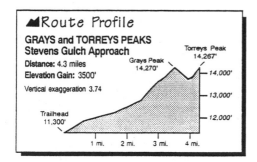

▲Route Profile

GRAYS and TORREYS PEAKS
Stevens Gulch Approach
Distance: 4.3 miles
Elevation Gain: 3500'

Vertical exaggeration 3.74

Torreys Peak 14,267'
Grays Peak 14,270'
14,000'
13,000'
Trailhead 11,300'
12,000'

1 mi.   2 mi.   3 mi.   4 mi.

Santiago mines on McClellan Mountain to the east and the National Treasure and Peruvian mines in Horseshoe Basin to the south. Perhaps the most famous, however, was the Stevens Mine in Stevens Gulch, northeast of the peaks, where Dick Irwin and his cronies first prospected in 1865. Several decaying buildings and a large tailings dump remain today as testaments to the once-booming operation that filled the innards of McClellan Mountain with a series of tunnels and shafts.

THE ROUTES

Stevens Gulch

From Georgetown, once the mining metropolis of the Clear Creek Valley, drive west on I-70 six miles to the Bakerville (once called Graymont) exit. En route, one passes the Georgetown Loop Historic Mining Area, a Colorado Historical Society project featuring the restored Georgetown Loop of the old Georgetown, Breckenridge & Leadville Railway. At Bakerville (what little there is left of it), a dirt road climbs south up Stevens Gulch for three miles almost to the Stevens Mine. One mile from Bakerville, the road forks as Kelso Mountain looms ahead. Take the left-hand (east) fork past a delightfully photogenic old millhouse. The road is passable in two-wheel-drive cars if it is dry, and it makes a fine cross-country-ski approach for winter ascents if one can avoid the snowmobiles that frequent the valley. From just below the Stevens Mine, a trail crosses the creek west (11,300 feet) and winds southwest two miles into the large cirque between Grays and Torreys. From here, the standard old horse trail (with some variations) climbs a circuitous one and one-half miles to the summit of Grays. Torreys is one-half mile north, with a five-hundred-foot drop.

The proximity to Denver and the easy nature of the main trail make the "GT" a natural for beginner and family climbs. Unfortunately, this also makes them among the most crowded. Try to avoid weekends or midsummer climbs, and please stay on the trail.

▲ *Stevens Mine to Grays and Torreys: 4.3 miles, 3,500 feet.*

Pikes Peak 14,110 feet (31st highest)

Pikes Peak requires no introduction, for even before the name "Colorado" was applied to the territory encompassing the highest part of the Rockies, Pikes Peak was almost a household word. Its massive rounded prominence from the Great Plains made its fame inevitable, and when gold was discovered well to the north in 1858, the subsequent rush became known as the Pikes Peak Gold Rush, as if the mountain held dominion from New Mexico to the high plains of Wyoming. Since that time, Pikes Peak has developed a unique history revolving around tourism; to many Americans, it remains the grandest symbol of the Colorado Rockies.

After Zebulon Pike's unsuccessful attempt to scale the peak in 1806, no further attempts were made until 1820, when the summit was reached by three members of Stephen Long's expedition. The leader of the summit party was Dr. Edwin James, a prominent botanist. On July 13, 1820, he and two others set out for the base of the great peak, prudently allowing three days for the climb. They reached the eastern foot of the mountain the first day, passing a group of large hot springs, which would one day become the nationally famous Manitou Springs. That evening they camped below timberline, but the next day they entered the magical world above the trees for the first time. The alpine tundra was an unexplored world for James, and he delighted in collecting and taking notes on the abundant alpine flowers of the peak's upper slopes.

On the afternoon of July 14, Edwin James and his two companions stood on the summit of the great peak—the first documented ascent of a United States Fourteener. James recorded a detailed description of the far-reaching vista, and after an hour of soaking up the view, the trio

37

Pikes Peak from the northeast. The Barr Trail climbs the gentle eastern flanks. *(Photograph courtesy Colorado Historical Society)*

descended to a makeshift camp for the night. The following morning, they descended to their base camp only to find that their smoldering campfire had set several acres of the surrounding forest on fire! Incapable of battling the blaze themselves, they hastily made their way back to the main body of Long's expedition, leaving the fire to burn itself out.

As a result of James's feat, Major Long christened the great mountain "James Peak." A great confusion of names resulted in subsequent years, however. "Pikes Peak" was more commonly used on an informal basis. Finally, in 1843, the issue was settled when explorer John Fremont used the name Pikes Peak on one of his maps. Since then, James's name has been given to a prominent thirteener in the vicinity of Berthoud Pass.

In the years that followed, it was natural that Pikes would become an enticing climb, because it was the first Fourteener to greet many flatlanders as they traveled west. A crude trail was constructed to the summit in the 1850s, and in 1858, Julia A. Holmes reached the summit, becoming the first woman to scale a United States Fourteener. Mrs. Holmes later went on to become a driving force in woman's suffrage, and in later mountaineering exploits she showed herself equal to men in climbing ability. Pikes became quite a popular goal for many women, and in 1893 Katherine Lee Bates was inspired to write the words to her immortal "America the Beautiful" from its summit.

In 1871, the Pikes Peak area became the resort center of the Rockies with the founding of Colorado Springs by William Jackson Palmer. His newly completed Denver and Rio Grande Railway brought many visitors to "Little London" to relax and enjoy the magnificent view of Pikes Peak. In 1874, the boiling springs James had seen were commercially developed, and Manitou Springs grew rapidly as an important resort and health center. A massive advertising campaign promoted the Pikes Peak region as the health capital of the United States, which, if not heaven itself, was close enough to heaven to make a one- or two-thousand-mile trip worthwhile.

Of course, Pikes Peak was at the heart of all this publicity, and better trails to its summit were constructed in the 1870s. The most popular trail was and is the Barr Trail, which starts directly from Manitou Springs and climbs 7,500 feet and eleven miles to the summit, more elevation gain than any other Colorado Fourteener. Improved access to the summit of Pikes did not stop with better trails, however. For those who did not want to climb the peak but preferred to sit all the way to the top, a carriage road was constructed in 1889. A scant one year later, the ultimate means of transportation comfort of the day reached the summit of Pikes via an easterly and southerly approach—the railroad.

The Manitou and Pikes Peak Cog Railway climbs 8.9 miles from Manitou Springs to the summit on a twenty-five percent grade. In 1890 it was the highest railroad in the world and today is still the highest standard-gauge line in the world (some narrow-gauge railroads in the Andes run over fifteen thousand feet). A small resort flourished for a short while at Halfway House Station on the railroad, but this lasted only until 1926. As if the railroad were not enough, the first automobile reached the summit of Pikes in 1901 via the crude carriage road.

Pikes Peak suffered its final humiliation when the old carriage road was converted into an automobile road in 1915. The major promoter of this construction was Spencer Penrose, a Harvard graduate who lived in Colorado Springs. Penrose built the road at a cost of a quarter of a million dollars, and to help offset this cost he organized the first Pikes Peak Hill Climb the following year. Twenty racers entered the first race, which was won by Rea Lentz in an eight-cylinder Romano. The tradition has continued, and today the Pikes Peak Hill Climb is one of the more unusual auto races in the United States. Penrose, meanwhile, did not stop

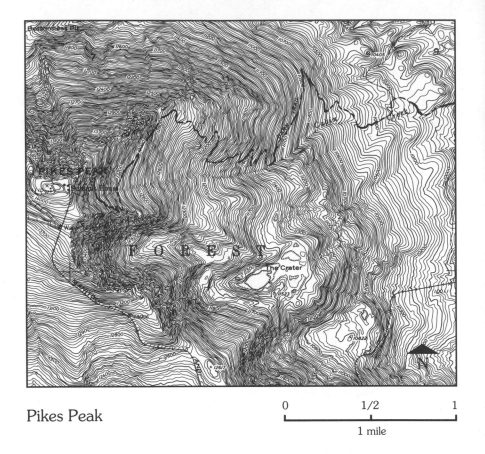

Pikes Peak

0   1/2   1

1 mile

his promotions with this race. In 1918 he put the icing on the cake of all his promotions with the completion of the two-million-dollar Broadmoor, the plushest of all Colorado's resorts, at the foot of Cheyenne Mountain.

Pikes Peak and the surrounding region remain a major recreation and vacation area today. The north side of the peak has attracted winter recreation in the form of a small ski area, and in the summer the health theme is further promoted with the annual footrace up the Barr Trail. Four divisions are represented, and the race is one of the most grueling in the nation. Another special event was initiated in 1921—the New Year's climb of the peak and associated fireworks from the summit. It is carried out annually by the Colorado Springs AdAmAn Club.

Each year in the summer months, when the road is open all the way to the top, more than 250,000 people drive to the summit and perhaps then enjoy a cup of coffee in the summit house while leisurely taking in the unparalleled view. Although it is in some ways objectionable to the mountaineer to have a road to the summit of what was once solely a climber's peak, perhaps it is justifiable that the legendary view from the summit of this legendary mountain is available to all Americans.

THE ROUTES

The Barr Trail

This is the classic route up Pikes Peak, but because of its length and 7,500-foot elevation gain it can be quite rugged as a one-day climb even

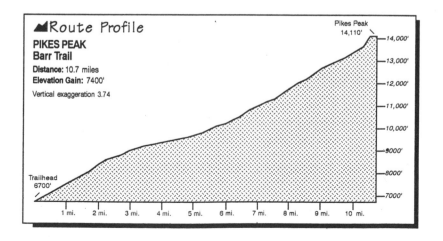

if one is superbly conditioned. For a two-day climb, the best camping site is at Barr's Camp, at 9,800 feet. In Manitou Springs, follow Ruxton Avenue west to the trailhead parking area just beyond the Pikes Peak Cog Railroad depot. The trail leaves from the parking lot, and then it is "merely" a trail climb to the summit.

   ▲ *Parking area to summit: 10.7 miles, 7,400 feet*

Quandary Peak 14,265 feet (13th highest)

Quandary Peak reportedly gets its name from a group of miners who were in a quandary over identification of a mineral specimen on its slopes. Indeed, however, the very fact that the peak was variously referred to as McCullough's Peak, Ute Peak, and Hoosier Peak may have left just about everyone in a quandary as to its name.

Although fur traders and trappers from South Park and the drainage of the South Platte River must surely have viewed the peak, the "Pathfinder of the West," John C. Fremont, got the first recorded close-up on June 22, 1844, when his second expedition to the Rockies crossed yet-unnamed Hoosier Pass from the drainage of the Blue River to the head-waters of the South Platte. Fremont's expedition solved a perplexing riddle of central Colorado geography by discovering the relationship of the Gore Range, the Blue Valley, and South Park to the headwaters of the Arkansas River.

As the mining rush of 1859 spilled beyond the Front Range, a homesick band of Indiana prospectors crossed the pass and, although it was some-times called Ute Pass, christened it Hoosier Pass. The riddle of names was finally solved in the Hayden Atlas, which correctly labeled the pass "Hoosier," and the mountain "Quandary."

In June of 1861, a party of eight wagons pioneered the first wheeled crossing of Hoosier Pass, going from Breckenridge to Fairplay. The Mos-quito Range soon felt the full brunt of the mining rush. Claims were staked on Quandary Peak and in the basin of the Blue Lakes and Monte Cristo Creek. Quandary City, two miles southeast of the peak, sprang up as a collection of tents and hastily constructed cabins.

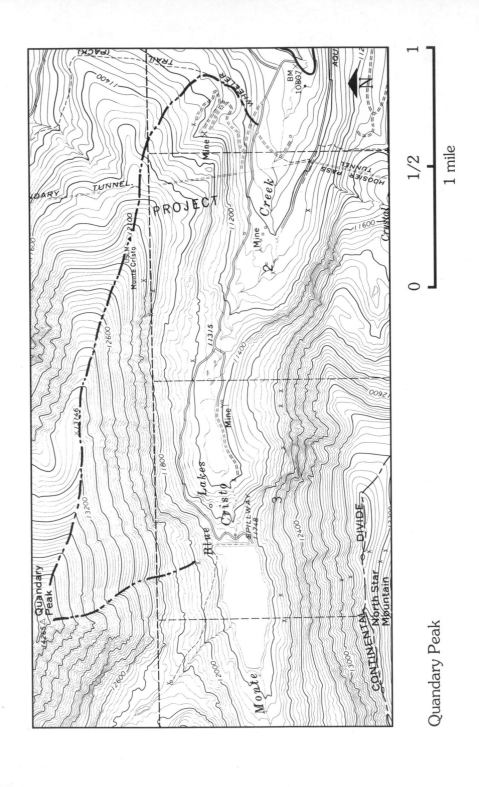

Quandary Peak

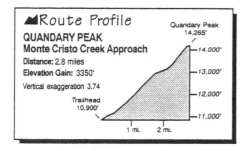

▲Route Profile

QUANDARY PEAK
Monte Cristo Creek Approach
Distance: 2.8 miles
Elevation Gain: 3350'
Vertical exaggeration 3.74
Trailhead
10,900'

Quandary Peak
14,265'
14,000'
13,000'
12,000'
11,000'
1 mi. 2 mi.

Quandary Peak viewed to the north across North Star Peak from Mount Lincoln and showing the prominent descent couloir from the summit. *(Craig F. Koontz)*

THE ROUTES

Monte Cristo Creek

Quandary is a fine family climb as well as an easily accessible winter ascent. On the north side of Hoosier Pass on Colorado 9, eight miles south of Breckenridge or fourteen miles north of Fairplay, on a prominent curve, a road leads west along Monte Cristo Creek to Monte Cristo

Reservoir. Quandary is easily recognizable from the summit of Hoosier Pass as the long-ridged mountain to the northwest. The long east ridge may be reached from any point along the Monte Cristo road. The most gentle approach climbs an old logging road a half-mile west of Colorado 9 to the broad ridge and then west two and one-half miles to the summit. The farther west one goes on the Monte Cristo road, the steeper the summit climb becomes. From the summit, a perfect couloir descends the south face, and in ideal spring or early-summer conditions, it will deposit one squarely at the Monte Cristo Reservoir dam after five minutes and one of the best glissades in the state. Ice axes are required, and careful scrutiny should be made of avalanche conditions.

▲ *Colorado 9 to summit: 2.8 miles, 3,350 feet*

From the summit of Quandary, rugged Pacific Peak (13,950 feet) is a fine view to the northwest. The Monte Cristo Valley also offers an approach to Fletcher Mountain (13,955 feet) to the west, as well as the spectacle of mine buildings clinging to the north slope of North Star to the south like sparrows to telephone lines in a gale.

Mount Lincoln 14,286 feet (8th highest)
Mount Democrat 14,148 feet (29th highest)
Mount Bross 14,172 feet (22nd highest)

If Longs Peak is known as a climber's mountain and Pikes Peak as a tourist's mountain, then history must justly accord Mount Lincoln the title of a miner's mountain. From the first flow of prospectors into the Mosquito Range in the early 1860s to the present, literally every inch of Mount Lincoln and its neighbors, from summit cairns to the valleys below, has felt the ring of miners' picks. All three summits were undoubtedly reached by prospectors and quite possibly by Indians before them.

In June of 1861, Wilbur F. Stone, whose pondering on a mining company title spawned the name "Mosquito" and who later helped to draft Colorado's constitution, ascended the highest peak above Hoosier Pass. After taking thermometer tests, he promptly pronounced it to be over 17,000 feet and returned to the mining camp of Montgomery at the mountain's eastern base to describe the peak's wonders and give it a name. In the best tradition of grand legends, the story is told that after a number of names were suggested, the name of the recently elected president was raised by the crowd as if in one voice, and Mount Lincoln it became.

Stone's estimate, perpetuated by boastful miners, of Lincoln's elevation influenced a number of later atypically high readings. Undoubtedly, casual observers were fooled into believing that Lincoln towered 6,000 to 7,000 feet above the broad expanse of South Park much as the Front Range does above the plains. South Park, however, is already a lofty 10,000 feet. As late as 1867, George Pine recounted in his travelogue *Beyond the West* that the peak was well above 15,000 feet. In style typical of the romantic adventure of the day, Pine wrote a vivid description of

47

Mount Bross (*left*) and Mount Lincoln (*right*) viewed west from Hoosier Pass across Montgomery Reservoir.

Lincoln rising above Montgomery City and concluded, "I never realized such poverty of language as when I stood upon that commanding peak."

Lincoln's two neighbors only broaden the massive appearance of Lincoln. Mount Bross, whose greatest claim to fame may be that it boasts the broadest, roundest summit of the fifty-four, was named for William Bross, who owned mining property near Alma. Bross owed his celebrity status largely to the fact that he served as lieutenant governor of Illinois from 1865 to 1869 and claimed Colorado mining legend "Commodore" Steven Decatur as his long-lost brother, much to the Commodore's denial. Bross made an ascent of Lincoln with Father John Dyer, the famed "Snowshoe Itinerant," in 1876 and was so enthusiastic about the view that local miners began referring to Lincoln's south peak as Mount Bross.

Mount Democrat bore the name of "Buckskin" in the Hayden Atlas, after the rip-roaring Buckskin Joe mining camp northwest of Fairplay. The name "Democrat" does not appear to be documented until the Land Office Survey of 1883. As elsewhere, the great influx of miners in the Mosquitos left countless stories, many bordering on legend if not outright fiction. By one account, however, "Democrat" came from a

Mount Democrat, viewed to the west from the slopes of Mount Bross. *(Lyndon J. Lampert)*

group of rebellious southerners during the Civil War who of course were strongly opposed to Abraham Lincoln.

Although in rapidly deteriorating condition, a number of mining buildings still dot the slopes of the three peaks, reminders of hard-rock miners working claims with names such as Dora, Addie, Crown, Reliance, Snowbird, Moscow, Russia, Alhambra, Balconia, and the Mary, which included the very summit of Mount Bross. Remnants of two of Bross's largest mines, the Dolly Varden and the Moose, still stand near 13,000 feet on the peak's northeast flank. Both silver producers, the mines produced three million dollars by 1878. The Russia Mine, located several hundred feet southeast of Lincoln's summit, was one of the largest operations on that peak and boasted silver ore worth up to five hundred dollars per ton. The Kentucky Belle was the premier operation between Democrat and Bross in the valley above Kite Lake and made its reputation on gold ore assaying out to almost nine hundred dollars per ton on choice loads.

Encircling the eastern slopes of Lincoln and Bross, from Hoosier Pass to Fairplay, was a string of mining towns: Montgomery, Quartzville, Buckskin Joe, Dudleyville, Mosquito, Park City, and Alma. Only Alma survives. Most of the towns were built to serve a particular group of mines.

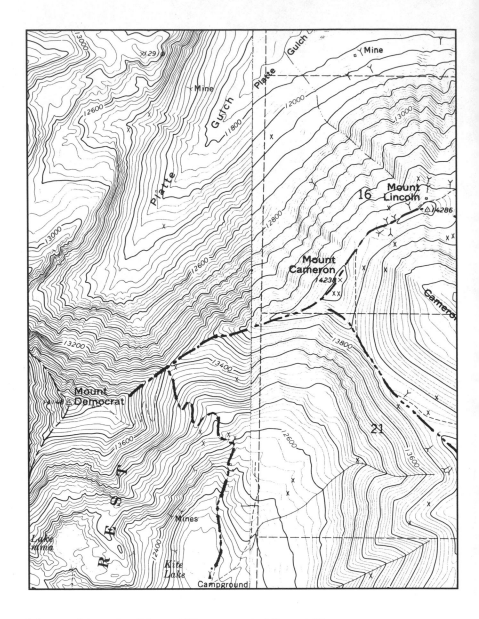

Mount Lincoln, Mount Democrat, Mount Bross

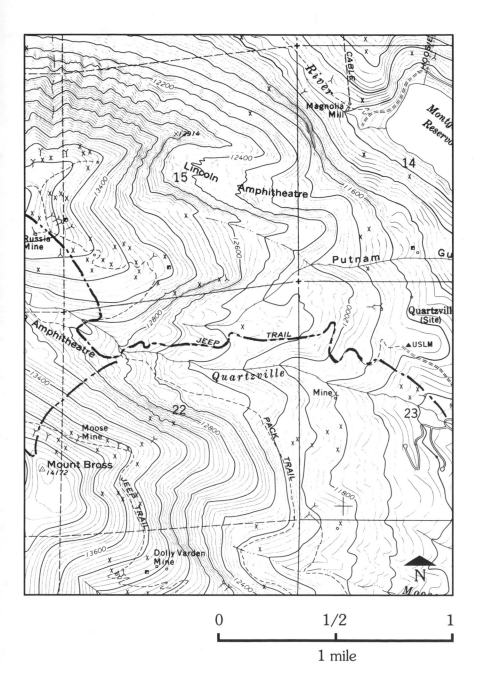

0   1/2   1

1 mile

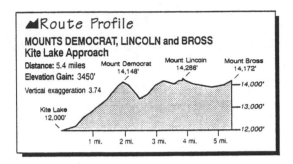

When the mines ceased operations or declined in production, the towns quickly died. Quartzville, for example, served the rich Moose and Dolly Varden claims on Bross. Today, only a few crumbling buildings remain in the shallow bowl at the mouth of the gulch between Lincoln and Bross as reminders of its existence.

THE ROUTES

Although rated as easy climbs technically, Lincoln, Democrat, and Bross all in one day for beginners or the ill-conditioned can be an exhausting experience. Two main approach routes are recommended for all or any combination of the three.

Kite Lake

You may want to have a delicious breakfast at the world-famous Fairplay Hotel before you drive seven miles northwest on Colorado 9 to Alma, then seven miles northwest up Buckskin Gulch on Park County 8 to Kite Lake (12,000 feet). Park County 8 in Alma may not be marked; it is the road leading west from the Texaco station intersection. If, within two or three blocks of Colorado 9, Buckskin Creek does not appear on your left, you are not on the road to Kite Lake. The road may be used by two-wheel-drives up to a steep hill just below the lake.

From the lake, Democrat is a one-mile climb northwest via the Cameron-Democrat saddle and Democrat's northeast ridge. At least one group chose to ascend via the jagged south ridge of Democrat and promptly christened the ridge with a name describing it as a pain in the posterior section of the anatomy. From Democrat, Cameron is one and one-half miles east after an agonizing drop of 750 feet, the greatest drop of the three saddles. From Cameron, Lincoln is an easy stroll northeast along a ridge that stays above 14,000 feet. Then it's back to Cameron and one mile southeast to big, broad Bross, whose summit cairn does stand out slightly in the midst of its spacious summit. The Cameron-Bross saddle dips to a livable 13,850 feet. From Bross's summit, descend southwest back to Kite Lake.

▲ *Kite Lake to Democrat, Lincoln, and Bross, and return: 5.4 miles, 3,450 feet.*

Hoosier Pass Approach

From Alma, continue north on Colorado 9 for two miles to where the road begins to climb Hoosier Pass in earnest. A dirt road leads left (west) on Roberts Lane (marked only with faint signs) across the flats for two-tenths of a mile and then west for two miles on a road that switchbacks and ends amid a housing development at the mouth of the gulch between Lincoln and Bross, a stone's throw from the site of Quartzville. From here, climb west-northwest up the broad southeast shoulder of Mount Lincoln either via the winding mine road that runs clear to 14,000 feet. Once on Lincoln, the geography of the route is the same as the Kite Lake approach save for the long pull back from Democrat and then the return northeast off Bross via a good glissade if conditions are right. Is it our imagination, or is it always windy and stormy in the Mosquitos? Be prepared.

▲ *Road end to Lincoln, Democrat, Bross, and return: 8.5 miles, 4,800 feet.*

Mount Sherman 14,036 feet (45th highest)

At the southern end of the Mosquito Range, inconspicuously situated near more prominent and easily recognizable Horseshoe Mountain, stands Mount Sherman. Sherman missed the early acclaim of the surveys directed toward Mount Lincoln, and it was apparently 1881 before its name appeared on a map of Colorado. Its namesake appears to have been Civil War general William Tecumseh Sherman. As was the case for all of the Mosquitos, mining activity on the mountain was frenzied, and a first ascent by miners in the 1860s is almost a certainty.

Sherman's greatest claim to fame lies with two once-roaring boom towns and one great mine that lay at its base. Horseshoe, incorporated in 1881, once boasted a post office, two stores, two hotels, a smelter, sawmill, and a population of three hundred. The real metropolis of the valley, however, was Leavick. Named for Felix Leavick, an early prospector, the town depended on the revenues of the Hilltop Mine, located on the southern slopes of Mount Sherman. A two-and-one-half-mile aerial tramway carried buckets of silver ore, four hundred pounds per bucket, from the mine shaft to a mill in Leavick. The mill still stands but is rapidly deteriorating. The silver crash of 1893 brought Hilltop operations to a halt almost overnight, but mine owners soon discovered the mine's potential for yielding high-grade zinc ore. Zinc production reached such levels by 1897 that the Denver, South Park and Pacific Railroad built a ten-mile spur from its main line in South Park to Leavick. Much of the grade is visible today.

In 1901, the Hilltop underwent a major renovation that completely electrified the operation and installed new machinery. The *Colorado Mining Directory* of that year showed the Hilltop boasting a 580-foot shaft,

Mount Sherman from campsite above Leavick. *(Gary Koontz)*

800 feet of drifts, and a work crew of thirty men. Production eventually declined until the railroad was abandoned in 1938. Now, only the main mill at Leavick and a few scattered foundations still stand, but as late as the 1940s, Muriel Sibell Wolle, the indomitable sketcher and preserver of ghost-town treasures, was able to visit and sketch a valley full of reminders of a bustling past.

Mount Sherman's broad summit plateau provided an unexpected landing field for a Cessna 310, which was forced down by severe downdrafts in a violent storm in January of 1967. Pilot Jimmy Williamson of Denver, flying a Clinton Air charter en route to Aspen, brought the aircraft to rest in deep snow with only minor injuries to his four passengers. Bitter Colorado weather thwarted rescue efforts for twenty hours until a helicopter piloted by Bob Green of Broomfield plucked the group from the peak.

THE ROUTES

Sherman in recent years has become a traditional "first Fourteener" for those wishing to sample the obsession of climbing. Among seasoned

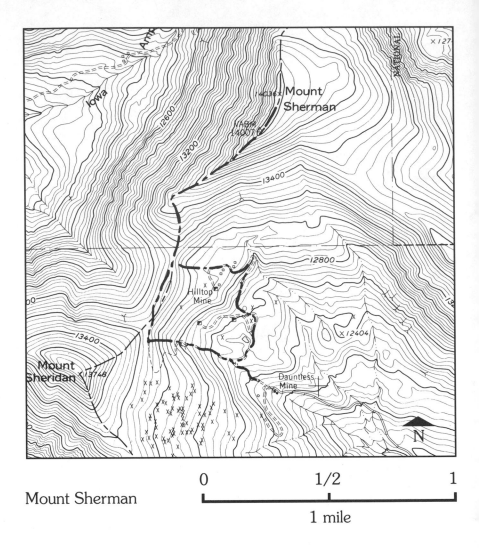

Mount Sherman

0   1/2   1

1 mile

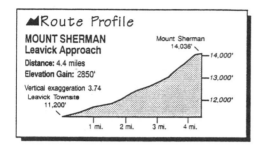

▲⁴Route Profile

MOUNT SHERMAN
Leavick Approach
Distance: 4.4 miles
Elevation Gain: 2850'

Vertical exaggeration 3.74
Leavick Townsite
11,200'

Mount Sherman
14,036'

—14,000'
—13,000'
—12,000'

1 mi.   2 mi.   3 mi.   4 mi.

Fourteener climbers, the mention of its name brings a chorus of hoots and, occasionally, cheers—take, for example, the intrepid climber on the Little Bear-Blanca ridge who, halfway across, came up with the bright idea, "Hey, let's do Sherman instead!" But a word of warning—the mountain is still 14,000 feet and the unpredictable weather of the Mosquitos makes it a mountain to be respected. (Come to think of it, all mountains should be respected.)

From Fairplay, drive south on U.S. 285 one mile to the Fourmile Creek national forest access road and then right (west) eleven miles on a reasonably good dirt road to Leavick (11,200 feet). At least one winter ski expedition reported the eerie presence of miners' ghosts moving silently about the deserted mine workings to the faint hum of machinery. Leavick is posted with No Trespassing signs, and camping is best done along the access road within the national forest boundary. From Leavick, a jeep road leads west-northwest two miles to the Dauntless Mine at 12,200 feet. Climb west to the low point of the Sherman-Sheridan saddle and then northeast up the southwest ridge for a total of one and one-half miles and eighteen hundred feet from the Dauntless. Yes, folks, there really is enough room up there for a football game!

▲ *Leavick to summit: 4.4 miles, 2,850 feet.*

Backbone of the Continent

The Sawatch Range

High, massive, and dominating are three terms that immediately come to mind when describing the Sawatch Range. Anyone who has traveled U.S. 285 and 24 from Salida to Leadville has received a spectacular impression of the Sawatch's nature. Like a row of tremendous granite mammoths, peak upon peak line up to confront the Arkansas Valley—scores of snow-clad summits tower up to 6,000 feet above the river. Fifteen Fourteeners rise in the Sawatch, including the three highest peaks of the Rockies, more than any other range in the contiguous forty-eight states. In a very real sense, the Sawatch is the backbone of the continent.

The Sawatch Range averages about twenty miles in width and stretches from the Eagle River south for ninety miles to Antora Mountain. Bounding the Sawatch are some of Colorado's great rivers: the Arkansas on the east, the Eagle on the north, the Roaring Fork on the northwest, and the Taylor and Gunnison drainages on the west. The Continental Divide is an integral part of the Sawatch's geography, entering the northern part near Tennessee Pass and running the remaining length of the range to south of Marshall Pass.

The Sawatch Range is indeed a physically impressive range, but unlike the Tetons, for example, Sawatch peaks are generally more impressive for their massiveness and overall altitude than for their ruggedness. Nevertheless, there are a number of localities in the Sawatch—such as the areas around Ice Mountain, La Plata Peak, and the Mount of the Holy Cross—that equal any of the ranges in Colorado for alpine ruggedness in the form of great rock faces and bristling ridges.

Geologically, the Sawatch Range is quite straightforward, being essentially a faulted anticline with Tertiary intrusions and one extrusion. The

59

largest and most important intrusion is the Princeton Batholith, which extends the width of the range from Mount Princeton to Mount Shavano. This batholith is composed largely of granite and quartz monzonite and is responsible for both the Chalk Cliffs of Mount Princeton and the gem field of Mount Antero.

Associated with this Tertiary igneous activity was the mineralization of much of the Sawatch Range. Silver, lead, gold, and other minerals crystallized into many of the cracks and fissures in the Precambrian core of the Sawatch, forming veins that became the attraction for hordes of fortune seekers beginning in the 1860s. Silver was the most commonly mined mineral in the Sawatch, but the best deposits of both silver and gold lay just beyond the outer slopes of the Sawatch peaks in such locations as Leadville, Aspen, and Tincup.

By 1880, numerous mining camps had grown up in almost every valley of the Sawatch. In addition, crude roads were constructed up the valleys and even across the range to connect with mining camps west of the Divide. Monarch, Tincup, Cottonwood, Independence, and Marshall passes were just a few of the routes used by miners to reach the vast country of the Western Slope.

Many of the Sawatch peaks were undoubtedly first climbed and named by miners in the 1870s. The name "Sawatch" appears as early as 1853, apparently a derivation from an Indian word meaning "water of the blue earth," and originally applied to a large lake that once existed in the San Luis Valley.

Concurrent with the mining activity was a comprehensive survey of the Sawatch, undertaken in 1873, as part of Ferdinand Vandeveer Hayden's larger survey of the West under the auspices of the United States Department of the Interior. Hayden's men climbed a number of Sawatch giants, including Elbert, Massive, La Plata, and Harvard.

The dire need for cheap transportation into the booming mining camps of western Colorado drew narrow-gauge railroads into the Sawatch by 1880. General William Jackson Palmer's Denver and Rio Grande Railway and John Evans's Denver, South Park, and Pacific became involved in a great race to be the first to throw rails across the Sawatch and tap the wealth of the Gunnison country. The only standard-gauge railroad to cross the Sawatch was the Colorado Midland, boring under the Continental Divide with Hagerman Tunnel, west of Leadville, in 1887.

Recent history in the Sawatch has focused on water-diversion projects. Small diversion ditches in the vicinity of Tennessee Pass captured and transported water from the Western Slope to the Arkansas Valley in the early 1900s. The largest diversion project in the range is the Twin Lakes facility, completed in 1935 as part of the New Deal. The Homestake Project was built to divert upper Eagle River water for use by the communities of Aurora and Colorado Springs. The proposed diversion project Homestake II, an attempt since the 1970s to divert even more water from the Holy Cross Wilderness, has so far been successfully challenged by the Holy Cross Wilderness Defense Fund.

Like the Front Range, the Sawatch has seen a heavy increase in tourism and accompanying development during the 1980s and 1990s. Whitewater rafting on the Arkansas River has burgeoned into an industry, and summer-home developments now reach well up the eastern slopes of parts of the range. The mining heritage of the Sawatch and all of the West is celebrated in the National Mining Hall of Fame, which established its home in Leadville.

The 1993 Colorado Wilderness Bill added the small but important Spruce Creek Wilderness Area west of Mount Massive to the range's existing wilderness areas. The Holy Cross, Collegiate Peaks, and Mount Massive wilderness areas, totaling almost 320,000 acres, are an important refuge at the core of the range. On its path from Denver to Durango, the Colorado Trail winds through much of the Sawatch, mostly on the path of the old Main Range Trail. The proposed American Discovery Trail will soon cross the range from Aspen to Leadville as it links the East and West coasts of our country and promotes local trail networks.

Mount of the Holy Cross 14,005 feet (52nd highest)

The aura of legend, history, and religious significance that has surrounded the Mount of the Holy Cross makes it one of the most notable
of all of the peaks in Colorado, and perhaps even the United States.
Isolated in the heart of the northern Sawatch and hidden from the east
by Notch Mountain, the peak was enveloped in an air of mystery for
years, and many felt that the huge white cross upon its side was more
legend than fact. Upon verification of its existence, however, the peak
vaulted into the national limelight, overnight becoming a grand symbol
of the Christian faith. Thousands of photographic reproductions and
paintings of the peak were circulated worldwide, and for a few years
Christians in the United States had a site to which they could make a
bona fide pilgrimage within their own country.

The cross itself lies on the northeast face of the peak and is composed
of a vertical couloir twenty-five to fifty feet wide and fifteen hundred feet
long. The horizontal arm of the cross is approximately 750 feet long and
is an outward-sloping bench that collects more snow than does the steeper
surrounding rock face. Geologically, the upright of the cross was formed
from the weathering of a seam of schist, which was much less resistant
than the gneiss that borders on either side. Although the cross has lost
some of its grandeur today, it is still obviously a cross formation and still
impressive.

The origins of the naming of the Mount of the Holy Cross are extremely
obscure, rooted more deeply in legend than in fact. A number of legends
deal with sightings of the cross by early Spanish explorers. Another legend
claims discovery by lost priests from New Mexico in the 1700s. Like most
legends, however, these stories are not supported by facts. Holy Cross

Looking south on the approach to the Mount of the Holy Cross. The cross couloir is out of sight behind the left-hand ridge, and the traditional route follows the right-hand ridge.

was probably first sighted from a distance by an unknown trapper or miner who reported his sighting to someone else who embellished the story, and gradually the mysterious mountain became known by word of mouth.

The first official sighting of the peak was by William H. Brewer, who ascended Grays Peak on August 29, 1869. He described the view from the summit, and his casual reference to the Mount of the Holy Cross, far in the distance, indicates that by 1869 the mountain was fairly well known, although its location was not yet pinpointed.

In 1873, the Hayden Survey made locating the Mount of the Holy Cross one of its primary objectives. The fascinating account of the discovery and the most complete work on the Mount of the Holy Cross is Robert L. Brown's *Holy Cross—The Mountain and the City*. William Henry Jackson, the famed western photographer, was the main character in the story. Jackson traveled with the Hayden Survey in 1873 as the official photographer, and on August 23, after numerous false starts and great difficulty passing through fallen timber, Jackson ascended Notch Mountain and took the now-famous first photographs of the cross.

Meanwhile, J. T. Gardner and W. H. Holmes made the first ascent of the mountain itself. When the team returned to civilization with the news of their discovery and the photographs, the fame of the peak was inevitable.

A measure of the peak's sudden rise to fame can be seen by noting its incorporation into the arts soon after its discovery. Thomas Moran, the noted English artist and painter of western scenes, was greatly inspired by Jackson's original photographs and made a trip to the peak in 1874. Afterward, Moran completed a number of paintings featuring the legendary mountain, the best of which measures seven feet, ten inches by six feet and now hangs in England. Other smaller originals also exist, and countless reproductions are found throughout the world.

In 1880, free gold was discovered not far to the east of the Mount of the Holy Cross, and placer discoveries were made along Homestake Creek, south of the mountain. With these discoveries the Holy Cross Mining District was established, and several hastily built communities appeared there. One community was located in the Homestake drainage just four miles south of the Mount of the Holy Cross. Although the peak itself was not visible from the camp, it soon acquired the name of Holy Cross City anyway. Mines such as the Pelican, Molly, Comstock, and Treasure Vault produced enough ore to attract about three hundred people to the community. The town consisted of two rows of houses, two general stores, the Timberline Hotel, two saloons, and a hodgepodge of other buildings.

Despite a promising beginning, Holy Cross City was doomed to fade after only four years because of the severe winters, poor transportation in the remote area, and a slowdown in mineral production. Brief resurgences of activity occurred in the late 1890s and in 1927, but these were minor, and Holy Cross City has been a true ghost town since about 1900.

In 1912, O. W. Daggett and Cole McDougal climbed the peak via the most direct route—the upright of the cross. Their hopes of a possible first ascent by this route were dashed, however, when they discovered a two-hundred-foot-long climbing rope that had been left in the upper part of the cross. Other ascents up the cross were made by experienced parties in the years that followed, and numerous rock routes were pioneered on the east face.

Also in 1912, the forerunner of the famous Holy Cross pilgrimages took place when three Episcopal priests held Eucharist on the summit of Notch Mountain. The organized pilgrimages began in the 1920s, largely due to the efforts of Father John P. Carrigan of Glenwood Springs. In 1928, 218 persons went on the pilgrimage to Notch Mountain; by 1932, the number had grown to two thousand. By this time, the entire area around the mountain had taken on a sacred air. A snow formation to the right of the cross became known as the Supplicating Virgin, and a lake at the base of the mountain was the Bowl of Tears. In addition, many miraculous healings were reported by either actual pilgrims or by those who had sent their handkerchiefs with pilgrims, a practice taken from scripture. Ironically, in 1938, just as these pilgrimages were at their height, they were halted by the United States Army, which controlled the surrounding area as a military reservation until 1950.

In 1929, the Mount of the Holy Cross National Monument was established by President Herbert Hoover, but it was abolished in 1950. The reason for this status loss was the reported deterioration of the right arm of the cross. Some claim that the arm has not deteriorated at all but that the quality of the cross merely fluctuates from year to year depending on sun, wind, and snow deposition. However, it is likely that some degree of deterioration has occurred from rock slides. Nevertheless, in 1951, a stamp honoring Colorado's seventh-fifth anniversary was issued that featured the peak with its cross in perfect form. Interestingly, in the more than one hundred years since its discovery, the cross has apparently never been in as fine form as when William Henry Jackson took those first photographs.

Earlier editions of this guide reported that the first winter ascent of Holy Cross occurred in January 1966. Some careful research by mountaineering historian Joe Kramarsic set the record straight. The January 21, 1944, edition of the *Camp Hale Ski-zette* reported that Corporal Russell Keene, Private William Ferguson, and Private Howard Freedman, all medics on duty at Camp Hale, reached the summit of Holy Cross on the day after Christmas 1943 after a three-day outing. Their route was from the south via Gold Park and Hunky Dory Lakes. At least three previous attempts by Camp Hale personnel to make a first winter ascent had been terminated the year before by strong winds. "The most fortunate part of the trip was the total absence of the winds which turned back last year's parties," the paper reported. An unusual occurrence indeed in Colorado's high country!

The January 2, 1966, ascent was made by three Holy Cross College students and Vail guide Jerry Sinkovec via Half Moon Pass. A fourth student became ill with the flu and remained at the old cabin on East Cross Creek. The climbers were all rugby players who had been prompted to make the climb by a challenge from the college newspaper, which offered a prize of $1,966 to any student who climbed the peak in winter.

The prize was quickly withdrawn to discourage reckless forays into Colorado's winter environment, but this climb took place nonetheless. With high winds and deep snow, it proved to be a four-day epic that Sinkovec later described as the toughest winter climb he had ever made. Winter ascents of the Mount of the Holy Cross are no longer rare, but they are frequently as grueling.

On July 8, 1973, a tragic fatality and a daring rescue took place on the upright of the cross. Dick Boss and Ron Dillon were roped together, descending the cross, when Boss slipped and began sliding down the treacherous couloir. Having lost control of his ice axe, he could not self-arrest, and Dillon prepared to arrest his partner's fall. The momentum of Boss's body was too great, however, and soon both were racing wildly down the snow. Near the bottom of the cross a cliff appeared, and both went hurtling over the edge. Boss was killed on impact but, miraculously, Dillon was thrown clear from the cliff and landed injured but alive in the snow two hundred feet below. Other climbers in the party went for help, and hours later a dramatic effort by helicopter pilot Len Casdorf rescued Dillon, who later spent a month recuperating in a Denver hospital. This incident reinforces the fact that the Mount of the Holy Cross, although a beautiful peak and one with a fascinating history, can be dangerous to those who venture onto its northeast face without adequate experience in mountaineering techniques.

THE ROUTES

Half Moon Pass

Extensive camping in fragile areas along East Cross Creek has resulted in the forest service initiating a permit system for camping here. There is also the possibility that day use may be limited. For the latest information, contact the Holy Cross Ranger District of the White River National Forest in Minturn at (303) 827-5717.

Because of the camping restrictions and fragile nature of wetlands in this area, it is highly recommended that this climb be done in one day. Please note, however, that this will be a significant undertaking, particularly in gaining almost a thousand feet of elevation on the return over Half Moon Pass. Make certain that everyone in your group is conditioned for the trip.

From two miles south of Minturn on U.S. 24, just before the highway crosses the Eagle River and begins to climb Battle Mountain, turn west

Mount of the Holy Cross

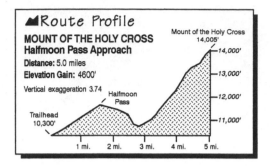

▲Route Profile

MOUNT OF THE HOLY CROSS
Halfmoon Pass Approach
Distance: 5.0 miles
Elevation Gain: 4600'

Vertical exaggeration 3.74

Mount of the Holy Cross
14,005'

Halfmoon Pass

Trailhead
10,300'

14,000'
13,000'
12,000'
11,000'

1 mi. 2 mi. 3 mi. 4 mi. 5 mi.

for six miles to Tigiwon Campground and two more miles to Half Moon Campground (at 10,400 feet). The road is rough but passable by two-wheel-drives and climbs on switchbacks through aspen and pine. From Half Moon Campground, the Half Moon Pass trail leads two miles to Half Moon Pass (at 11,600 feet) and then descends two miles and nine hundred feet to East Cross Creek—a rather discouraging way to begin a climb!

From the crossing of East Cross Creek, follow the trail west. This trail skirts west of the cliffs at the end of Holy Cross's north ridge and then climbs up to and traverses the broad north ridge. Follow the ridge south to the final summit cone, which is climbed from the west. Descend the same way, taking care to stay on the trail.

A direct approach via the cross involves a series of cliffs at its base and a fifteen-hundred-foot technical snow and ice climb. It should be attempted only by experienced parties fully cognizant of rock and avalanche conditions. Do not attempt a descent of the cross couloir if you have climbed the standard route.

▲ *Half Moon Campground to summit: 5 miles, 4,600 feet, plus 900 feet on the return to Half Moon Pass.*

Mount Massive 14,421 feet (2nd highest)

Massive—there's really no other name for it. With five main points above 14,000 feet and a broad three-mile summit crest, the mountain *is* massive. Henry Gannett climbed, named, and mapped the mountain for the Hayden Survey in 1873. Little did he know that the name he gave it, despite its appropriateness, would cause so much fervor in the years ahead.

By 1880, Leadville, at the mountain's base, was a booming silver camp eagerly awaiting the arrival of not just one but two railroads. As the fortunes of Horace Tabor, Molly Brown, and Baby Doe rose and fell, Leadville residents became quite fond of "old Massive." Its presence was felt on the town year-round—from the warm sunbeams of a cool summer morning first kissing its summit to the bone-chilling below-zero nights when bitter winds from its slopes sent snow piling up a dozen feet. Yup, it was massive all right!

With such an appropriate name, it was only a matter of time before someone would suggest changing it. The first attempt occurred in 1901, when the *Denver Post* thought it would be "most appropriate" to rename the peak "Mount McKinley" after the recently assassinated President William McKinley. The *Leadville Herald-Democrat* immediately championed a petition drive against the change. The petition, which soon boasted a thousand local signatures, was sent to the U.S. Board of Geographic Names. The board's chairman replied that he agreed with local sentiment—after all, there already was one Mount McKinley, and the name "Massive" was very descriptive. The chairman's name was Henry Gannett.

Doubtless Gannett would have voiced a similar opinion some twenty years later, when an attempt was made to rename the peak none other

69

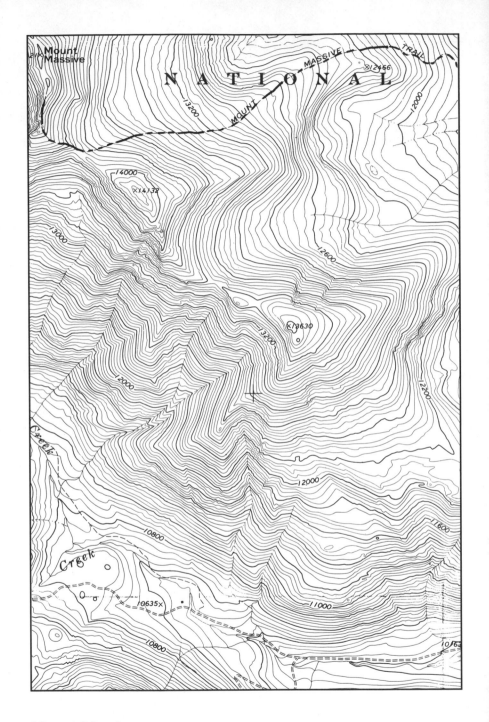

Mount Massive

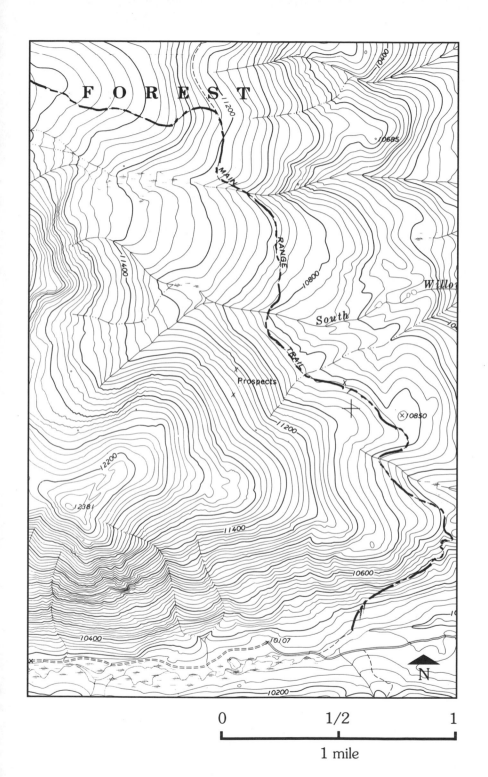

Mount Massive from the east; the mountain is indeed massive. *(Photograph courtesy Colorado Historical Society)*

than "Gannett Peak." A six-year fight by the Colorado Mountain Club and Leadville residents finally reversed a preliminary decision to call the peak Gannett, and the name Massive was restored.

In 1965, State Senator John Bermingham, R-Denver, tried to turn a "Third-Time's-the-Charm" by seeking to rename the peak "Mount Churchill," in honor of the late Sir Winston Churchill. Although Massive's character is well suited to that of England's most famous bulldog, local sentiment again prevailed, and the proposal was defeated. It is hoped that, once and for all, Massive's name is secure.

THE ROUTES

Mount Massive Trail

From Malta, three miles west of Leadville on U.S. 24 at the collection of trailers, take Colorado 300 west three-quarters of a mile to Lake County 11. Turn south (left) on Lake County 11 and follow it six and one-half miles to the trailhead, bearing right at the Y in the road at the gravel pit after one mile; pass Halfmoon West Campground after five

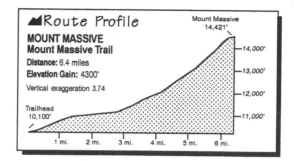

▲Route Profile

MOUNT MASSIVE
Mount Massive Trail
Distance: 6.4 miles
Elevation Gain: 4300'
Vertical exaggeration 3.74

Trailhead
10,100'

Mount Massive
14,421'

14,000'
13,000'
12,000'
11,000'

1 mi. 2 mi. 3 mi. 4 mi. 5 mi. 6 mi.

miles. Elbert Creek Campground is just east of the trailhead. This is the old Main Range Trail, now designated the Colorado Trail. Heading north leads to Mount Massive and hiking south climbs toward Mount Elbert.

From the trailhead, the Main Range/Colorado Trail rolls along Massive's eastern flank, crossing several small streams in the process. Hike north on it for three miles to a west (left) junction with the Mount Massive Trail at 11,250 feet. The Mount Massive Trail climbs steeply to timberline and then proceeds west through willows and rolling tundra up broad slopes and into the cirque between Massive's main summit and 14,132-foot South Massive. Follow the trail all the way to the saddle between these two peaks before turning north (right) along the final summit ridge. Follow the ridge north over small rocky steps to the summit. On the descent, unless snow affords an appropriate glissade southeast to the trail, return all the way to the saddle before descending. Many people have shortcut this section of trail; consequently, the slopes here are heavily eroded.

The western approaches to Mount Massive via North Halfmoon Creek should be avoided except by small groups on extended backpacks because of the severe environmental impacts caused by climbers.

▲ *Trailhead to summit: 6.4 miles, 4,300 feet.*

Mount Elbert 14,433 feet (Highest point in Colorado)

Of the three thousand miles of Rocky Mountain peaks, only one can claim the honor of being the highest: Colorado's Mount Elbert. In addition, only California's 14,495-foot Mount Whitney is higher in the contiguous forty-eight states. Mount Elbert rises above the Arkansas Valley in a gigantic mass with its distinguishing long, smooth ridges. Consequently, Mount Elbert gives the appearance of a mountain at rest, seemingly comfortably confident of its status as the monarch of the Rockies.

Although some question surrounds the exact date of its naming, it was the namesake of Samuel Elbert, who first came to Colorado Territory in 1862 as secretary to Governor John Evans. Elbert furthered his political fortunes in 1865 by marrying Evans's daughter, Josephine. In March of 1873, after serving in the territorial legislature, he was appointed territorial governor by President Ulysses S. Grant. Elbert served an inglorious term of less than one year between two controversial terms of Edward McCook—terms marked by the worst of the Grant administration scandals. Such service by Elbert hardly deserved recognition on Colorado's tallest mountain, but Elbert did go on to serve twenty years on the state supreme court after statehood was granted in 1876.

Not only has Mount Elbert's role as the Colorado high point made it suffer the indignity of countless tests of its altitude, but the peak also has witnessed just about every assault imaginable. Elbert's first documented ascent was by H. W. Stuckle of the Hayden Survey, in 1874. In recent years, however, its summit has been reached by jeep, bicycle, all-terrain vehicle, and even helicopter, when a *Denver Post* photographer left an evening edition under a rock at the summit cairn, presumably for a literate

Mount Elbert with its prominent eastern cirque and northeast ridge.

Mount Elbert from U.S. 285 near Granite.

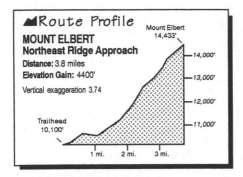

pika. Despite years of talk, Elbert never has had a road built to its summit. We hope this is one indignity it will never have to suffer.

THE ROUTES

Despite the fact that Mount Elbert can be, and has been, climbed from almost every point on the compass, the Forest Service recommends the Halfmoon Creek approach, with the Mount Elbert Trail as a strong second choice.

Halfmoon Creek, Northeast Ridge Trail

From the Main Range/Colorado Trailhead (10,060 feet) on the Halfmoon Creek road (see page 72), hike south on the trail, climbing steeply southeast to the top of a ridge (10,600 feet). Here, the trail levels out for about one-half mile, and you can relax in preparation for the remaining 3,800 vertical feet. When the Main Range/Colorado Trail appears to drop steeply into the Box Creek valley, don't panic; just continue following it on down for another quarter-mile, where a right-hand fork angles up-slope. Follow the right-hand fork (which may or may not be signed) west as it climbs steeply to timberline, one mile distant. From timberline, the trail continues and gains Elbert's northeast ridge at about 12,700 feet. From here, it is simply a climb up the northeast ridge to the right (northwest) of the Box Creek cirque and on to the gentle summit, one and one-half miles.

▲ *Trailhead to summit: 3.8 miles, 4,400 feet.*

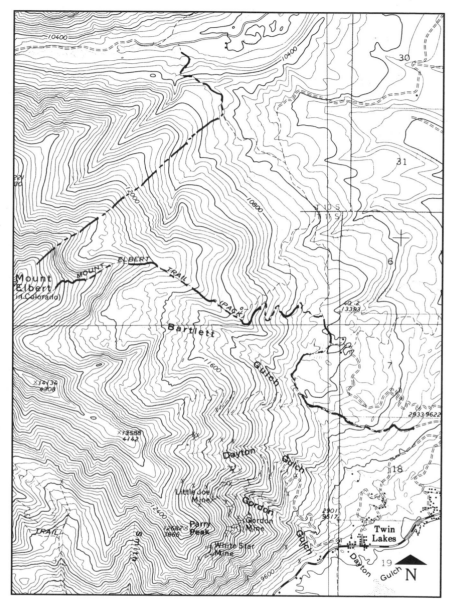

Mount Elbert

1 mile

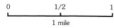

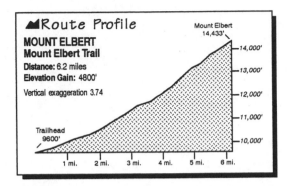

▲Route Profile

MOUNT ELBERT
Mount Elbert Trail

Distance: 6.2 miles
Elevation Gain: 4800'

Vertical exaggeration 3.74

Mount Elbert
14,433'

Trailhead
9600'

14,000'
13,000'
12,000'
11,000'
10,000'

1 mi. 2 mi. 3 mi. 4 mi. 5 mi. 6 mi.

Colorado Trail, Mount Elbert Trail

From U.S. 24 south of Leadville, head west on Colorado 82 for four miles to Lake County 24. Turn north (right) on Lake County 24 and follow it one mile to Lake View Campground. The Colorado Trail passes through the western end of the campground. Hike west and then north on the Colorado Trail for two miles, to its junction with the Mount Elbert Trail. Several recent guidebooks direct you to a series of roads that climb about another six hundred feet and bring you about a mile closer; however, this route leads through some pristine wetlands and is not very well defined. Please use the established Colorado Trail.

From the Colorado Trail/Mount Elbert Trail junction, the Mount Elbert Trail switchbacks west, steeply at first, and then contours northwest to the long ridge separating the Box Creek cirque from the Bartlett Gulch cirque. As the trail breaks timberline, it is actually a two-track road. More switchbacks lead farther west with views north into the Box Creek cirque. Once above the cirque, the trail again contours south of the main summit before the final set of switchbacks lead directly north to the summit. Staying on the trail during this final approach may be impossible early in the season, when snow will cover much of this stretch, but later in the season please follow the trail.

▲ *Lakeview Campground trailhead to summit: 6.2 miles, 4,800 feet.*

La Plata Peak 14,336 feet (5th highest)

La Plata Peak rises six miles south of Mount Elbert among the row of mountains that separates Lake and Clear creeks. Unlike many of its neighbors, La Plata has a rugged personality all of its own, and thus stands out in the midst of many less dramatic Sawatch peaks. Being such an impressive mountain, La Plata has long captured the attention of both the casual traveler and the serious mountaineer.

It is probable that La Plata was first ascended by miners in the late 1860s or early 1870s, for numerous high silver mines were located in its vicinity, especially to the south. However, the first recorded climb was made by members of the Hayden Survey on July 26, 1873. They gave the peak its name, which means "silver" in Spanish. William N. Byers, the colorful editor of the *Rocky Mountain News,* and no stranger to mountaineering, accompanied this portion of the survey and sent running accounts to be published in his Denver paper. Byers followed chief topographer James Gardner and others to the summit via the northwest ridge and noted with vivid description the abundance of raspberries, strawberries, and sky blue forget-me-nots found far above timberline. Upon reaching the summit, Byers was awed by the magnificent view and wrote, "The world seems made of mountains; a chaotic mass of rocky ridges, peaks and spurs," a description *every* Colorado mountaineer readily understands.

The most spectacular single feature of La Plata Peak is its northeast ridge, an incredibly narrow, rugged, and exposed two-mile collection of pinnacles, cuts, and rock faces. This ridge was quite naturally avoided by the early climbers of La Plata, but as climbing techniques became more sophisticated in the 1900s, it was destined that the challenge of this ragged

Looking south to La Plata Peak from the summit of Mount Elbert. Ellingwood Ridge is in the foreground. *(Lyndon J. Lampert)*

ridge would soon lure some daring climber into attempting it. That daring climber was Albert R. Ellingwood.

Albert Ellingwood probably contributed more to the development of technical climbing in Colorado than did any other person. Born in 1888 in Iowa, Ellingwood attended high school in Colorado Springs; in 1910 he was awarded a Rhodes Scholarship. After being graduated from Oxford with a degree in civil law, Ellingwood taught as a professor of political science in Colorado and Illinois, and from 1931 until his death in 1934 he was an assistant dean at Northwestern University.

While in England attending Oxford, Ellingwood engaged in rock climbing and soon learned the virtues of safe climbing techniques with the use of a rope. He brought this invaluable knowledge back to the States, and in the years that followed he was able to pioneer many climbs previously thought to be impossible. Included in these were the first ascents of the Crestones, Lizard Head, Middle Teton, South Teton, and what was only the third ascent of the Grand Teton. In addition, Ellingwood pioneered many new routes on other peaks, such as the Ellingwood Arête on the Crestone Needle and the threatening northeast ridge of La Plata Peak, now appropriately named "Ellingwood Ridge."

Ellingwood met the challenge of the ridge that would one day bear his name in 1921. Climbing with Robert Ormes and two others, Ellingwood departed from the rest of the party to attack the ridge solo and was not heard from until he showed up at camp late in the evening. Ellingwood had conquered the ridge and gleefully reported that he had dangled from a finger ledge for two full minutes. He obviously enjoyed the tricky problems of technical mountaineering, and it was not long before Ellingwood Ridge became renowned as one of the classic technical climbs of the Sawatch.

In the years that followed, numerous parties succeeded in making summer ascents of Ellingwood Ridge, but all attempts at a grueling winter ascent failed. On March 19, 1960, Karl Pfiffner, George Hurley, and Ron Bierstadt began climbing Ellingwood Ridge, but they were forced to retreat due to oncoming darkness. On the descent, at about timberline, the trio entered a small, steep basin. An extremely cold winter followed by a sudden warming trend had produced a deep layer of unstable hoar snow beneath the surface crust, and the snow of the basin slid, carrying with it all three men. Hurley and Bierstadt quickly extricated themselves, but their partner Pfiffner could not be found. His body was finally located by a rescue party at the foot of the three-hundred-foot-long slide the following morning.

The Pfiffner accident put a damper on winter attempts of Ellingwood Ridge until January 12, 1974, when Craig Koontz, Gary Kocsis, Chuck Tolton, and John Lafferty began an assault on the ridge. The experienced team had planned a two-day climb but, hampered by strong winds, snow-covered pitches, and difficult route-finding, they extended it far longer. Finally, on the afternoon of January 15, after four days on the ridge, the four men stood on the summit of La Plata Peak.

Approximately seven miles to the west of La Plata Peak is Grizzly Peak, lying on the Continental Divide. Grizzly was formerly rated at an even 14,000 feet, but in 1965, the U.S. Geological Survey revised this figure to 13,988 feet. Nevertheless, even though it is now out of the Fourteener club, Grizzly deserves mention as a notable mountain well worth climbing.

Grizzly Peak, like La Plata, was probably first climbed by miners in search of silver, but the first recorded ascent was made by members of the Hayden Survey. Reportedly, they observed a grizzly bear floating on an iceberg in a lake at the base of this peak, resulting in the name. Unfortunately, the several Colorado mountains that bear the name Grizzly are anachronisms, because the silvertips may be extinct in the state.

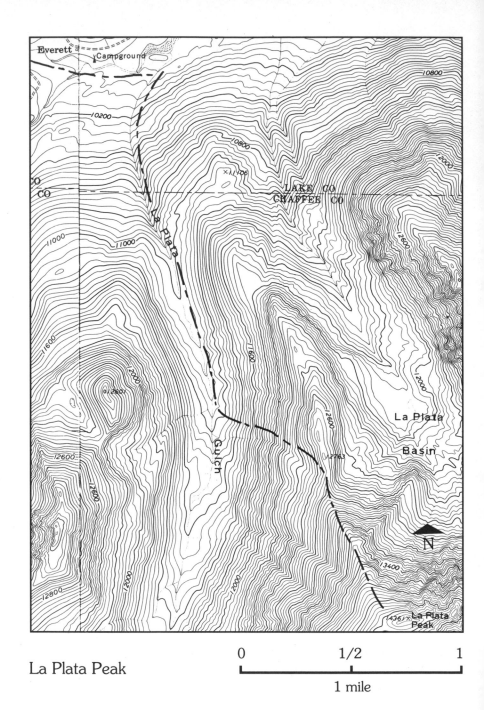

La Plata Peak

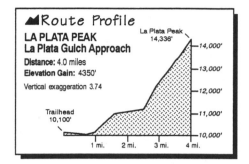

▲▲Route Profile
LA PLATA PEAK
La Plata Gulch Approach
Distance: 4.0 miles
Elevation Gain: 4350'
Vertical exaggeration 3.74

La Plata Peak
14,336'
—14,000'
—13,000'
—12,000'

Trailhead
10,100'
—11,000'
—10,000'

1 mi.   2 mi.   3 mi.   4 mi.

THE ROUTES

La Plata Gulch

From the junction of U.S. 24 and Colorado 82, drive west on Colorado 82 for fourteen miles to the junction of Lake Creek and its South Fork. Here, a dirt road leads south across a wooden bridge over Lake Creek. Park in the wide area just west of the intersection and walk south on the dirt road. Immediately across the bridge, an unmarked path leads east (left) along the south side of Lake Creek. Follow the path or its minor variations for a quarter-mile to near the major obstacle of the climb—the South Fork of Lake Creek. The described path network ends on the old campground road as it curves south perhaps several hundred yards south of Lake Creek. Do not follow the road south, but rather, at its easternmost point, hike east several hundred yards toward the sound of the South Fork. (Do not follow main Lake Creek to the South Fork confluence.) The South Fork has cut several different channels over the years, but currently the main eastern channel is crossed by a crude and exposed log bridge just before the stream plunges into a small gorge above its confluence with Lake Creek. Given the exposure, a fixed rope across the log may be desirable. Once across the South Fork, continue east along the south side of Lake Creek for almost one-half mile to La Plata Gulch Creek. A trail runs south along the east side of the gulch for two miles to timberline. Then, angle east (left) to La Plata's northwest ridge, 1,600 steep feet above. Once on the ridge, the summit is less than one mile south. Hard work by a Colorado Mountain Club trail crew during the summer of 1993 made real progress improving one well-defined trail from timberline to the summit ridge. This area is badly eroded from overuse and is crisscrossed by a myriad of braided trails. Please stay on the main trail during your descent.

▲ *South Fork Bridge to summit: 4 miles, 4,350 feet.*

Mount Oxford 14,153 feet (27th highest)
Mount Belford 14,197 feet (19th highest)
Missouri Mountain 14,067 feet (36th highest)

While the attention of the surveys focused on Mount Elbert and Mount Harvard, a ridge of three fourteen-thousand-foot-plus points rising between the two was largely ignored. The three peaks, resembling the gentle rolling humps of a camel's back, were mapped in the Hayden Atlas but not named. Indeed, a key reason for the scant attention they received is their lack of any distinctive or striking features.

During the silver boom of the early 1880s, miners rode up Clear Creek north of the peaks and established a string of boom towns: Beaver City, Silverdale, Vicksburg, Rockdale, and Winfield. Today, only the remnants of Vicksburg and Winfield survive, testaments to the preservation work of the Clear Creek Canyon Historical Society of Chaffee County. Society members have restored a number of buildings in an attempt to keep souvenir hunters from carrying the towns off piece by piece to a thousand backyards scattered across the country.

Sometime during the mining rush, miners from the Show Me state of Missouri decided to show locals their fondness for the folks back home, and Missouri Gulch, Missouri Basin, and Missouri Mountain, the western-most of the three peaks, were named. Which came first is a case of the proverbial chicken and egg; history has recorded no better explanation.

Likewise, history cannot pinpoint a date when some barrel-chested miner swung his pick into the ground and declared, "By gum, let's name that thar peak for old Jim Belford." James B. Belford was Colorado's first congressman after statehood was achieved and a powerful voice for the free coinage of silver. Belford's flaming red hair and fiery oratory earned him the nickname "The Red-Headed Rooster of the Rockies." The miners followed Belford's silver speeches with keen interest, and in

Mount Belford viewed to the south from Missouri Gulch.

time his name became associated with the peak identifiable by its reddish rock outcropping on the summit. Prospect holes cover the mountain, including the very summit, and are evidence that the miners were very familiar with the land above timberline.

Recognition of the Oxford, Belford, and Missouri massif received a boost in 1925 when Albert Ellingwood (see page 80) and Stephen H. Hart took transit sightings on "an unnamed mountain with three summits of 14,000 feet altitude north and east [sic] of Mount Harvard" from the summits of Harvard and Columbia. Six years later, in 1931, John L. Jerome Hart, brother of Stephen, pondered over naming the peak while compiling his classic *Fourteen Thousand Feet*. In keeping with Collegiate Peaks tradition, he christened it Mount Oxford after the university attended by Ellingwood and Stephen Hart. By no small coincidence, John Hart was also a Rhodes Scholar. Both Hart brothers became eminent Denver lawyers and public servants, Stephen Hart as chairman of the board of the Colorado Historical Society and John Hart as president of the American Alpine Club.

Although their broad ridges and gentle slopes make Oxford and Belford rather dull mountains for the adventurous climber, both peaks are exceptionally good beginner or family climbs. Missouri Mountain, however,

Mount Oxford viewed to the southeast from Belford's north ridge. Mount Harvard is visible over the Oxford-Belford saddle at the extreme right. *(Gary Koontz)*

offers an exception to the broad, gentle ridge description, and on one occasion it tragically snuffed out the lives of two climbers. On Saturday, July 3, 1976, Kim Wickholm, twenty-one, and Sharon Barnes, twenty-nine, fell to their deaths down a northeast-face couloir. Some mystery surrounds the accident; one possible explanation is that the couple reached the summit in the fading twilight via an easy route and then, in an attempt to get off the mountain by darkness, tried to descend the steep couloir. The fact that Wickholm was an experienced climber and that both were well equipped only deepens the mystery.

THE ROUTES

Missouri Gulch, Oxford and Belford

From U.S. 24 fourteen miles north of Buena Vista, turn left (west) at Clear Creek Reservoir and drive eight miles to Vicksburg (9,700 feet) and a trailhead parking area on the south side of the road. Cross Clear Creek on a forest service bridge and hike two miles south into upper

Missouri Mountain as seen to the west from the slopes of Mount Belford. The summit is the hump above the prominent C-shaped snowfield.

Missouri Gulch Basin. The first half-mile is steep, but abundant Colorado columbines make for enticing rest stops.

From the basin, a trail network leads southeast up Belford's northwest ridge to the right (southwest) of the prominent couloir. The erosion and overuse suffered by these slopes caused Mount Belford to be ranked as the forest service's number-one priority in the construction of new trails on Sawatch Range Fourteeners. Until this trail is finished, hikers are asked to stay on a cairned route up this slope.

From Belford's summit, Oxford is a one-and-one-half-mile walk northeast via a climber's trail through a saddle with a 700-foot loss of elevation. From both Oxford and Belford, a particularly impressive view of Harvard appears to the south. Rising above broad Missouri Basin, Harvard's size and dimensions are far more accented than when viewed from the south.

From Oxford, do not be tempted to glissade northwest into Belford Gulch; this will lead to a narrow canyon, complete with waterfalls. Backtrack over Belford. From its summit, instead of descending your ascent route, the forest service suggests that you descend via a cairned route

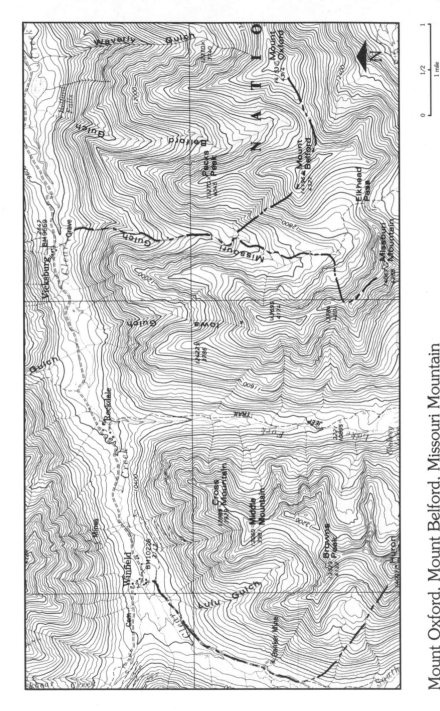

Mount Oxford, Mount Belford, Missouri Mountain

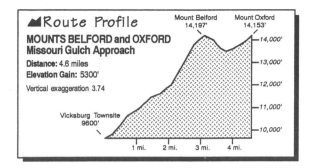

▲Route Profile

MOUNTS BELFORD and OXFORD
Missouri Gulch Approach

Distance: 4.6 miles

Elevation Gain: 5300'

Vertical exaggeration 3.74

Mount Belford
14,197'

Mount Oxford
14,153'

Vicksburg Townsite
9600'

14,000'

13,000'

12,000'

11,000'

10,000'

1 mi.   2 mi.   3 mi.   4 mi.

south down the summit ridge and then southwest to the trail near Elkhead Pass. This will mitigate the impact on the northwest ridge route until that trail is fully completed. This descent route may also be used on the ascent.

▲ *Vicksburg to Belford: 3.1 miles, 4,600 feet.*

▲ *Vicksburg to Belford and Oxford: 4.6 miles, 5,300 feet, plus another 700 feet on return over Belford.*

Missouri Gulch, Missouri Mountain

From the high basin at the head of Missouri Gulch, Missouri Mountain is the long ridge to the southwest. The highest point is barely discernible as the third point to the right (west) of Elkhead Pass, the low pass at the head (south) of the basin. Well into the basin, where the trail turns abruptly east (left) to climb toward Elkhead Pass, turn west (right) and climb grassy slopes to Missouri's northwest ridge, aiming for the low point between points 13,784 and 13,930. This slope suffers from erosion, and care should be taken to stay on established trails as much as is possible, particularly on the descent. From the ridge, hike southeast to Missouri's summit, bypassing a couple of minor points just below the summit on the west side. The couloirs on Missouri's north face should be avoided except by those who are properly experienced and equipped.

▲ *Vicksburg to Missouri: 4.3 miles, 4,500 feet.*

Missouri seems a good peak from which to preach the gospel of the ice axe. Although definitely not needed on a number of summer climbs, ice axes are invaluable to the serious climber. Although their presence is frequently sneered at by people not understanding their importance, they are part of the authors' climbing gear 365 days a year. In 1972, Omar Richardson and Walt Borneman were caught in a mid-July thunderstorm (one

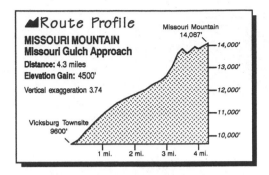

◢Route Profile

MISSOURI MOUNTAIN
Missouri Gulch Approach

Distance: 4.3 miles
Elevation Gain: 4500'

Vertical exaggeration 3.74

Missouri Mountain
14,067'

Vicksburg Townsite
9600'

14,000'
13,000'
12,000'
11,000'
10,000'

1 mi. 2 mi. 3 mi. 4 mi.

that struck at 11:00 A.M.) atop Missouri. After failing to find a route off the peak east toward Elkhead Pass (there are several pitches requiring rope), the pair reclimbed several hundred feet in freezing rain to the summit. With lightning flashing around them, they made a hurried exit down a long shoestring couloir just east of the summit. The snow was hard-packed with an icy crust, but a thousand-foot glissade with ice-axe heads buried through the crust dropped the climbers out of danger within several minutes. Descending the couloir without an ice axe would have resulted in a thousand-foot death ride.

Ice axes make for safer, surer climbing and also have numerous supplemental uses. So carry an ice axe, and know how to use it!

Huron Peak 14,003 feet (53rd highest)

Bounded on three sides by beautiful valleys, Huron Peak was probably first climbed by prospectors from one of the mining camps in the Clear Creek Valley. Many substantial mines were located in the area, and numerous prospect holes dot the mountain. Although not a particularly historic peak, Huron does offer one of the best views in the Sawatch Range.

The exact origin of Huron's name is unknown, but John L. J. Hart reported that it was probably named for a Huron Mine somewhere in the vicinity. A relative latecomer to the Fourteener rolls, Huron was not given official U.S. Geological Survey designation until 1956.

From the summit of Huron, the valleys of Clear Creak drop away in three directions, but the climber's eye is immediately drawn to the jagged mass of snow and ice to the south. Sitting atop the Continental Divide, Ice Mountain and the Three Apostles almost make you stop and quickly check the map to be certain you are still in the Sawatch. The peaks' sharp ridges and deep couloirs are dramatic exceptions to normal Sawatch geography. The name Three Apostles refers to a group of three summits: two peaks, one of 13,570 feet to the southwest, and one of 13,863 feet to the northeast, flank the main summit of 13,920 feet, called Ice Mountain. Here indeed is as challenging a climb as any Fourteener. Although miners scoured the upper basin of the South Fork of Clear Creek and broad Harrison Flats for silver, no documented evidence of a climb of Ice Mountain existed until John L. J. Hart's climb of October 4, 1931.

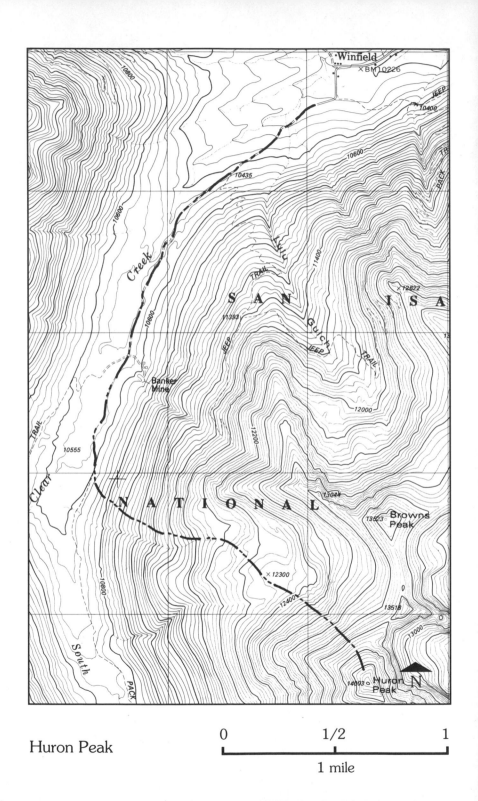

Huron Peak

Huron Peak viewed to the south with Ice Mountain to the right. *(Lyndon J. Lampert)*

THE ROUTES

South Fork Clear Creek

Four miles beyond Vicksburg (see page 84) is Winfield, which still bears a flavor of the silver boom of the 1880s, thanks to the Clear Creek Canyon Historical Society. At Winfield, the north and south forks of Clear Creek meet. A dozen surrounding thirteeners and the beauty of the valley make Winfield an ideal headquarters for a week of backpacking. For Huron, hike southwest from Winfield for two miles along the South Fork to the Banker Mine, in its day a key silver producer of the valley. The road is passable by four-wheel-drive to just south of the Banker; take the right (west) fork one-half mile south of Winfield.

A half-mile beyond the Banker and round the west shoulder of Browns Peak, grassy slopes lead southeast to moderate talus and eventually Huron's summit. Because of heavy use, most of these slopes are heavily eroded and crisscrossed by a myriad of trails. In David Duffy's 1993 "Sawatch Range Fourteener Impact Study," he recommends the following route, which at some future point may become an officially sanctioned "Mount Huron Trail."

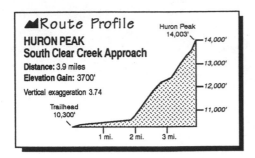

Route Profile

HURON PEAK
South Clear Creek Approach
Distance: 3.9 miles
Elevation Gain: 3700'
Vertical exaggeration 3.74

Huron Peak
14,003'
— 14,000'
— 13,000'
— 12,000'

Trailhead
10,300'
— 11,000'

1 mi. 2 mi. 3 mi.

"From the end of the South Fork Clear Creek Road (approximately 2.5-3 miles from Winfield and past the old Banker Mine) park and hike south less than 100 yards to the large wooden Collegiate Peaks Wilderness Area sign. Fifty yards past the sign, look sharp for an unmarked trail to the east (left). Follow this unmaintained path up the first small hill. To the right (south) a very faint trail begins. Follow this game trail-like path through the timber, contouring at 10,800 feet parallel to the old road to a small gushing creek. At the creek, turn east (left) on a larger well established dirt trail up the steep slopes. Near 11,800 feet the trail breaks timberline, angling slightly northeast to a large grassy bench at 12,300.

"From this point Huron's summit and large basin are plainly visible. Continue following the trail (faint at times) above the grassy plateau into the basin. Browns Peak, 13,523 feet, and its steep northwest ridge define the northern wall of the basin. Hike east through the basin towards Point 13,518 located on the connecting ridge between Browns and Huron. Just to the south of Point 13,518 is a small saddle. Reach the saddle and continue on the rocky ridge of Huron's north ridge. Remain on the ridge to the summit avoiding the urge to contour below Huron's summit into the large scree and talus filled bowl. Multiple trails, all heavily eroded, are the cause of significant resource damage found in this section. Remain on the ridge for the descent and regain the trail for the return trip."

Please pay close attention to any signs posted at the trailhead, which will provide the latest information on this route, and please treat this special little valley with an extra measure of respect.

▲ *Winfield to summit: 3.9 miles, 3,700 feet.*

Mount Harvard 14,420 feet (3rd highest)
Mount Columbia 14,073 feet (35th highest)
Mount Yale 14,196 feet (21st highest)

Mount Harvard's story begins in California in 1864. In that year, members of the California Geological Survey mapped what they thought to be the highest peak in the Sierra Nevada and named it after the Survey's director, Professor Josiah Dwight Whitney. A year later, Whitney, an 1839 graduate of Yale University, accepted a position as Professor of Geology at Harvard. In the course of his work, Whitney made plans for an expedition to the central Colorado Rockies to provide field experience for his students and particularly to obtain altitude readings of the higher peaks. His desire to explore the inner Rockies was fired by rumors, largely the result of barroom guesses by miners near Fairplay, of peaks in central Colorado exceeding 17,000 feet.

In 1869, Whitney led the first class of the Harvard Mining School, a grand total of four eager young men, and accompanying support personnel west to explore the Sawatch Range. Notable among the expedition were William H. Brewer, Whitney's assistant and a colleague from the California survey days, and Henry Gannett, in 1869 a student, who would later gain fame with the Hayden Survey and have the highest peak in Wyoming named after him.

Whitney's party traveled west from Denver, across South Park, and into the Arkansas Valley near Trout Creek Pass. At some point between an ascent of Mount Lincoln and their descent into the Arkansas Valley, their attention focused on two prominent peaks of the central Sawatch. The northern summit Whitney named Mount Harvard, after the expedition's sponsoring institution. The south summit was named Mount Yale after Whitney's alma mater, a christening that undoubtedly pleased Brewer, also a Yale graduate (class of 1852) and at that time professor

Mount Columbia (*right*) and a portion of the Harvard-Columbia ridge from the southern slopes of Mount Harvard.

of agriculture there. Whitney's act of naming the peaks after universities initiated the Collegiate Peaks section of the Sawatch.

William Brewer recorded the events of the Whitney expedition in a series of letters to his wife. Unfortunately, while flowing with general scenic description, the letters are sparse in specific geographic routes. Brewer's letters do indicate, however, that Whitney, Brewer, William M. Davis, S. F. Sharpless, and Robert Moore made the first recorded ascent of Mount Yale on August 18, 1869. A logical reading of Brewer's letters suggests that the ascent was probably from North Cottonwood Creek via some combination of the northeast ridge and the drainage of Silver Creek.

From the summit of Yale, Whitney and his companions calculated its elevation at just over 14,000 feet but observed that Mount Harvard was the higher of the two peaks. The following day, Davis and Sharpless battled rain and fog to make the first recorded ascent of Mount Harvard. Logistics with supplies and pack animals prevented Whitney and Brewer from joining them, much to Brewer's recorded chagrin. The Whitney expedition returned to Harvard certain that no 17,000-foot giants rose in the Sawatch Range and with the distinction of being the first scientific survey to penetrate the inner Colorado Rockies.

A view north up Horn Fork Basin to Mount Harvard.

A scant four years later, Henry Gannett was back in the Sawatch Range with the Hayden Survey. Hayden's men used Mount Harvard as a tri-angulation station for mapping the central Sawatch.

Little attention was paid Harvard's nearest neighbor until 1916, when Roger W. Toll, who was placing Colorado Mountain Club registers on the Sawatch peaks, named it Mount Columbia. It was no coincidence that Toll, an early pioneer of Colorado climbing, was a 1906 graduate of Columbia University. Toll went on to a notable career with the National Park Service, serving as superintendent of three national parks: Mount Rainier, Rocky Mountain, and Yellowstone.

Toll's naming of Columbia was in keeping with Whitney and Brewer's lead, but little could any of them suspect that collegiate rivalry would reach the "heights" it did in the early 1960s. On July 13, 1962, three Harvard men, David Owen (class of '61), Henry Faulkner ('63), and Steve Potter ('62), attempted to reach the summit of Mount Harvard carrying a long metal pole topped with a sign reading: "Mt. Harvard, 14,434. This sign erected at an altitude of 14,434 making it the second highest point in the contiguous United States . . ."

Although their intent to make the sign higher than Mount Elbert was obvious, approaching darkness forced the trio to cache the pole several hundred yards beneath the summit and abandon the climb. The pole and sign lay untouched until the following June, when Hugh E. Kingery (Cornell class of '54) and John and Tim Wirth (Harvard '58 and '61, respectively) chanced on the material. They lugged it the remaining distance to the summit. Kingery evidently convinced the Wirths that one Cornell man with seniority took precedence over two junior Harvard men, because Kingery was able to sign the register by noting that "Cornell finished Harvard's effort today." The story, however, does not end there.

On July 11, 1963, a month after the Kingery-Wirth climb, the original Harvard lads, Owens, Faulkner, and Potter, were again in the Sawatch determined to take their pole the remaining distance to Harvard's summit. Their dismay at finding the pole gone turned to relief when they found it securely anchored in the summit rocks. Owens promptly noted a thank you in the register to the two Harvard men and the "one from Cornell, who being deprived of any Mt. Cornell, helped us make this the highest in Colorado and 2nd highest in the U.S." The entry was signed with the admonition: "Fight fiercely, Harvard!"

The pole was visible to a sharp eye from Horn Fork Basin, and it remained on the summit of Harvard until sometime in the early 1980s, when it disappeared, perhaps as part of the campaign to clean up the Fourteener summits. One of the pole planters, Tim Wirth, went on to represent Colorado in the United States Senate.

With all of the Ivy League pomp and glory, the histories of Harvard and Yale have at least one episode with a homespun touch. In February of 1956, Gordon B. "Rocky" Warren, one of the pioneer pilots of the Colorado high country, was flying over the Harvard-Yale vicinity when he observed a horse stranded by deep snowdrifts on a saddle on the Continental Divide northwest of Mount Yale.

At his home base of Gunnison, Warren's report of the animal's predicament prompted Gunnison Mayor B. H. Jorgenson to provide bales of hay for the horse. Warren and fellow pilot Ned Wallace were to drop it to the animal. On a subsequent flight, Warren took a photograph showing the horse standing contentedly over one of the bales of hay. The photograph soon focused nationwide attention on the Harvard-Yale area. The news media dubbed the horse "Elijah," after the biblical prophet who was fed by ravens in the wilderness. Airline pilots of mountain-hopping Frontier Airlines went out of their way to show their passengers the newfound celebrity. Soon, donations for the animal's welfare were pouring into Jorgenson's office from all over the country, and Warren was able to add oats to the horse's diet.

A view of Mount Yale north up Delaney Gulch from the Denny Creek Trail.

When spring melted the snows from Elijah's timberline palace, Elijah the celebrity turned out to be none other than "Bugs," the packhorse of local residents Al and Bill Turner. Bugs was a cantankerous beast with a particular aversion to parked cars and women in skirts. Evidently, Bugs had headed to the high country to get away from it all. Just goes to show how hard it can be to get a little peace and quiet!

THE ROUTES

Horn Fork Basin, Harvard and Columbia

Half the battle on this approach is finding one's way out of Buena Vista. From the town's main intersection and traffic light where the Cottonwood Pass road and U.S. 24 intersect, drive north .4-mile on U.S. 24. Turn left (west) on Chaffee County 350 for two miles, then continue north and northwest one mile. At the Forest Service sign "North Cottonwood Creek," turn south for .2-mile and then continue west five miles to the end of the road and the trailhead. The road is a washboard—what dirt side road isn't?—but it is passable by two-wheel-drives after it has dried

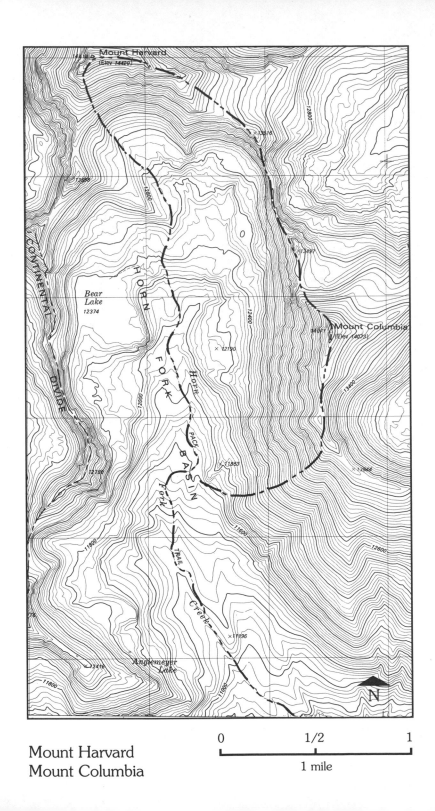

Mount Harvard
Mount Columbia

0   1/2   1

1 mile

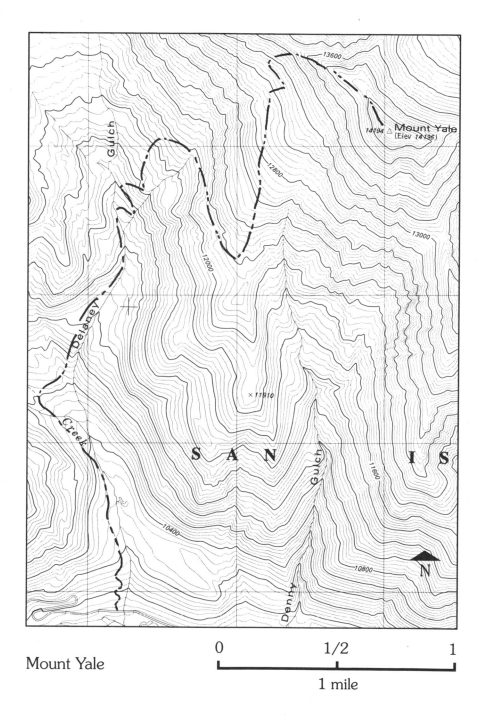

Mount Yale

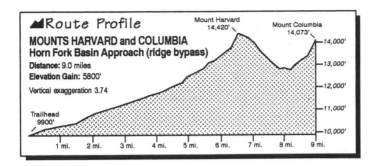

▲Route Profile

MOUNTS HARVARD and COLUMBIA
Horn Fork Basin Approach (ridge bypass)
Distance: 9.0 miles
Elevation Gain: 5800'
Vertical exaggeration 3.74

out each spring. There is room to camp near the trailhead at 9,850 feet or lower along the road.

From the trailhead, go west two miles to a trail junction. The left-hand (west) trail winds to Kroenke Lake, Elijah's winter pasture, and the Continental Divide. The right-hand fork (north) climbs three and one-half more miles to Horn Fork Basin and Bear Lake, one of the prettiest spots in the Sawatch but one that has seen severe environmental damage caused by climbers.

From the basin, Harvard dominates the view to the north and Mount Yale rises in broad Sawatch form to the south. A climb up the grassy slopes and drainages of Harvard's south shoulder and a mild scramble over the summit boulders bring you to the granite blocks on the top. Unless you are committed to doing the entire Harvard-Columbia ridge, descend the same way. Please stay on this route instead of cutting across fragile Horn Fork Basin.

For Columbia, avoid the scree slopes immediately west of the peak. This area has seen far too many feet and is severely eroded. Instead, from the vicinity of the last trees at the mouth of the basin, hike east, staying just south of the prominent rock outcrop. This leads to Columbia's south ridge, about a half-mile south of the summit. Follow the ridge north. If you have climbed Columbia from the Harvard-Columbia ridge, descend this same route and avoid the scree slopes to the west.

The Harvard-Columbia ridge is long, with many ups and downs and a number of places with hard third-class climbing. The final towers on the ridge, "the Rabbits," are best skirted to the left (east). Then, continue up the final scree slopes to Columbia's summit. This is a very long undertaking and should only be attempted by experienced and well-conditioned parties.

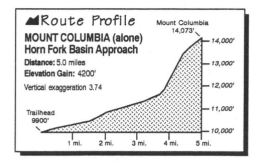

▲ *Trailhead to Harvard: 6 miles, 4,400 feet*
▲ *Trailhead to Columbia: 5 miles, 4,200 feet.*
▲ *Trailhead to Harvard and Columbia via connecting ridge: 8 miles, 5,300 feet; 5 miles on return.*

Denny Creek, Mount Yale

The southern approach to Mount Yale is a good example of what overuse can do to a moderate route. For years, the standard route was via Denny Gulch, but heavy traffic on the slopes leading to the saddle between Yale and its southern subpeak caused extensive erosion and created significant loose-rock hazard. Overuse changed a relatively straightforward route into a dangerous approach for large parties and resulted in severe environmental damage. In 1992, the forest service closed the Denny Gulch route and now directs climbers to a route via Denny Creek and Delaney Gulch.

From Buena Vista's main intersection, drive west on the Cottonwood Pass road, Colorado 306, for eleven miles to Collegiate Peaks Campground and then one more mile to the Denny Creek trailhead on the north (right) side of the road. The Denny Creek Trail leads north up moderate switchbacks and after one mile crosses Denny Creek. Mount Yale is momentarily visible to the northeast, and you may feel as though you are heading away from the mountain rather than up Delaney Gulch. Take heart and continue northwest for another quarter-mile to an intersection that should be signed.

The right-hand fork points to Mount Yale and leads northeast back into Delaney Gulch. After almost a mile, the trail crosses Delaney Gulch to the east and then switchbacks up Yale's broad southwest ridge separating Delaney and Denny gulches. Once atop this ridge, at 12,200 feet,

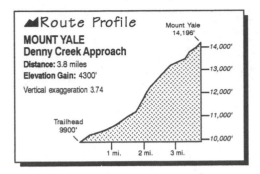

▰Route Profile

MOUNT YALE
Denny Creek Approach
Distance: 3.8 miles
Elevation Gain: 4300'

Vertical exaggeration 3.74

Mount Yale
14,196'

—14,000'
—13,000'
—12,000'
—11,000'
—10,000'

Trailhead
9900'

1 mi.   2 mi.   3 mi.

Mount Yale is again prominently visible to the northeast. The trail climbs north on the ridge and after more switchbacks it reaches a saddle at 13,500 feet on Yale's northwest ridge. From here, it is a half-mile climb southeast to the summit. A faint trail stays to the south (right) of the ridge crest, and one prominent rock step just above the saddle may either be climbed directly or passed on the south.

On the return, it is very critical to return all of the way northwest to the 13,500-foot saddle and the trail before starting your descent. Although this route is relatively new, the slopes below the northwest ridge are already showing signs of erosion because of parties shortcutting the trail. Either climb this route early in the season when a glissade will take you across this area, or return via the trail. Let's not create another Denny Gulch situation! If you do climb early in the season, remember that on the descent you must cross the southwest ridge at the 12,200-foot level to get back into the Delaney Gulch drainage—otherwise, you end up in Denny Gulch.

▲ *Denny Creek trailhead to summit: 3.8 miles, 4,300 feet.*

Mount Princeton 14,197 feet (18th highest)

The southernmost of the Collegiate Peaks, Mount Princeton rises in grand majesty with a graceful symmetry quite unique among Colorado's Fourteeners. Seen from the east, the peak presents three summits, with the two lower ones flanking the highest central peak in almost perfect balance. Mount Princeton is considered by many to be the most attractive of the Sawatch peaks as seen from the Arkansas Valley and in many ways is symbolic of the Colorado Rockies as a whole—dramatic in its abrupt rise from the valley floor yet attractive in form and rich in legends and the history of surveys, mining, and tourists.

The south slope of Mount Princeton drops off abruptly in an escarpment known as the Chalk Cliffs. In reality, the cliffs are not chalk at all but are composed of white quartz monzonite in a crumbling state, thereby giving early visitors the impression of chalk. These striking cliffs have long been a prominent feature of Mount Princeton and have given rise to at least one legend concerning lost Spanish treasure. This legend purports that approximately two hundred years ago a small group of Spaniards from settlements in New Mexico raided an Indian village and escaped with a large amount of valuable items. The Indians quickly pursued the thieves, and the Spaniards were forced to stash the treasure somewhere in the Chalk Cliffs. The treasure achieved its "lost" status when the Indians caught up with the raiders and killed them but could not locate their stolen goods. The search has continued for two hundred years, but the treasure, if it exists, will probably remain lost forever among the dangerous cliffs.

The white cliffs also inspired the Wheeler Survey to give the peak its original name, "Chalk Mountain." However, Mount Princeton is found in use as early as 1873, and it is suspected that this name was given by

Mount Princeton from the east, above the Arkansas River Valley.

Henry Gannett of the Hayden Survey, in keeping with the other nearby Collegiate Peaks. It is not recorded that members either of the Hayden or Wheeler surveys ascended Mount Princeton, but it is a possibility.

The first recorded climb of Mount Princeton was accomplished in 1877 by William Libbey, Jr., of Princeton University. Libbey had just received his degree, and he accompanied other students and a professor on what amounted to a practicum in scientific study and surveying in the mountains of Colorado and Utah. Mount Princeton proved to be an irresistible goal for obvious reasons, and on July 17, 1877, William Libbey reached the summit on a solo ascent. Appropriately, Libbey later became a professor of geography at Princeton, and no doubt he enjoyed telling many times of the day he conquered the mountain that bears the name of his alma mater.

The possibility that Princeton was first ascended by miners is supported by the fact that the Hortense Mine was discovered at about 12,000 feet on the southern peak of Mount Princeton in July of 1872 by J. A. Merriam and E. W. Keyes. The Hortense became one of the finest silver producers of the Sawatch Range, but access was extremely difficult over a narrow, twisting, ledge trail. However, the mine was producing one hundred dollars per ton of ore, and such a figure was ample incentive for the manager, Eugene Teats, to construct a five-mile wagon road. Before long, the burro pack trains were replaced by oxen-drawn wagons, and this improvement enabled the Hortense to operate profitably for many years, until the ore finally played out.

Most of the miners who worked at the Hortense commuted from residences at the southeast foot of Mount Princeton. This settlement centered around a group of seven hot springs that had been known to the Utes long before the miners entered the area. It was inevitable that the hot springs would be commercially developed, for in the latter part of the 1800s Colorado was developing a reputation as a health-spa paradise. By 1884 the Mount Princeton Hot Springs were sporting a newly completed hotel, but due to financial problems and the fading of the Chalk Creek boom towns, no paying guests were received for a number of years. Finally, the property changed hands in 1915, and it then blossomed into a first-class resort. When completed, the hotel had one hundred rooms, stained glass windows, and a huge ballroom. In addition to the hot springs, other outdoor facilities included tennis courts and a nine-hole golf course, undoubtedly one of the highest in the nation at that time.

Mount Princeton Hot Springs flourished for about fifteen years, with high-class guests arriving in glistening chauffered Cadillacs from the train depot at Buena Vista. The bubble burst, however, with the great crash of 1929. In the 1930s the property was renamed the Antero Hotel, but it led a struggling existence until finally the once grand building was razed in 1950. The hot springs still survive, however, and are experiencing something of a revival in business today.

THE ROUTES

Mount Princeton Road

From Buena Vista, drive south on U.S. 285 for eight miles to Colorado 162 and west four miles to the site of the famed Mount Princeton Hot Springs. Turn right (north) on Chaffee County 321 for about one mile and then left on Chaffee County 322 for another mile. Young Life's Frontier Camp is on the left, and the Mount Princeton Road is on the right. Passenger cars should park here, at 8,900 feet.

The road switchbacks three miles to a series of radio towers at 10,900 feet. There is very limited parking here and along the rougher jeep trail just to the west. Hike the rough jeep trail west to timberline. Eventually,

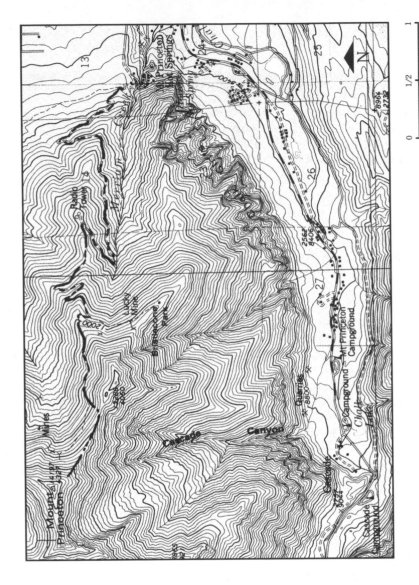

Mount Princeton

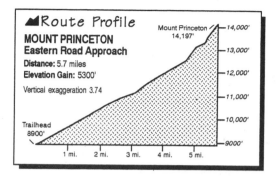

▲▲Route Profile

**MOUNT PRINCETON
Eastern Road Approach**

Distance: 5.7 miles
Elevation Gain: 5300'

Vertical exaggeration 3.74

Trailhead
8900'

Mount Princeton
14,197'

14,000'
13,000'
12,000'
11,000'
10,000'
9000'

1 mi.　2 mi.　3 mi.　4 mi.　5 mi.

it leads south across the face of the southeastern subpeak to a Young Life chalet. As the road turns south, a trail branches off it to the right (west) and leads first north to the crest of a small ridge and then west directly toward the summit. The trail leads all of the way to a mine at almost 13,000 feet, but it is best to angle south to the 13,040-foot saddle between Princeton's summit and its southeast subpeak. Follow the ridge three-quarters of a mile west to the summit. This avoids steep talus slopes between the summit and mine. Return the same way. Princeton may be a good one to do later in the fall, perhaps even mountain-biking the lower road, as a way to avoid summer crowds.

▲ *Parking lot trailhead to summit: 5.7 miles, 5,300 feet.*

Mount Antero 14,269 feet (10th highest)

No Colorado Fourteener, not even any of the mineral-rich peaks of the Mosquitos, can come close to matching the wealth of gems Mount Antero has produced. Many a Fourteener can claim one or two great mines on its flanks that have produced fabulous amounts of gold or silver, but Mount Antero has cornered the market on aquamarine, topaz, and clear and smoky quartz crystals.

Mount Antero rises south of Mount Princeton across Chalk Creek, which was the scene of extensive mining activity during the 1870s. It was probably climbed by prospectors during this time, but the specifics of any first ascent have not been recorded. While these early silver prospectors may have noticed Mount Antero's rich gem field, they staked no claims on it and made no mention of the gems.

Part of the reason for the neglect of Mount Antero's gems was the discovery of a number of promising silver mines in the area, mainly to the west of Mount Antero. These discoveries lured hopeful prospectors into the Chalk Creek Valley, and in 1879 the community of Alpine was incorporated; it is located directly below Mount Antero's northwest flank. In many ways, Alpine was a classic mining camp, with about one thousand people, its own newspaper (the *True Fissure*), three banks, two hotels, no church, but twenty-three saloons. Alpine's earliest and principal silver mine was the Tilden, which was located on the slopes of Boulder Mountain, just west of Mount Antero.

Alpine was the major supply point for the area and a booming town with a bright future until 1881, when the Denver, South Park, and Pacific Railroad arrived in the Chalk Creek Valley. The narrow-gauge rails pushed rapidly through Alpine and soon reached the rival town of St. Elmo, about

A view west to Mount Antero from the Arkansas River Valley.

five miles up the valley. This was just what struggling St. Elmo needed, and the population skyrocketed, drawing many of its residents from Alpine. As a result, by 1882 Alpine was little more than a memory, providing a classic history of a short-lived but rip-roaring mining camp of the Colorado Rockies. Today a few summer homes mark the site of Alpine, but St. Elmo is a superbly preserved ghost town, thus outdoing its former rival even now.

As Alpine faded and St. Elmo blossomed, a lone prospector by the name of Nathaniel D. Wanemaker combed the slopes of Mount Antero far above the bustling activity of the valley. Wanemaker had forgotten about silver prospecting in the Sawatch ever since he had discovered crystals of blue aquamarine high on the mountain in 1884. Wanemaker soon realized the great potential in mining Antero's gems and proceeded to construct a small stone cabin at about 13,400 feet on the south side of the peak. Reportedly, he found six hundred dollars worth of gems his first year on Antero and lived on the mountain many years thereafter, single-handedly collecting what gems he could find.

Wanemaker's discovery attracted many others to the peak, and in the years that followed, a number of impressive finds were made, both by professional prospectors and amateur rock hounds. The most popular of

Antero's gems was the aquamarine, which ranged from pale blue-green to deep blue in color. Many of the better aquamarine specimens were sent to Germany to be cut into jewelry-quality gems and then returned to the United States. In addition, Mount Antero has yielded huge clear quartz crystals, including a seven-inch specimen that is currently located in the Harvard Mineralogical Museum. One of the largest clear quartz crystals from Mount Antero was shaped into a crystal sphere nearly six inches in diameter and displayed at the 1893 Columbian Exposition. Smoky quartz is more common than clear quartz on the mountain, with some specimens weighing as much as fifty pounds.

Recognizing the value of Mount Antero as a mineral site, the Colorado Mineralogical Society held ceremonies on the peak on August 1, 1949, creating the Mount Antero Mineral Park. A bronze tablet was placed in a granite boulder near the summit of the peak, officially making Mount Antero the highest mineral locality in North America. Recently, the only commercial mining on the mountain has been for beryllium, and this activity was responsible for the construction of a road to 13,500 feet on Mount Antero's south shoulder in the 1950s.

Mount Antero was named for Chief Antero of the Uintah band of the Ute Indians. The situation surrounding the naming of the peak is somewhat obscure, for although the name is given in the 1870 atlas of the Hayden Survey, it is not mentioned in any of the Hayden reports. As a Uintah chief, Antero spent most of his time in Utah, but he was one of the chiefs to sign an 1878 treaty that ceded portions of Ute land in the San Juans to the silver-hungry white men. In addition, Chief Antero helped to quell an uprising of another band of Utes in 1867, and he kept his own band peaceful during the White River Utes's uprising in 1879. John Jerome Hart suggests that Antero's peaceful cooperation with the whites at that time may have been responsible for the peak's being named for him.

THE ROUTES

Baldwin Gulch

From Buena Vista, drive south on U.S. 285 for eight miles, then west on Colorado 162 about twelve and one-half miles to just west of the old site of Alpine, where the Baldwin Gulch road enters from the south (9,383 feet). Turn left (south) and climb a rocky jeep road two and one-half miles into Baldwin Gulch to a fork in the road and creek crossing. Follow the trail left (east) across the creek to its end on Antero's south shoulder

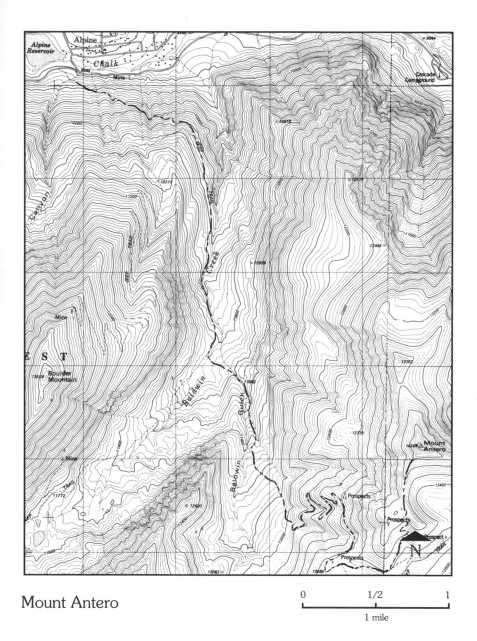

Mount Antero

0   1/2   1
|—————————————————————|
1 mile

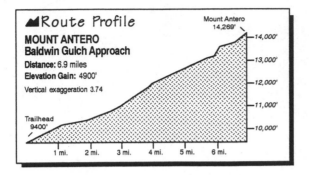

near the gem mine at 13,500 feet. Climbing directly east from the creek crossing only takes you onto one of the most "mobile" talus slopes of the Sawatch. From the mine, the summit is a half-mile north along the ridge.

▲ Baldwin Gulch Creek crossing to summit: 3.5 miles, 3,300 feet.

Mount Shavano 14,229 feet (17th highest)
Tabeguache Mountain 14,155 feet (26th highest)

Mount Shavano and Tabeguache Mountain are two of only four Colorado Fourteeners to bear names of Indian origin. Appropriately, Shavano was a prominent chief of the Tabeguache branch of the Utes, and to add even more Indian character to the peaks, a number of Ute legends have been born concerning a mysterious snow formation that appears on the east flank of Mount Shavano each spring. However, like much of the West, the Indian heritage remains in name and legend only. The Indians themselves were forced from the area by miners in the 1870s, who brought more permanent "civilization" to the area and left their marks upon the peaks.

Chief Shavano was prominent among Ute leaders and therefore was often an important figure in Indian-white relations. He first gained favor with the whites when he helped to capture Kaneache, another Ute who began a small-scale rebellion in 1867. In 1873, Shavano was among 133 Utes who signed the Brunot Treaty, which ceded most of the San Juans to the whites. Trespassing violations by miners took Shavano and others to Washington, D.C., for negotiations, and finally, in 1878, Shavano, Ouray, Antero, and others signed a second treaty that settled the problem in favor of the miners. Shavano continued to demonstrate loyalty to the whites when he helped to rescue the white women captured by the White River Utes following the Meeker Massacre in 1879. For all of his efforts, Shavano was favored by Chief Ouray as his possible successor, but after Ouray's death in 1880, political manipulations prevented Shavano from taking the position; five years later, he died also.

Shavano's name as applied to the mountain appears on maps as early as 1875, indicating his popularity with the whites at that time. However,

115

The summit of Tabeguache Mountain from the west ridge. Mount Shavano's summit is visible behind and to the right. (R. Omar Richardson)

the Wheeler Survey named the mountain "Usher Peak," after Judge J. P. Usher, Chief Counsel for the Denver and Rio Grande Railway, but his name never gained acceptance. Tabeguache Mountain was surveyed at more than 14,000 feet as early as 1913, but it was not named or recognized as a separate peak from Mount Shavano until 1931, when the Colorado Mountain Club officially recognized it as such.

Mount Shavano and Indian legends are inseparable, for each spring a figure of snow with upstretched arms, known as the Angel of Shavano, appears on the eastern flank of the mountain. Like the Holy Cross, this formation has bred a multitude of legends. It is virtually impossible to determine which of these legends is of the greatest antiquity, or which are even genuinely Indian in origin.

Numerous legends concerning the alleviation of drought reflect natural associations with a snow formation that produces precious life-giving water. One legend says that long ago a severe drought was forcing the Indians from the area. As a last resort before leaving, an Indian princess knelt at the foot of Mount Shavano and prayed for rain. The Indian god to whom she prayed demanded that she sacrifice herself for the sake of her tribe. She did so, and every year thereafter, the princess appears

Mount Shavano and the angel from the southeast. *(Photograph courtesy Colorado Historical Society)*

as the Angel of Shavano. The Angel weeps for her people, and her tears in the form of melting snow, symbolic of her sacrifice, provide valuable moisture to the land below.

Another legend, obviously of relatively recent origin, is of interest because it involves Chief Shavano himself and the great scout, Jim Beckwourth. This legend contends that Shavano and Beckwourth were close friends, and when Beckwourth was fatally injured in 1853, Shavano went to the mountain to pray for Beckwourth's soul. Each spring afterward, the Angel appears to indicate that Shavano's prayers have indeed been answered.

Mining activity in the vicinity of Shavano and Tabeguache dates as early as 1863, when a few gold seekers staked claims on the eastern side of Mount Shavano. These claims never amounted to much, but in the 1870s, better finds of gold were made to the west and south of Tabeguache Mountain. In 1879, a mining camp sprang up at 11,000 feet at the southwest foot of Tabeguache Mountain, and it was christened Clifton. Before long it was renamed Shavano, and by 1880 the camp held about one hundred people.

Over the years, Shavano had three general stores and three mills, but only one saloon. As mining camps went, Shavano was quite placid, experiencing only one murder and one hanging, both revolving around the same incident. Apparently, the mining activity around Shavano was quite placid as well, for the town lasted only about three years. In the years that followed, a few individual mines continued to operate, but after 1907, Shavano proper was never inhabited. Some prospecting continued, and in 1913 the Shavano Mining and Milling Company was busy drilling a tunnel at 13,400 feet on the south shoulder of Mount Shavano. The tunnel was cut into a lead that had been opened on the surface in the saddle above and that had yielded forty dollars per ton in gold. The mine was never profitable, but the remains of the workings are still clearly evident on Mount Shavano's broad south saddle.

Shavano and Tabeguache were probably first scaled by miners, but one climb in 1888 by Charles Fay had widespread publicity through the magazine *Appalachia*. Fay climbed Mount Shavano, hardly a noteworthy mountaineering landmark, but the readers of *Appalachia* devoured any sort of outdoor adventure, and the fact that Fay began climbing at 2:30 A.M. gave his account some added dramatic appeal.

Barely missing the 14,000-foot mark is Mount Ouray at 13,971 feet, located approximately fourteen miles south of Mount Shavano. While not a Fourteener, the massive cone of Mount Ouray is nonetheless impressive enough to easily deserve the name of the great Ute chief. No one man did more to preserve peace between the Utes and the whites than Chief Ouray.

While Mount Ouray is not rich in mining history, it is closely tied with narrow-gauge railroad history. Marshall Pass, at 10,846 feet, is located on the southern flank of the peak and is the lowest crossing of the Sawatch Range. Discovered in 1873 by William Marshall, the pass became a route for one of Otto Mears's toll roads in 1879 and then was occupied by Palmer's Denver and Rio Grande Railway in 1881. The pass proved to be the best railroad route into the Gunnison country, and for more than seventy years the Marshall Pass line was a featured part of "The Scenic Line of the World."

THE ROUTES

Jennings Creek, Tabeguache and Shavano
AVOID MCCOY GULCH! AVOID MCCOY GULCH!! AVOID MCCOY GULCH!!! No route in the first edition caused us more consternation than

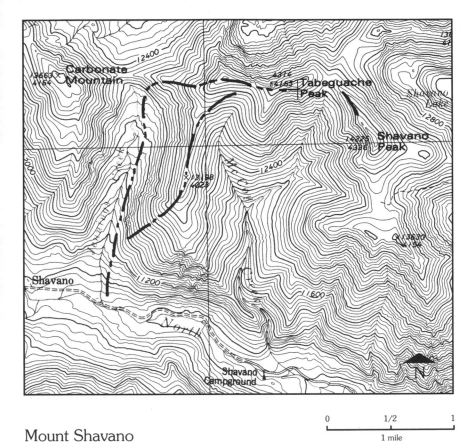

Mount Shavano
Tabeguache Mountain

0   1/2   1
1 mile

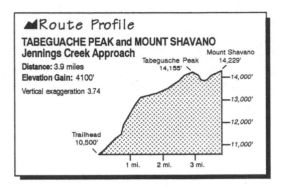

▲Route Profile

TABEGUACHE PEAK and MOUNT SHAVANO
Jennings Creek Approach
Distance: 3.9 miles
Elevation Gain: 4100'
Vertical exaggeration 3.74

Mount Shavano 14,229'
Tabeguache Peak 14,155'

Trailhead 10,500'

14,000'
13,000'
12,000'
11,000'

1 mi. 2 mi. 3 mi.

this one! We recommended a route up Jennings Creek and over Tabeguache to Shavano, specifically warning against McCoy Gulch. Despite this, some parties returning from Shavano have been suckered into descending easy-looking McCoy Gulch. Out of sight from above, McCoy Gulch is blocked by steep cliffs and a maze of downed timber. Numerous search and rescue operations have plucked unprepared and uninformed hikers from McCoy's cliffs. There is now a fairly well established trail up Tabeguache's south ridge from Jennings Creek, and one dropping west from the saddle south of Shavano. This allows you to traverse upper McCoy Gulch and skirt Tabeguache on the return from Shavano, but you must still remember to exit the gulch before dropping too low. Popular use to the contrary, we continue to describe our original route, which, if followed, will keep you entirely clear of McCoy Gulch.

From Maysville, west of Poncha Springs on U.S. 50, take the North Fork road north-northwest for eight miles to Jennings Creek at 10,500 feet. Climb north up Jennings Creek almost to the head of the gulch and angle east (right) to the broad end of Tabeguache's west ridge. Follow the ridge with several scrambling cuts east one mile to the summit. Shavano is one mile east and southeast, via an easy ridge with a 400-foot drop. Return via the same route; DO NOT descend McCoy Gulch.

▲ *Jennings Creek crossing to Tabeguache: 3 miles, 3,600 feet.*

▲ *Jennings Creek crossing to Tabeguache and Shavano: 3.9 miles, 4,100 feet, with 400 feet on the return over Tabeguache.*

Mount Shavano Southeast Couloir

A more direct route to Shavano is available for winter ascents. From Maysville, drive almost four miles up the North Fork road to about

9,200 feet. As the road swings west, a prominent couloir dominates the southeast flank of Shavano. This couloir is in line with the 13,611-foot subpeak south of Shavano's summit. Climb the eastern ridge of this steep couloir to the subpeak. The cone of Shavano's summit is one mile to the north and 800 feet above the 13,400-foot broad saddle. The final eight hundred feet to the summit is easy talus-hopping unless the wind is blowing a steady fifty-five miles per hour with gusts to seventy miles per hour, as it was on one March ascent by the authors. From Shavano's summit, Tabeguache may be climbed via the ridge described above. The return is via the ascent route with the possibility of a glissade down the southeast couloir if avalanche conditions permit.

▲ *Foot of couloir to Shavano: 3 miles, 5,200 feet.*

▲ *Foot of couloir to Shavano and Tabeguache: 4 miles, 5,600 feet, with 500 feet on return over Shavano.*

Red, Rugged, and Rotten

The Elk Range

For many, the epitome of Colorado mountain grandeur lies in the heart of the Elk Range: the Maroon Bells. Indeed, few Colorado sights can match the combination of colors presented by the Maroon Bells flanked with stands of flaming golden aspen and set against a crystalline blue sky, but the Elk Range is far more than the Maroon Bells. Many other peaks share the unusual red-layered nature of the Bells, while the thin, sweeping ridges of Capitol and Snowmass peaks provide mountain beauty of another sort. In addition, winter transforms the Elk Range into an incredible collection of snow-frosted peaks that appear to be taken directly from a Christmas card. The beauty of the Elk Range, regardless of the season, and the unmatched quality of its light powder snow have made it one of the nation's foremost recreation areas.

The Elk Range is one of the smallest ranges in the state, only about forty-five miles long and thirty miles wide. Topographically, it is connected to the Sawatch Range to the southeast. It lies on the western side of the Continental Divide; it is drained on the north by the Roaring Fork and Crystal rivers, and on the south by the East and Taylor rivers, tributaries of the Gunnison. The valleys of the Elk Range are generally steep-sided and narrow, and the rule for the higher elevations of the range is ruggedness. Only one of the six Fourteeners of the range has a walk-up route to the summit, and even the passes are high and rugged. No regular automobile road has dared venture across the southern crest of the range, and those passes that do connect with the Gunnison country—such as Schofield, Pearl, and Taylor—are occupied only by jeep or foot trails and are legendary for their toughness.

At the heart of the beauty of the Elk Range is its geology. Unlike most

Colorado ranges, which are predominantly of Precambrian igneous rock, the Elk Range displays Paleozoic sedimentaries on many of its peaks. During the last part of the Paleozoic era, the area of the Elks was apparently part of a large mud flat and delta that accumulated sediments eroded from the surrounding uplands. Eventually, sediments from this erosion reached thicknesses of as much as ten thousand feet; these were compacted and metamorphosed into what is called the Maroon Formation. It is this formation that composes the greater portion of the Maroon Bells, Castle Peak, and Pyramid Peak.

During the Laramide Orogeny, the sedimentary rocks of the former mud flat were greatly uplifted in association with the uplift of the Sawatch Anticline to the east. This caused the layers of the sedimentary rocks to be tilted at an angle, and in some places thrust over one another. As a result, today the general angle of the sedimentary rocks in the Elks slopes upward to the east. During and after uplift, igneous intrusions invaded parts of the Elks, and this activity explains why sedimentary peaks rise virtually next door to igneous peaks. The Snowmass Stock is the largest of these intrusions; it contains the granite rock granodiorite, which composes Snowmass and Capitol peaks.

As in all other Colorado ranges, glaciation made great changes in the Elk Range. Large glaciers formed in the higher valleys and ground away at the slopes of peaks to leave the narrow and beautiful ridges of the Snowmass-Capitol area as well as the classic glacial lakes in the Pierre Lakes Basin. The upper Roaring Fork Valley remains a characteristically U-shaped glacial valley.

E. G. Beckwith named the Elk Range when he saw it from a distance in 1853, but in 1874, Henry Gannett made note that until the surveys, the Elk Range was "as little known as any part of the western territories." Both the Hayden and Wheeler survey teams entered the Elks in 1873 and were deeply impressed by its unique and complex geology and unmatched beauty. Castle and Snowmass were the only two Fourteeners ascended by the Hayden Survey, while the Wheeler men climbed no peaks above 14,000 feet.

After the Leadville silver boom of the late 1870s, prospectors filtered across the Sawatch Range via Independence Pass to search for similar lodes. By 1879, four small mining camps had been established in the Elk Range, including Ute City, which became Aspen the following year. An incredible amount of high-grade silver ore was found on the hillsides south of town, and when Independence Pass was improved to wagon-road status in 1881, Aspen's boom was on. By 1889, the area had produced approximately ten million dollars, and Aspen's population was more than eight thousand.

By the early 1900s, the silver mines of the Elk Range operated only sporadically, and it appeared that the area would never regain the economic status it had enjoyed in the 1880s. During World War II, however, ski troopers from Camp Hale, near Tennessee Pass, skied the hills near Aspen and became intrigued with the idea of developing a downhill ski area. By the late 1940s, the fame of Aspen's deep powder snows was beginning to spread—and the rest is history.

But as that history has made Aspen a mega-resort, the Elks have become a textbook case of a region grappling with the "being loved to death" syndrome. The inherent beauty of the region attracts huge crowds winter and summer, and the crowds have spawned thousands of garish condominiums, noisy traffic jams, and a significant air pollution problem. In response, the forest service has imposed use restrictions to protect the backcountry, including shuttle buses to Maroon Lake and camping restrictions in the Castle Creek Valley. For now, the Elks hang in a tenuous balance and, ironically, the culprits are those who have come here because of the beauty of the land.

Castle Peak 14,265 feet (12th highest)

The highest mountain in the Elk Range, Castle Peak dominates the upper reaches of the Castle Creek Valley. Somewhat isolated, the peak is seldom seen by the casual traveler, but the hiker and climber who venture into its vicinity are rewarded with splendid views of its rich coloration and pinnacled ridges. Although the peak is not well known today, it was familiar to many miners of the 1880s, and no Fourteener in the Elk Range can match its rich mining history.

Although one may walk to the summit of Castle relatively easily if the right route is taken, it is doubtful that the peak was climbed until 1873, when the Hayden Survey passed through the Elk Range. Members of the party were impressed with the numerous rock towers and spires along the peak's south ridge, and the descriptive name was born. Realizing that Castle Peak was probably the highest summit in the Elks, they chose to climb it, but from the difficult south side. The party began their climb from a timberline camp southwest of the peak and were soon confronted with several bands of small cliffs. Henry Gannett related in a 1902 article in *Everybody's Magazine* that they made their way through the cliffs via a series of chimneys in which they used a counterforce technique involving climbing with their backs and feet on opposite sides of the chimney— quite an advanced climbing technique for 1873! Gannett and his partners found the ridge they gained to be extremely narrow in places, so much so that they sometimes had to straddle it and move along in a sitting position. Finally, however, the team reached the top, and they can almost surely be credited with a first ascent as well as having completed what may have been the most technically difficult climb made in the Rocky Mountains until that time. Not surprisingly, Gannett reported that Castle

The north face of Castle Peak. The traditional route follows the right-hand skyline. *(Gary Koontz)*

"afforded more of a climb than any other Colorado mountain with which I have any acquaintance."

By 1880, a small mining camp had grown up about twelve miles up Castle Creek from Aspen; it was known as Castle Forks City. In January of 1882 it became known as Ashcroft but did not appear to have much of a future as a silver camp. In the spring of 1882, however, the Fitzgerald brothers and Jake Sands found rich silver ore in the Montezuma Mine, at 12,700 feet in the basin on Castle's northeast flank. Immediately there was quite a legal battle for the rights to the mine. Eventually it ended up in the hands of none other than H.A.W. Tabor of Leadville.

The rich strikes at the Montezuma and the Tam O'Shanter mines, also owned by Tabor, caused Ashcroft to boom, and its population grew from five hundred to two thousand in one year's span. In time, a mill and aerial tram were built to serve the Montezuma Mine. Even though the two mines produced up to twenty thousand dollars a month, Tabor poured more money into them than he ever received, and the 1893 silver crash spelled final doom for the operations. By 1900 the Montezuma had virtually ceased operation, and today only scattered remains of the mine and mill survive to remind the hiker and mountaineer of the once-promising

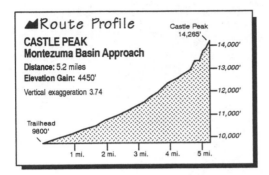

▲Route Profile

CASTLE PEAK
Montezuma Basin Approach
Distance: 5.2 miles
Elevation Gain: 4450'
Vertical exaggeration 3.74

Castle Peak
14,265'
—14,000'
—13,000'
—12,000'
—11,000'
Trailhead
9800'
—10,000'

1 mi.   2 mi.   3 mi.   4 mi.   5 mi.

business venture. The town of Ashcroft lives again today, thanks to the restoration efforts of the U.S. Forest Service, the Aspen Historical Society, and numerous others.

THE ROUTES

Montezuma Basin

From Aspen, drive northwest a half-mile on Colorado 82 to the junction of the Ashcroft and Maroon Lake roads. Turn left and then immediately take the left-hand fork, which leads up Castle Creek. Drive eleven and one-half miles to Ashcroft and then one and one-half miles farther to a fork where the main road continues up the valley toward mining operations, and the right-hand fork (west) climbs southwest into a stand of aspens. Due to previous overuse by campers, camping is no longer permitted in the Castle Creek Valley within one-quarter mile of any stream. This regulation effectively prohibits any car camping in the valley, and those climbing Castle are advised to seek camping at developed campgrounds elsewhere in the Aspen area.

Although high clearance four-wheel-drives can continue up this road to well over 12,000 feet in Montezuma Basin, most vehicles should be parked just before the road leaves the flat-bottomed Castle Creek Valley and begins to climb to the southwest at 9,800 feet. Hike southwest from here for about two and one-half miles, past the site of the old Montezuma Mill, across the creek, and to the junction of the road to Pearl Pass (11,100 feet). Take the right-hand fork and proceed another one and one-half miles into the flats in the basin. From the basin, two routes are possible, either via Castle's northeast ridge or via the bowl directly northwest

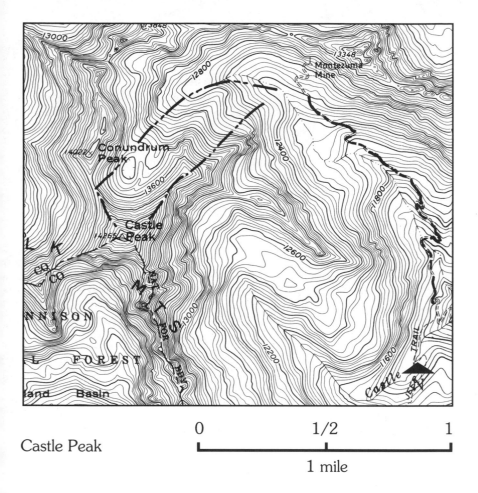

Castle Peak

0   1/2   1

1 mile

of this ridge. For the ridge, continue up the valley a quarter-mile to about 12,400 feet, about a quarter-mile south of the Montezuma Mine. Climb southwest up the shallow gully on the northeast ridge, which leads to the visible false summit of Castle (13,760 feet). The northeast ridge can also be reached by continuing into the bowl described below and then angling south onto the ridge. From the false summit, it is another three-eighths of a mile southwest along the ridge to the summit.

The bowl route, which is not so steep, leaves the road at about 12,400 feet, almost to the Montezuma Mine. Continue west up the main drainage a half-mile and then follow it southwest another half-mile into the bowl. Scramble southwest to the low point in Castle's northwest ridge (13,800 feet). Continue up the ridge a quarter-mile southeast to the summit. From the saddle, you may want to make the side trip a quarter-mile northwest to the subsidiary summit of 14,022-foot Conundrum, one of those points above 14,000 feet that has not officially been verified as a separate Fourteener. From the summit of Castle, a good but steep glissade may be found off a north-face couloir and into the bowl, or descent may be made by either of the above-described ascent routes.

The forest service strongly recommends against any other approach to Castle Peak than Montezuma Basin, particularly from the Conundrum Creek Valley to the west, because of severe environmental degradation attributed to recreational overuse.

▲ *Trailhead (9,800 feet) to summit (either route): 5.2 miles, 4,450 feet.*

Pyramid Peak 14,018 feet (47th highest)

Driving south from Aspen toward Maroon Lake, many an expectant eye eagerly awaiting the Maroon Bells is first treated to the towering mass of crumbling spires dominating the valley above the confluence of East and West Maroon creeks. To be sure, its rugged symmetry deserves the name "Pyramid."

In general, the surveyors of the Hayden and Wheeler surveys kept their distance from the crumbling walls of Pyramid and the Maroons. Wheeler's eminent geologist, Professor John Stevenson, did, however, report an ascent by the team's topographer, a man named Young, to within several hundred feet of a peak that could easily have been either Pyramid or North Maroon, from Stevenson's description. While some sources credit Young with the first near-miss on Pyramid, these writers conclude that Young ascended to near the top of North Maroon. There is ample room for discussion, and folks wishing to draw their own conclusion should consult *Roof of the Rockies* for Stevenson's description.

Regardless of Young's exploits, the first complete ascent of Pyramid appears to have been the August 31, 1909, climb of Percy Hagerman and Harold Clark. Hagerman was the son of J. J. Hagerman, entrepreneur extraordinaire of Colorado Midland Railroad and Hagerman Tunnel fame. Percy followed in his father's footsteps and developed a number of business and mining interests. Harold Clark was a prominent Aspen lawyer who also had a number of mining interests. Busy as they were in their individual pursuits, Hagerman and Clark teamed together during the summers of 1908, 1909, and 1910 to climb virtually every major summit in the Elks. Hagerman was 39 in 1908 and Clark was 46, no young ages for accomplishing feats that must rank with Dwight Lavender's

131

Pyramid Peak viewed to the east from Buckskin Pass. The route climbs into the large amphitheater with the patch of snow and then diverts either left to the north ridge or right to the west-face "couloir and ledges" approach as described. *(Glen Gebhardt)*

and Mel Griffith's pioneering of the San Juans. Hagerman Peak near Snowmass Peak, and Clark Peak east of Capitol were named for the climbers.

Hagerman and Clark's climbing legacy became *Notes on Mountaineering in the Elk Mountains,* which Hagerman compiled in 1912. In it, Hagerman stressed a fact well known to later Pyramid climbers—the loose rock hazards of the mountain, particularly in the chimneys and couloirs.

A route on Pyramid's crumbling 1,800-foot north face was pioneered in June of 1952 by a team led by Harvey Carter. The first winter ascent of the peak was made in February 1969 by Gordon Whitmer and Fritz Stammberger.

THE ROUTES

Pyramid must rank as one of the toughest of Colorado's Fourteeners on anyone's list because of technical difficulties, loose-rock hazard, and the fact that the mountain is a very complex network of couloirs and ridges. A wrong turn on Pyramid does not bring one to a broad, grassy,

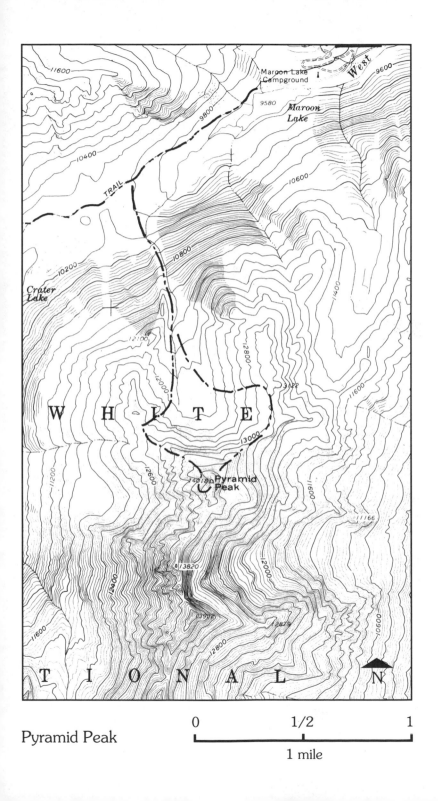

Pyramid Peak

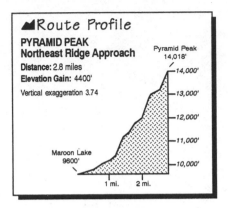

▲Route Profile

PYRAMID PEAK
Northeast Ridge Approach

Pyramid Peak
14,018'

Distance: 2.8 miles
Elevation Gain: 4400'

Vertical exaggeration 3.74

—14,000'

—13,000'

—12,000'

—11,000'

Maroon Lake
9600'

—10,000'

1 mi.   2 mi.

"Oh-well-we'll-go-down-this-way" slope but rather to a frequently hazardous situation.

The approach to Pyramid is the same approach as to the Maroon Bells. From Aspen, drive west on Colorado 82 to just across Castle Creek, a distance of one mile, then turn south in nine and one-half miles to Maroon Lake Campground (9,600 feet). In recent summers, the Maroon Lake road has been closed to private vehicles from approximately 8:30 A.M. to 5:00 P.M., and a shuttle bus is in operation. Climbers should arrive well before 8:30 A.M., of course, but anyone planning an afternoon arrival for camping is advised to contact the White River National Forest Office in Aspen at (303) 925-3445 for the latest information. In addition, backcountry camping in the immediate vicinity of Crater Lake is restricted to designated campsites only.

From the parking lot at Maroon Lake (see Maroon Peak), hike up the trail toward Crater Lake for almost one mile to an area of downed timber and rock, where an increasingly used trail wanders southeast across the drainage from Crater Lake and then south up the prominent couloir that drains the huge amphitheater of Pyramid's north side. After one mile of steep climbing into the amphitheater, contour south (right) around the amphitheater bowl to the low point of the ridge running from Pyramid's summit to a small western subpeak. Pass southwest across the ridge at about 12,700 feet and work immediately east across ledges and then up a long narrow couloir full of loose and sliding rock. The couloir ends abruptly beneath a large rock face to the south (right of the couloir exit). To the east, the view drops off into the many couloirs circling the amphitheater. Climb south up the rock steps. Party members unfamiliar with exposure may wish to use a rope here. Keep to the west of the main summit buttress. Continue south across a series of ledges, exposed and tricky if snow-covered, then east up another section of rock face, but with a good crack, to finish on the peak's south ridge a hundred feet below the summit.

For the descent, follow the north ridge around the amphitheater until a shallow couloir gives exit from the ridge to the amphitheater, at about 13,000 feet. The ridge is loose and includes at least one relatively exposed down-climb section but is generally less exposed than the western route. Once in the amphitheater, return to Crater Lake Trail via the exit couloir from the amphitheater. Climbers may wish to ascend via the descent route described or make a round-trip climb via one route. On any route of Pyramid, climbers should be especially cognizant of other parties above and below them and of both causing and becoming a target of falling rocks.

▲ *Maroon Lake to summit and return with traverse as described: 5.6 miles, 4,400 feet.*

Maroon Peak 14,156 feet (25th highest)
North Maroon Peak 14,014 feet (50th highest)

Immortalized on seemingly countless calendars, placemats, notecards, and other assorted memorabilia, for many tourists the Maroon Bells *are* Colorado. To be sure, it is the Bells's popularity and easy access more than their technical difficulties that have led inexperienced parties into trouble and earned the peaks the name "The Deadly Bells." A combination of poor rock, complex routes, and bad weather has also spelled disaster for the most competent of parties. Tourists and mystique aside, the Maroon Bells are without a doubt two of the most picturesque of Colorado's high peaks and two of the most difficult Fourteeners to climb.

The Hayden and Wheeler surveys mapped and admired the Bells but did not reach their summits. It is possible, however, that one member of the Wheeler Survey did come within several hundred feet of the summit of North Maroon, a climb that some have reported to be an early attempt on Pyramid (see page 131). The Hayden men correctly named the Bells formation "Maroon Mountain" and regarded the North Bell as merely a subpeak. Later usage prompted a change to "Maroon Peak" in an attempt to identify two distinct summits. Indeed, it seems that counting the Bells as two distinct Fourteeners stems far more from their popularity than geography. The maximum drop from the north Bell to the saddle separating it from the peak is only 234 feet in a total distance of 2,100 feet.

Hart and Bueler speculate on a possible ascent of Maroon Peak by a local boy in the 1890s, but the first documented ascent of the peak came on August 28, 1908, when Percy Hagerman reached the summit solo via the south ridge. This ascent came three days after Hagerman and Harold Clark reached the summit of North Maroon Peak via a difficult route angling up the north face.

136

The Maroon Bells in April from the northeast on the approach to Crater Lake. *(Lyndon J. Lampert)*

Following Hagerman's and Clark's pioneering climbs, the Maroon Bells became a favorite for Colorado Mountain Club parties. A particular highlight came during the club's 1928 annual outing, when an overnight excursion over Buckskin Pass from a Snowmass Lake base camp was made to climb the two peaks. One marvels that more injuries did not occur in these early years, given the large numbers usually in the climbing party. The Colorado Mountain Club Labor Day outing of 1940 put seventy-three people into base camp; forty people were in the climbing party to attempt to ascend the Bells. On this climb injuries did occur when two climbers strayed from the main group and were struck by falling rocks.

More often than not, the recent history of the Bells has been one of tragedy—tragedy brought about not so much by inexperience as by lack of respect for the unforgiving nature of the peaks. Rarely do they give a second chance. A September 1952 tragedy took the life of Gordon Schindel and severely injured his climbing companion, Larry Hackstaff. Both experienced climbers, they began a traverse from North Maroon to Maroon Peak late in the afternoon and lost control while descending the treacherous snow-filled couloir running northeast off the first main subpeak south of Maroon Peak. Only one climber carried an ice axe.

The east face of the Maroon Bells from Pyramid Peak. If the traverse from North Maroon to Maroon Peak looks exposed, it is!

The year of "The Deadly Bells" was 1965. In July, an Outward Bound instructor was knocked to his death off a ledge by falling rock. Several weeks later, three scientists from the University of California's Los Alamos Scientific Laboratory in Los Alamos, New Mexico, all experienced climbers (one was Herbert E. Ungnade, author of *Guide to the New Mexico Mountains*), fell to their deaths while roped together on a snowfield west of Maroon Peak. A fourth member survived the 1,000-foot fall only because he wore a hard hat.

During the following April, two Western State College students were killed in a fall while descending the standard northeast couloir route. A third member survived the fall. Incredibly, the climb to the summit had taken fourteen and a half hours; then, when cold discouraged a high-altitude bivouac, they began a moonlit descent to their deaths. Although each set of tragedies had multiple causes, the elements of ice axe, hard hat, and time schedule should be evident.

In the early 1970s, attention in the Elks focused on German-born skier and mountaineer Fritz Stammberger. He climbed North Maroon solo in February 1971 and Maroon Peak with Mike Pokress in December 1971, but the act that had Aspen buzzing was his daring ski descent of the North

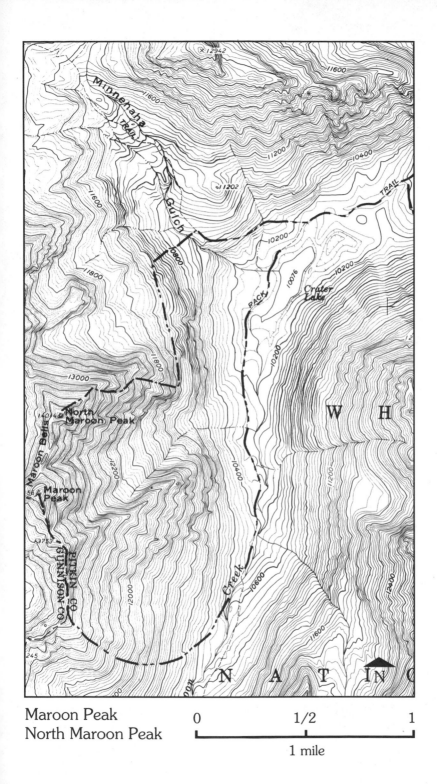

Maroon Peak
North Maroon Peak

0   1/2   1

1 mile

Bell. On June 24, 1971, after carefully calculating a line of snow-filled ledges and gullies, Stammberger climbed the route first and then made a forty-eight-minute descent down the north face.

THE ROUTES

The route-finding challenges, steepness, and exceptionally loose rock of the Maroon Bells make these peaks no place for beginning climbers. The disproportionate number of accidents and fatalities on these peaks should serve as a warning to those who would venture onto their slopes inexperienced or ill-equipped. At the very least, those who are contemplating a climb of the Bells should consider climbing with a competent guide who knows the peaks well.

From Aspen, drive west on Colorado 82 to just across Castle Creek, a distance of one mile, then turn south nine and one-half miles to Maroon Lake Campground (9,600 feet). In recent summers, the Maroon Lake road has been closed to private vehicles from approximately 8:30 A.M. to 5:00 P.M., and a shuttle bus is in operation. Climbers should arrive well before 8:30 A.M., of course, but anyone planning an afternoon arrival for camping is advised to contact the White River National Forest Office in Aspen at (303) 925-3445 for the latest information. In addition, backcountry camping in the immediate vicinity of Crater Lake is restricted to designated campsites only.

From the campground, hike southwest along a well-beaten path for one and one-half miles to Crater Lake, then west for just over a half-mile on the trail up Minnehaha Gulch to Buckskin Pass. Where the trail begins to level, descend south one hundred feet to the creek and climb south up a prominent gully topped by what in summer looks like a round, rocky island surrounded by a sea of green grass.

Cross the huge rock glacier beneath the north face of the North Bell southeast to a cairn-marked (the cairn is difficult to see) trail along the first prominent ledge below the face. Follow the ledge across the strata of the northeast face to a rocky couloir. Although they are not always visible, orange dots mark the route from here. In recent years, small rock cairns have sprung up all over the North Bell, constructed by parties making their own routes. As a result, following rock cairns is not a substitute for knowing the route from described landmarks or climbing with someone who knows the mountain.

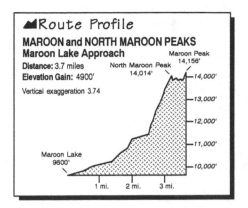

▲Route Profile

MAROON and NORTH MAROON PEAKS
Maroon Lake Approach
Distance: 3.7 miles
Elevation Gain: 4900'

Vertical exaggeration 3.74

Maroon Peak 14,156'
North Maroon Peak 14,014'
14,000'
13,000'
12,000'
11,000'
10,000'

Maroon Lake 9600'

1 mi. 2 mi. 3 mi.

Make a mental note of the exit point where the ledge intersects the couloir for the return trip and climb up the couloir, through a crack at its head, and then left (southwest) to a ridge separating it from another couloir. From the ridge separating the two couloirs, keep to the south (left) of the main ridge to the top of the second couloir and then cross the ridge onto the upper part of the north face at 13,800 feet. A twenty-foot crack with an orange dot and a large boulder at its head mark the route onto a short catwalk ridge and then up the remaining ridge to the summit. On a clear, dry day the route is obvious, but the complexity of the mountain can spell disaster in inclement weather. For the North Bell only, return the same way.

For the traverse, descend south from the North Bell down a loose and steep section and then along the ridge, staying on top or just to the west to the lowest saddle. At the low point, traverse slightly to the east, and then take a clear shot for the summit of Maroon Peak. No cairns or paint dots mark the traverse. The traverse takes at least one and one-half hours and should be attempted only if time and weather permit the long haul off Maroon Peak. Many parties desire the protection of a rope. Jim Gehres notes that the traverse from south to north is easier because one climbs up rather than down the most exposed portion and then has a shorter descent off North Maroon, although care must be taken in locating the correct descent route.

From Maroon Peak, descend via the south ridge, remaining on top of the ridge amid possibly the worst rock of the trip: loose and rotten! Circle the deep cut of the couloir, which descends east from the 13,753-foot subpeak, on the west, and drop several hundred feet off the

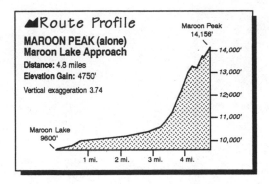

◢Route Profile

MAROON PEAK (alone)
Maroon Lake Approach

Distance: 4.8 miles
Elevation Gain: 4750'

Vertical exaggeration 3.74

Maroon Lake
9600'

Maroon Peak
14,156'

14,000'
13,000'
12,000'
11,000'
10,000'

1 mi.   2 mi.   3 mi.   4 mi.

ridge to the west for about a half-mile. Regain the ridge and follow it south for a half-mile to a ridge just south of a broad but crumbling couloir leading east to West Maroon Creek, two miles above (south of) Crater Lake. A descent via the 13,753-foot subpeak couloir should be made only by experienced parties equipped with ice axes and only after careful scrutiny of avalanche conditions. For the South Bell alone, follow the descent route.

▲ *Maroon Lake to North Bell summit: 3.2 miles, 4,400 feet.*

▲ *Maroon Lake to North and South Bell (traverse): 8.2 miles, 5,000 feet.*

▲ *Maroon Lake to South Bell summit (alone): 4.8 miles, 4,750 feet.*

Capitol Peak 14,130 feet (30th highest)

Like a giant throne—the capitol, indeed, of some noble monarch—
Capitol thrusts its summit skyward amid an intricacy of long, narrow
ridges. It is a mountain easily recognized from a distance and one on
which the summit is usually in view to climbers scaling its heights. The
mountain was named by the Hayden Survey for its resemblance to the
U.S. Capitol building, but no attempt was made to climb it because, in
Henry Gannett's words, its "prism-shaped top and precipitous sides forbid
access."

Apparently, Gannett's assessment of the peak held true until the days
of Percy Hagerman and Harold Clark's (see page 131) forays into the
Elks. Hagerman and Clark climbed Capitol on August 22, 1909, and
Hagerman later reported that "as far as we can learn no other party has
ever been on Capitol Peak. There was no evidence on the summit of
any previous ascent and the peak was reputed to be unclimbed and unclimbable by ranchmen living in its neighborhood." Their route was via
the northeast ridge, which Hagerman described as doubtless the easiest,
despite the fact that they negotiated the knife edge on hands and knees—
a procedure familiar to numerous later climbers of the peak.

Capitol is without a doubt one of the most difficult of the Fourteeners
to climb and one that offers nontechnical climbers only one approach—
the knife-edge ridge. Yet, there are those who would dispute a 1946
Rocky Mountain News headline hailing it Colorado's *most* difficult peak.
Certainly the question is more academic than practical when one considers such variables as routes, rock stability, and weather. What is true
is that Capitol's firmer rock (when compared to the Bells) has led to a
number of fine technical climbs.

143

The summit prism of Capitol Peak as viewed southwest from K2. The knife-edged ridge is running directly toward the camera.

Capitol's dramatic 1,800-foot north face has lured a number of rock climbers, beginning with the 1937 ascent by Carl Blaurock, Elwyn Arps, and Harold Popham. Although subsequent climbs were made, for years the standing winter debate of Aspen barrooms centered around who would be the first to scale Capitol's north face in winter and the godlike qualities such a person would have to possess. The gods turned out to be Aspen's own Fritz Stammberger (see page 138) and Gordon Whitmer, who reached the summit after eleven hours of face climbing on March 10, 1972. The north-face ascent came only six years after the first winter ascent of Capitol via the knife edge, in January of 1966.

THE ROUTES

Capitol Lake

The Capitol Lake approach to Capitol Peak is the route now recommended to minimize the environmental impacts of climbing parties on Capitol. Capitol Lake is a popular destination, and climbers should expect company if camping near the lake.

From the Snowmass Post Office on Colorado 82, take the paved road south up Snowmass Creek for 1.8 miles, then the right-hand (west) fork up the Capitol Creek road 8.3 miles farther to the trailhead. The final one and one-half miles of this road are very rough and can be slippery when wet—four-wheel-drive is necessary during wet conditions. The spacious parking and camping area at the end of the road offers a superb view up the Capitol Creek Valley and of Capitol Peak at its head. The Capitol Lake trail leads generally south from this point (9,400 feet) for five and one-half miles to Capitol Lake at 11,600 feet. Wood fires are banned within one-half mile of the lake.

From the lake, it is a steep scramble east to the Capitol-Daly saddle at 12,500 feet. In the summer of 1993, the Forest Service constructed a clearly cairned route up this slope and revegetated much of the rest of it. Remain on the cairned route ascending *and* descending. From the saddle, drop into the basin to the east rather than tackle the tough ridge directly to the south, and angle southwest up the basin to K-2's summit (13,664 feet). Here the fun begins! Take care not to lunge immediately for the knife edge! K-2 drops off sharply into Pierre Lakes Basin! Instead, contour around K-2's north side to the ridge and proceed to negotiate one of Colorado's most-noted routes—Capitol's knife edge. Although some daredevils insist on tightrope-walking the entire route, on a clear day

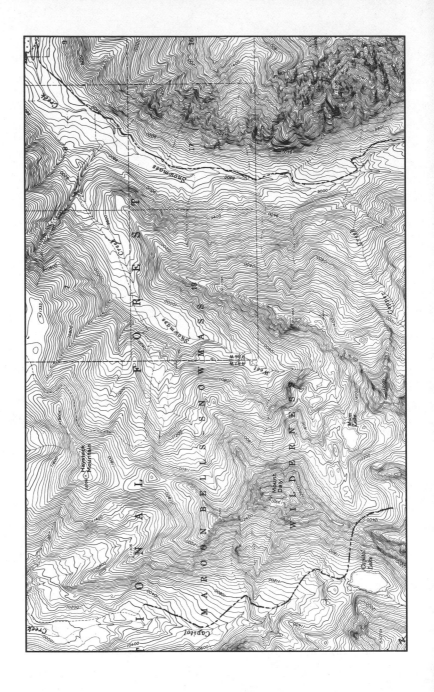

Capitol Peak

Climbers returning across Capitol Peak's knife-edge ridge.

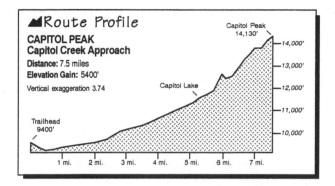

▲Route Profile

CAPITOL PEAK
Capitol Creek Approach
Distance: 7.5 miles
Elevation Gain: 5400'
Vertical exaggeration 3.74

Capitol Peak
14,130'

Capitol Lake

Trailhead
9400'

14,000'
13,000'
12,000'
11,000'
10,000'

1 mi. 2 mi. 3 mi. 4 mi. 5 mi. 6 mi. 7 mi.

(a welcome though uncommon occurrence in the Elks) the firm rock of the ridge requires little more than a steady pair of hands and a little gusto. As always, however, poor weather can turn it into a nightmare. Once across the knife edge, Capitol's rock becomes loose and dangerous for the remainder of the route, which crosses the east face and then climbs west to the summit. Climbing to the northeast ridge when it is practical avoids the section of extremely loose rock southeast of the summit.

▲ *Capitol Lake trailhead to summit: 7.5 miles, 5,400 feet.*

Snowmass Mountain 14,092 feet (32nd highest)

The great snowfield that lies on the eastern flank of Snowmass Mountain has long made it one of the most prominent summits seen from peaks well to the east. The striking beauty of the peak is furthered by its graceful upward-sweeping ridges, which encircle the better portion of the snowfield. Appropriately, this great peak is also a wilderness peak, and the eight-and-one-half-mile trip into base camp at Snowmass Lake is the longest required into any Fourteener in the state and also affords one of the most scenic backpacking trips.

Because of its prominent but isolated location, Snowmass was sighted and used as a landmark long before it was climbed. The first recorded sighting of the peak was from Grays Peak in August 1869 by William Brewer, who noted "a great Snow Peak" on the western horizon just to the left of the Mount of the Holy Cross. Oddly enough, no formal name was given to this prominent summit until the Hayden Survey of 1873, but as miners penetrated the Elk Range, the two summits of Snowmass were known to them as "The Twins."

In 1873, a Hayden Survey team led by James Gardner entered the unknown valleys near Snowmass Mountain from the south, with a climb of the peak as one of their primary objectives. Although their ascent route was from the south and not via the snowfield on the east, they were nonetheless very aware of the great expanse of snow, and they dubbed the mountain Snowmass. Henry Gannett, however, overstated the nature of the snowfield when he reported that it had an area of five square miles and was probably the closest thing to a true glacier in the Rocky Mountains. In reality, the snowfield has an area of perhaps only one square mile, and large true glaciers were later found in Wyoming's Wind River

Snowmass Mountain in the spring. This view is west from Snowmass Lake across the snow-filled basin for which the peak is famous.

Range. Nevertheless, Snowmass is an accurate and descriptive name for the peak. The name persisted, despite some discussion among members of the survey to name it "Whitehouse" as a complement to nearby Capitol Peak.

The first recorded ascent of Snowmass, on August 7, 1873, was well documented and reported by members of the climbing team. William Byers climbed and carried the original account in his *Rocky Mountain News* later in the month. In the article, he quoted James Gardner as remarking that Snowmass was "the most difficult and dangerous climb he ever made," an understandable assessment considering that he carried a forty-pound transit while rock-scrambling to the summit! Another account was later written by English author W. H. Rideing, guest of the survey, who commented that some of the party amused themselves by toppling over large boulders that went crashing down the slope, a practice definitely not recommended.

Before their work was completed on the peak, three separate ascents of Snowmass were made by the survey team. Snowmass provided an excellent vantage point into the heart of the Elks and would have been a prime location for photographic work by William Henry Jackson, but the day he climbed, inclement weather set in, spoiling potentially high-quality photographs. Since Snowmass was one of only two Elk Range Fourteeners climbed by the Hayden Survey, triangulation work from its summit was extensive, but they calculated Snowmass's height at only 13,970 feet, a figure not corrected until the twentieth century.

There was little mining activity in the immediate vicinity of Snowmass Mountain, but some silver mines operated in the 1880s and 1890s in Lead King Basin, southwest of the peak and above the town of Crystal. Miners may have climbed Snowmass Mountain, but probably not before the Hayden team in 1873. After the silver crash in 1893, the mines in Lead King Basin faded, and Snowmass Mountain returned to being one of the most isolated and least-climbed Fourteeners in the state; that is, until the tremendous backpacking boom of the 1960s.

Although James Gardner found Snowmass to be a tough climb, it is not difficult by the normal route when one is not carrying a forty-pound transit, but neighboring 13,841-foot Hagerman Peak, which thrusts 2,800 dramatic feet above Snowmass Lake, has seen some classical technical climbs. Technical routes on Snowmass have usually been traverses from either Hagerman or Capitol. Harold Clark made the first traverse of the difficult ridge between Snowmass and Hagerman in 1919. The first attempt at traversing the jagged four-mile-long ridge connecting Snowmass and Capitol was made in 1951 by Bob Allen and Karl Gustafson, but they were turned back by lightning when almost to the summit of Snowmass. The traverse was finally successfully completed by Bill Forrest and Glen Denny in 1966.

THE ROUTES

Snowmass Lake

The backpack into Snowmass Lake is one of the most popular trips in the Elk Range for the backpacker, fisherman, photographer, and climber. As a result, the area is very heavily used in the summer; take extra care to leave as little trace as possible. Use of Snowmass Lake is not under a permit system yet, but such a measure may eventually be necessary to protect the environment around the lake as well as the wilderness experience of its visitors.

The community (post office) of Snowmass is on Colorado 82, about twenty-eight miles south of Glenwood Springs and fourteen miles north of Aspen, and should not be confused with the ski area of the same name.

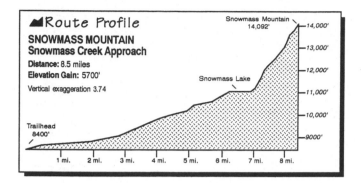

▲Route Profile

SNOWMASS MOUNTAIN
Snowmass Creek Approach

Distance: 8.5 miles
Elevation Gain: 5700'

Vertical exaggeration 3.74

Snowmass Mountain
14,092'

Snowmass Lake

Trailhead
8400'

14,000'
13,000'
12,000'
11,000'
10,000'
9000'

1 mi. 2 mi. 3 mi. 4 mi. 5 mi. 6 mi. 7 mi. 8 mi.

Drive south from the post office on a paved road for 1.8 miles to a T junction. At this junction, turn left on the Snowmass Creek road and drive 9.7 more miles to the Snowmass Lake trailhead (keep right at the junction at mile 9.3). The old Snowmass Campground once located here has been closed for years, but the forest service permits low-impact car camping near the trailhead.

Backpack up the excellent Snowmass Lake Trail past the Snowmass Falls Ranch and continue on the east side of the creek to about mile 6, where a large series of beaver ponds have dammed up the stream. Remain on the east side of the valley until the trail reaches a large logjam, which it crosses to the west side of the stream. Shortly thereafter, the trail switchbacks up the hillside and gains eight hundred feet in the final one and one-half miles to Snowmass Lake, at almost 11,000 feet. Wood fires are prohibited within one-half mile of the lake, as is camping within one hundred feet of water.

The conspicuous peak rising directly southwest of the lake is Hagerman Peak, and Snowmass Mountain is the hump directly above the rolling expanse of the snowfield basin to the right of Hagerman. The actual summit is the central high point of this hump. Pick your way around the left (southeast) shore of the lake and up the steep talus slope at the southwest end of the lake and into the snowfield basin. Until late summer, a great amount of snow may lie in this basin, and the reflection of the sun's rays can be unbearably hot—skin and eye protection is vital.

Cross the basin west for about one mile until you are below the rocky southeast ridge of Snowmass. If steep snow lies along the east side of this ridge an ice axe is handy, and spring climbers will do well to be extremely wary of avalanche danger when gaining the ridge. The rounded

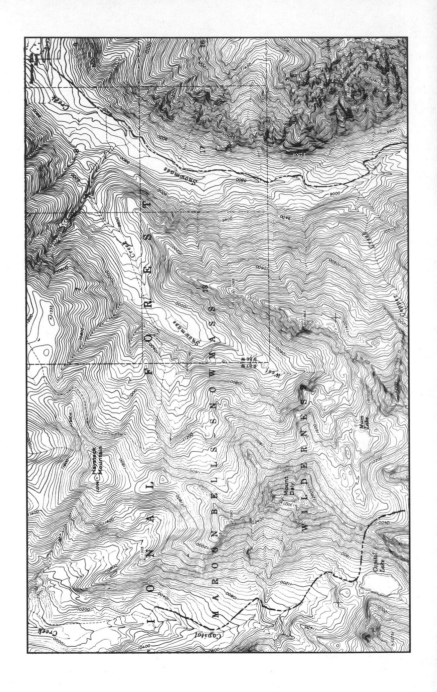

Snowmass Mountain

end portion of the ridge to the left of the summit is the easiest route to gain the crest of the ridge. Scramble up this rounded hump where it appears gentlest, and you'll wind up on the southeast ridge about one-third mile from the summit. The summit ridge may look tough, but the rock is generally sound and offers handholds when they are needed. Snowmass is a good introduction to bouldering without the necessity of a rope. Stay on top of the ridge or just to the left (west) of it the remaining distance to the summit.

▲ *Snowmass Lake to summit: 2.2 miles, 3,100 feet.*

▲ *Snowmass Lake trailhead to Snowmass Lake: 6.3 miles, 2,600 feet.*

▲ *Snowmass Lake trailhead to summit: 8.5 miles, 5,700 feet.*

Sentinels of a Spanish Legacy

The Sangre de Cristo Range

Unique in many respects, the Sangre de Cristo Range defies comparison with other ranges in Colorado. While other Colorado ranges have histories intimately tied with the Anglo mining rushes of the 1800s, the Sangre de Cristo Range is tied more closely with the history and culture of the Southwest; indeed, its snowcapped peaks may have been known to the Spanish as early as 1600. Geographically, the Sangre de Cristo is long and narrow, rising to a sharp crest with a minimum of foothills, quite unlike the more massive, rolling character of most of the other ranges in the state. Finally, even the geology of the Sangre de Cristo Range does not fit the mold of most of the state's ranges. Many of its geologic complexities are still being unraveled.

The southernmost range in the Rocky Mountain chain, the Sangre de Cristo Range runs for about two hundred miles from south of Salida well into New Mexico, terminating in the vicinity of Santa Fe. Approximately 115 miles of the range lie in Colorado, and it averages only 10 to 20 miles in width. To the west, the Sangre de Cristos are flanked by the expansive San Luis Valley, which is drained by the Rio Grande River; to the east, the Wet Mountain Valley and Huerfano Park border a substantial portion of the range.

The crest of the Sangre de Cristos lies almost 7,000 feet above the San Luis and Wet Mountain valleys, making it one of Colorado's steepest ranges overall. As a result, though the range is highly visible, few roads penetrate it and even fewer cross it.

The geology of the Sangre de Cristos has not been studied thoroughly, but the northern part of the range is basically a fault block structure. A fault block range differs from an anticlinal range in that it is lifted as a

157

block with complete breaking of overlying rock layers along at least one side, rather than arched and folded. These overlying Paleozoic layers have been eroded from the crest of the range north of Hayden Pass but are present on the very crest of the range to the south. The most notable of these sedimentary layers for the mountaineer is the Crestone Conglomerate, whose plentiful nubs and projections make for a rock climber's delight on Crestone Needle.

About twenty thousand years ago, long after the major glaciers had disappeared, Colorado became semi-arid in climate. This warming and drying had the greatest effect on vegetation, and once-lush valley floors became only sparsely vegetated. As a result, winds blowing across the wide valley floor of the San Luis Valley picked up a tremendous amount of topsoil and sand. In the San Luis Valley, winds have a tendency to funnel toward Mosca and Music passes and, as they rise, they are unable to carry all the sand over the mountains and so deposit it along the western foothills of the Sangre de Cristos. In twenty thousand years, these deposits of sand have accumulated to depths of up to seven hundred feet and formed one of the most interesting and distinctive features of the Sangre de Cristos, the Great Sand Dunes.

Following the founding of Santa Fe in 1609, Spanish missionaries and explorers gradually penetrated the country to the north. As they went, they gave names to prominent geographic features. The most common explanation for designating the range Sangre de Cristo, or "Blood of Christ," is that an unknown explorer or missionary viewed the reflection of a deep red sunset upon its peaks and in a moment of inspiration gave the range the religious name. It is not known exactly how early the Spaniards used this name, but Anglo references to the name appeared in the early 1800s.

In 1820, Mexico declared its independence from Spain, and the new government granted large parcels of land along its northern frontier to encourage settlement. Six of these grants were wholly or partially in what is now Colorado, and two of these encompassed sizable portions of the Culebra Range. The Vigil and St. Vrain Grant occupied the eastern slope of the Culebra Range, the southern one-half of the Blanca massif, and a tremendous amount of land to the east. The Sangre de Cristo Grant bordered the Culebra Range on the west and included much of the southeastern San Luis Valley. Both of these grants were given in 1843, but attempts at settlement two years later were thwarted by Indian raids. In 1849, permanent settlement began in the San Luis Valley; in 1851, the community of San Luis, Colorado's oldest town, was founded.

Most of the recent history in and around the Sangre de Cristos has revolved around agriculture and real estate development. In 1867, the Sangre de Cristo Grant was bought and divided into the Costilla and Trinchera estates, two of Colorado's first major real estate developments; the trend has continued ever since. Large land sales in the area have made access difficult into parts of the range and have also allowed for the only sole ownership of a Fourteener in the United States, Culebra Peak.

The best thing to happen in the Sangre de Cristos in the last several decades was the 1993 passage of the Colorado Wilderness Bill. It created the Sangre de Cristo Wilderness Area, a 226,455-acre preserve running almost the entire length of the range from south of Salida to the Great Sand Dunes National Monument, and including the four Fourteeners of the Crestone group. It was by far the largest new area created by the 1993 law and is exceeded in size in the entire Colorado wilderness system only by the Weminuche and Flat Top areas. Unfortunately, the heavily traveled road into South Colony Lakes was exempted from the legislation; but overall, if each of us does his or her part, the wilderness designation will go a long way toward preserving the sanctity of this special range.

Crestone Peak 14,294 feet(7th highest)
Crestone Needle 14,197 feet(20th highest)
Kit Carson Peak 14,165 feet(23rd highest)
Humboldt Peak 14,064 feet(37th highest)

Search Colorado for the sheer and abrupt grandeur of Wyoming's Tetons and one name immediately comes to mind—the Crestones. Rugged, isolated, and unforgiving, Crestone Peak and Crestone Needle dominate an area of the central Sangre de Cristo that until 1967 did not even have an adequate topographic map. A certain veil of mystery and mystique surrounding the peaks dates from the earliest Spanish forays into the San Luis Valley. De Anza's 1779 ride around the Sangre de Cristos is well documented, but for every factual account, a dozen or more legends of wandering adventurers, lost mines, and buried treasure have come down through the years with just enough historical fact to give them credence.

Many of the legends center on the large and complex underground labyrinth of Marble Cave in Marble Mountain just southeast of the Crestones. Tales of Spaniards using Indian slaves to mine gold and silver and of entrances to the cave on both sides of the range have sent spelunkers probing its depths.

While "who did what where" will probably remain veiled in mystery, some Spanish adventurers and prospectors did scour the valleys of the Sangre de Cristo. The word Crestone itself is of Spanish derivation, meaning "the top of a cock's comb," "the crest of a helmet," or in mining parlance, "an outcropping of ore."

If the Spanish presence in the Sangre de Cristo is somewhat bewildering, equally so are Anglo attempts over the next century to name and map the peaks. Mountain men noticed the similarity between these peaks and Wyoming's Tetons and gave the name "Trois Tetons" to the Crestones and one of their neighbors, either Kit Carson Peak to the northwest or

160

Crestone Peak from the north, high on Kit Carson Peak. The summit to the right (west) is the true summit, and the cliffs at the prominent couloir's base graphically demonstrate the need to exit before the couloir bends west. *(R. Omar Richardson)*

Broken Hand Peak to the south, depending on which account you prefer. The name "Trois Tetons" was duly recorded by Captain John Gunnison in his journal as he passed south of the peaks in 1853, seeking a transcontinental railroad route. Here, however, the story becomes a labyrinth of confusion. Until well into the 1900s, a wide variety of surveys placed Crestone Peak and Kit Carson in just about every location imaginable, interchanged the names, and even gave them just about every name imaginable! One 1882 map did nothing to ease the Crestone-Trois Teton confusion by adding the names "Mount Celeste" and "Mount Julia" to the group. Even today, some old-timers in the town of Crestone on the San Luis Valley side insist on calling Kit Carson "Crestone Peak." Thus, tales of naming the peaks are almost as boundless as are tales of buried Spanish treasure.

One bright light does shine through the veil to illuminate the naming and first ascent of Humboldt Peak. In sharp contrast to the rugged Crestones, Humboldt sprawls like a giant anthill east into the Wet Mountain Valley from the high plateau separating Crestone Peak and Kit Carson. In the spring of 1870, Carl Wulsten, a Prussian immigrant and one-time

Crestone Needle from Humboldt Peak: The nontechnical route gains the saddle at left and then climbs to the summit via the second rib west of the skyline. Ellingwood Arête descends straight down from the summit. *(R. Omar Richardson)*

Civil War general, led a band of German settlers into the Wet Mountain Valley in an attempt to establish the first cooperative community in Colorado. The group built homes, plowed fields, and planted crops to the southwest of present-day Westcliffe, naming their hoped-for utopia Colfax, after the then vice-president of the United States. The promises of spring, however, were unfulfilled, and a series of problems, not the least being Wulsten's tactless leadership and a devastating fire, scattered the settlement.

In subsequent years, however, a large influx of German settlers continued to such valley towns as Ula, Rosita, Querida, Silver Cliff, and Westcliffe. Although primarily farmers, these newcomers mined the eastern slopes of the Sangre de Cristo. In 1874, Leonard Frederick located the Humboldt Mine near the slopes of what became known as Humboldt Peak. The name honored Alexander von Humboldt, an eminent German geographer, explorer, and mountaineer who gained particular fame in mountaineering circles with an unsuccessful 1802 assault on Ecuador's Mount Chimborazo, then thought by some to be the highest peak in the world. As part of the Land Office Surveys of 1883, the peak was climbed,

The view southeast to Crestone Needle from the summit of Crestone Peak. As is obvious from the photograph, the traverse is nothing to mess with in bad weather. *(Craig F. Koontz)*

probably by surveyor T. P. Momson, and clearly recorded as Humboldt Peak. No serious attempt was made to penetrate the mountain walls to the west.

By 1916, the names of Crestone Peak, Crestone Needle, and Kit Carson Peak were reasonably well established on the peaks we know today and, perhaps most significantly, were the only 14,000-foot peaks in Colorado that were unclimbed. In the summer of 1916, Albert R. Ellingwood, the grand master of early Colorado climbing, and seven others made camp in the drainage of Willow Creek, northwest of the peaks, in high spirits, in Ellingwood's words, "fed by tales of peaks unclimbed and peaks unclimbable." The party ascended the northwest ridge of Kit Carson, scrambled over the northwest subpeak (14,080 feet), and made the first documented ascent of Kit Carson.

Kit Carson, of course, was named for the famous scout who, in the mid-1860s, commanded the garrison at Fort Garland at the foot of Blanca Peak. Here too, local legend and lore run deep, with some asserting that the great scout lived in a cabin near the peak's base for several years. A rip-roaring contemporary of old Kit's was Indian agent Thomas FitzPatrick, whose Indian name, Broken Hand, is remembered in 13,573-foot Broken Hand Peak, southeast of Crestone Needle. Broken Hand is the first prominent landmark that climbers see as they navigate the South Colony road, and more than one group has mistaken it for Crestone Peak—a mistake that is soon apparent when the Needle looms in view.

With one down and two to go, "the more energetic of the party," Ellingwood, Eleanor Davis, Frances "Bee" Rogers, and Joe Deutchbein, moved their camp south to the Spanish Creek drainage to test, in Ellingwood's words, "the unclimbability of the Crestones." On July 24, 1916, the quartet got an exceptionally late (8:10 A.M.) start and proceeded up Crestone's north arête and into the north couloir, reaching the summit of the main peak at 12:40. After constructing a cairn on each of the twin summits (Ellingwood incorrectly guessed the eastern point was higher), the party gingerly began the traverse to the Needle. Ellingwood found, as have later climbers, that "progress on the ridge was most encouraging, for the gendarmes that stood up like Cleopatra's Needle on the east were of a gentler aspect on the other side, and lent themselves to prudential circumvention." Halfway across, Deutchbein, who was troubled with a bad knee, and Miss Rogers returned to the Spanish Creek camp, but Ellingwood and Miss Davis continued the traverse, finishing on the conglomerate-studded northwest wall of the Needle. Here, Ellingwood and Davis built a third cairn and claimed the last unclimbed Fourteener in

Kit Carson Peak viewed to the north from Crestone Peak. *(Craig F. Koontz)*

the state. As twilight approached, the pair hurried down the southeast ridge, glimpsed the prominent eastern arête, skirted the South Colony Lakes, and returned to their campsite via the Crestone-Humboldt saddle, arriving at 11:15 P.M.

Once conquered, the peaks continued to lure only a handful of climbers during the next decade. Eleanor Davis and Albert Ellingwood with Stephen H. Hart and Marion Warner returned in August of 1925 to pioneer the classic eastern arête of Crestone Needle, now known as "Ellingwood Arête." The 1925 Annual Outing of the Colorado Mountain Club made a traverse of Crestone Needle to the Peak, only its fifth recorded ascent. As late as September of 1929, *Trail and Timberline* reported only the fifth ascent of Kit Carson.

With climbing interest increasing, the peaks withstood one more attempt to confuse their names. In 1923, the Colorado Mountain Club officially added the name "Crestone Needle" to its list of high points. A year later, club member Roger Toll suggested changing Crestone Needle to "Mallory Peak" and North Maroon Peak to "Mount Irvine." Mallory and Irvine's names were on the lips of the climbing world for their mysterious disappearance the preceding spring while high in the

The plaque placed atop Challenger Point on Kit Carson Peak. This view is to the south, to the Sand Dunes and Blanca massif. *(Alan Silverstein)*

Humboldt Peak as seen from the west, across the pinnacles of the Crestone Needle to the Peak ridge. *(Craig F. Koontz)*

mists of Mount Everest. Nothing was done, however, and the matter quickly dropped; yet Crestone Needle was again suggested for a name change in 1976 when members of the Colorado Centennial-Bicentennial Commission were searching for a peak to christen "Centennial Peak." A visit by one commission member to the town of Crestone revealed that old-timers might call Kit Carson "Crestone" and vice versa, but they did not want any part of "Centennial Peak." The name was finally bestowed on Banded Mountain, an inconspicuous subpeak of Hesperus Peak in the La Platas.

The thousand-foot northeast wall of the Crestones has become a favorite for rock climbers, with such climbing greats as Bob Ormes, Bill House, Dick Pownall, and Bill Forrest pioneering technical climbs. The face must rank with the north faces of Blanca and Capitol as one of Colorado's most challenging rock climbs. The challenges of winter ascents were met in the 1960s, culminating in a traverse of the Needle to the Peak on March 17, 1972, by a party of Pat McGrane, Charles Campbell, and John Rehmer, which ended with a forced bivouac at 13,300 feet on Crestone Peak.

The unforgiving nature of these peaks was dramatized in June 1979, when four young climbers plummetted to their deaths while making a roped descent on Kit Carson's north face. The three teenage boys and their young-adult leader were members of an expedition from a Missouri-based troubled teen program. The four were roped and equipped with ice axes and were apparently descending the snowfields above upper Willow Lake after an attempt on the northwest ridge of Kit Carson when they got off route and fell to their deaths.

In recent years, the death toll on the Crestones has been every bit as grim as that of the "deadly Bells." John Holyoke, an experienced and veteran climber, died on Crestone Peak in 1981. The following year, Matthew O'Connor, Dave Madsen, and D. Evan Best, Jr., died in separate accidents involving long falls on Crestone Needle. Douglas Hunt died in a fall on Crestone Needle in 1992. At least one search and rescue mission, and frequently many more, takes place on these peaks every year. These mountains are unforgiving.

In 1987, the 14,081-foot northwest subpeak of Kit Carson was named Challenger Point, commemorating the crew members of the space shuttle Challenger who lost their lives on January 28, 1986. A bronze plaque was placed on the summit on July 19, 1987, by a party led by Alan Silverstein.

THE ROUTES

South Colony Lakes

When the nominations are made for the paradise of Colorado, the Wet Mountain Valley rolling up the green flanks of the Sangre de Cristo Range to the summits of the Crestones must surely be among them. From Westcliffe, drive south on Colorado 69 for about four and one-half miles to Colfax Lane, then right (south) on Colfax Lane for five more miles until it comes to a T intersection and turns west, climbs through several fence lines, and becomes increasingly rocky. Most cars stop at the forest boundary, although jeeps and an occasional Volkswagen have made it six miles more to the end of the trail beneath Broken Hand Peak.

The South Colony Lakes road was exempted from wilderness designation in the 1993 legislation creating the Sangre de Cristo Wilderness Area, so it will remain open to vehicles. In many respects this is unfortunate, because the road is rough, heavily traveled, and brings too many people into what would be a relatively remote area without it. The forest service plans to construct a new trailhead a short distance farther east on the

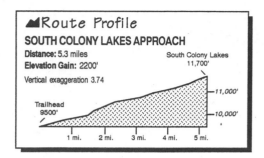

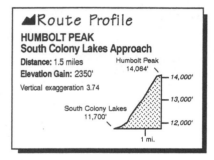

road in an attempt to reduce the impact on the area immediately below Broken Hand Peak.

From the end of the road, lower South Colony Lake is one-half mile north along a well-used trail. Large parties should use any number of campsites along the road, but smaller groups will find several campsites near the lakes. Minimum-impact camping is a must! This is definitely one of those spots that should be visited, if at all possible, during the week. Weekends have seen major traffic jams.

From South Colony Lakes, Humboldt is the easily distinguishable anthill-type mountain one mile to the northeast. It is an easy climb from the lakes, providing one puts up with combinations of talus and scree. Farther down (east) the valley from the lakes, the climb gets steeper and leads one into the very prominent avalanche chutes that frequently discharge their burden of white death in the early spring.

The minimum-impact route is to follow the trail north from the upper lake to the saddle west of Humboldt, turning right (east) at the saddle and climbing to the summit via the west ridge. Returning the same way—all of the way to the saddle—will prevent further erosion and deterioration

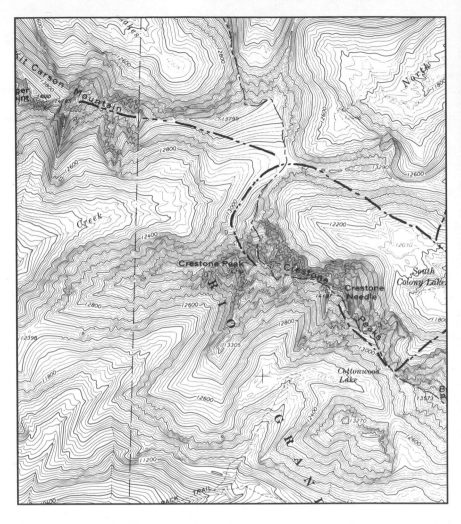

Crestone Peak, Crestone Needle
Kit Carson Peak, Humboldt Peak

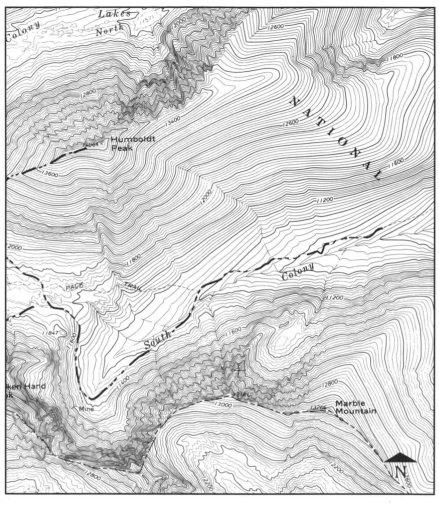

0   1/2   1

1 mile

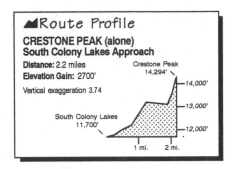

▲Route Profile
CRESTONE PEAK (alone)
South Colony Lakes Approach
Distance: 2.2 miles
Elevation Gain: 2700'
Vertical exaggeration 3.74
Crestone Peak 14,294'
14,000'
13,000'
South Colony Lakes 11,700'
12,000'
1 mi.   2 mi.

of the peak's southwest slopes. Humboldt offers an unparalleled view of the Crestones and the routes on Crestone Peak and Kit Carson.

▲ *Lower South Colony Lake to Humboldt: 1.5 miles, 2,350 feet.*

Ah yes, the Crestones! What a contrast in rock stability within yards! The route up the Needle from the south is on solid rock with plenty of handholds. The route in the north-face couloir of Crestone Peak is crumbly and frequently icy and slick. The Needle and Peak are frequently climbed together; the south to north (the Needle to Peak) traverse is the easier way. Individual climbs do best to follow the directions given for that peak in the traverse description. From the lakes, climb southwest to the low point of the Needle's southeast ridge, a route marked with cairns. Atop the ridge, a cairn-marked trail leads north into the second prominent rock gully. The first gully is steeper and airier, but it also ends up on the summit. The couloir is steep and a little airy, but the rock is superb and handholds are plentiful once the summer sun has emptied the place of ice and snow. The couloir climbs straight up to just southeast of the summit, and then it's northwest on the ridge several hundred feet to the top. For the Needle only, return the same way.

The traverse to the Peak is long but not particularly difficult once one is down the first pitch northwest of the Needle's summit. A fixed rope or rappel will make the one hundred feet from Needle summit to ridge more secure. The rock is conglomerate with ample handholds, but since one false step will deposit climbers a thousand feet down the east face, more timid and frequently wiser souls enjoy the use of a rope. The trick to the Needle-Peak traverse is to drop down the southwest couloirs of the ridge just enough to avoid the spires on the ridge proper but not so far that one loses precious elevation. The goal is the red couloir and saddle,

▲Route Profile

CRESTONE NEEDLE and PEAK
South Colony Lakes Approach

Distance: 1.8 miles

Elevation Gain: 3200'

Vertical exaggeration 3.74

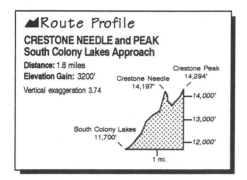

very visible from most of the ridge, which runs within two hundred feet of the Peak's summit. Climbing to the ridge before the red couloir will require skirting the 14,000-foot point east of the red saddle. Upon reaching the red saddle, climb left (west) to the summit.

From the summit of the Peak, return to the red saddle and descend the north couloir, a painful array of smooth slab rock sprinkled with sand, ice, and loose rock. As the couloir swings increasingly northwest, exit to the north at the first opportunity. The point is about a thousand feet in elevation below the saddle and a few hundred feet above the sharp cliffs at the couloir's foot. (This makes a spectacular photograph from Kit Carson.) The exit drops one into a large plateau, the Bears Playground, between Kit Carson and the Peak. From here, the route swings east, skirts the Peak's northeast ridge, offers a fantastic silhouette of the Needle with Ellingwood Arête on the left-hand skyline, and drops down a scree-filled couloir to the upper lake.

For Kit Carson, climb to the Bears Playground via a couloir leading northwest from the upper lake. Contour across the north side of the plateau, angling for the highest visible point, which is the east false summit of Kit Carson (not the 13,800-foot point directly north of the plateau). With steep sides to the north and south, it is just as easy to climb over the false summit as to traverse. Then descend on the west-southwest side of the subpeak via a series of chutes and cracks into the bottom of a rather dramatic cut. The climb is steep, but the route obvious and the rock firm. Scramble across the cut and up the final five hundred feet to Kit Carson's summit, amid generally loose talus and scree.

▲ *Lower South Colony Lake to Crestone Needle: 1 mile, 2,500 feet.*

▲ *Lower South Colony Lake to Crestone Peak: 2.2 miles, 2,700 feet.*

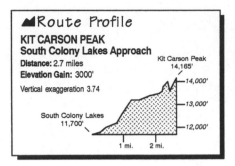

▲Route Profile

KIT CARSON PEAK
South Colony Lakes Approach
Distance: 2.7 miles
Elevation Gain: 3000'
Vertical exaggeration 3.74

Kit Carson Peak
14,165'

14,000'
13,000'
12,000'

South Colony Lakes
11,700'

1 mi.   2 mi.

▲ *Lower South Colony Lake to Needle-Peak traverse, round-trip: 4 miles, 3,200 feet, but hard.*
▲ *Lower South Colony Lake to Kit Carson: 2.7 miles, 3,000 feet, plus 350 feet on return over subpeak.*

A number of routes also exist on Kit Carson from the Willow Creek and Spanish Creek drainages of the San Luis Valley. Similar approaches for the Peak and Needle still involve the described upper routes, although from Cottonwood Creek an easier route ascends the gully leading to the red couloir on the Peak.

Blanca Peak 14,345 feet (4th highest)
Ellingwood Peak 14,042 feet (43rd highest)
Little Bear Peak 14,037 feet (44th highest)

The Sierra Blanca abounds in those things that make great mountains great—a dominating position overlooking the vastness of the San Luis Valley, steep peaks whose great rock faces beckon the mountaineer, and a rich and colorful history. The king peak of the Sierra Blanca is Blanca Peak, and it is encircled with a number of lesser summits creating such a striking hierarchy of form that Franklin Rhoda noted in 1875 "such a beautiful subordination of parts we had not seen before anywhere among the mountains of Colorado." Over one hundred years later, few mountaineers who stand upon Blanca's summit would disagree with Rhoda's assessment of the magnificent Sierra Blanca.

A landmark since the prehistoric settlers of the San Luis Valley, the Sierra Blanca has watched the march of the Ute, Spanish, and Anglo cultures across the valleys around its base. Spanish influence is seen in the name *Sierra Blanca,* meaning simply "White Mountain," and probably applied because snow is visible high on the massif throughout the year. The name appears as early as E. G. Beckwith's report of the Gunnison expedition of 1853, but it may have been used much earlier by the Spanish. Blanca became the name of the highest summit of the Sierra at an early date, but "Little Bear" and "Ellingwood" were not given as names until much later.

The first recorded ascent of Blanca Peak was on August 14, 1874, by Gilbert Thompson and Frank Carpenter of the Wheeler Survey; yet, much to their surprise, they found a man-made stone breastwork on the summit. Undoubtedly, the Utes had climbed the peak and used it as a lookout, or perhaps it was the work of some adventuresome Spaniard out to see what was up there. Blanca was one of the few Fourteeners

The north face of Blanca Peak from the upper Huerfano Valley. Ellingwood Peak is to the right. *(Photograph courtesy Colorado Historical Society)*

on which the Wheeler Survey preceded the Hayden Survey; yet, characteristically, it is the Hayden Survey's record, thanks again to the recording detail of Franklin Rhoda, that is more complete. Rhoda climbed the peak with A. D. Wilson and Frederic Endlich on June 19, 1875. His account is rich in detail and is published in some length in Bueler's *Roof of the Rockies*. Rhoda made note of Old Baldy (Lindsey), and without naming it, Little Bear. Another Hayden party climbed Blanca the following year, and in the 1876 report, Wilson gave the peak an elevation of 14,413 feet, then thought to be the highest in the state.

After the survey ascents of Blanca, the possibility that the peak was the highest in the Rockies made it a natural goal for the venturesome mountaineer. In 1888, Charles Fay and J. R. Edmands set out to ascend Blanca, but in the confusion of ridges and valleys found themselves standing on the summit of West Peak instead. Between West Peak and Blanca itself lay a one-and-one-half-mile narrow ridge that Rhoda had described as being "perfectly impassable to man." Although Fay disputed Rhoda's opinion, he and Edmands decided that time did not permit attempting a traverse, and so they descended. Although Fay and Edmands failed to reach Blanca on this climb, what they perhaps did not realize was that their climb of West Peak (now Little Bear) was certainly a first ascent. A difficult peak, Little Bear was seldom climbed until the mid-1900s. The name change was made in 1916, and John Jerome Hart states that the peak acquired the name of "Little Bear Creek" at its foot, but the 1965 Twin Peaks Quadrangle shows no sign of Little Bear Creek, only Little Bear Lake, suggesting that the name of the creek has been changed since 1916.

The spectacular ridges and great faces of the Sierra Blanca inevitably attracted some of the foremost rock climbers of the twentieth century. The greatest face in the Sierra is the one-mile-wide and 1,500-foot-high north face of Blanca and Ellingwood peaks. The first ascent of this face was by Robert Ormes and Harold Wilm in 1927. A more direct route up this face was pioneered by a Colorado College team in 1948, and other routes have become increasingly popular in recent years. Blanca's tough northeast ridge may have been first climbed by Enos Mills in an early 1900s winter ascent, but details in his *Spell of the Rockies* are extremely sketchy—so much so that it is not certain whether he climbed Blanca or some other peak in the vicinity. The first verified ascent of the northeast ridge was made by Carl Blaurock and Mary Cronin in 1937. Blanca's southeast face remained unclimbed until 1938, when Joe Merhar and others successfully scaled it.

Although most of the attention has focused on Blanca, neighboring Little Bear has also seen some technical climbing. Little Bear's most imposing side, its 1,200-foot east face, has impressed many climbers, but as of 1993 it remained unconquered, perhaps the highest unclimbed face in Colorado. In 1931, Rhoda's "impassable" ridge between Little Bear and Blanca was first traversed by Joe Merhar and Dale Norton, who thereby conquered what may be the toughest connecting ridge between any two Fourteeners in the state. In the early days, Little Bear was climbed by its south ridge, probably the easiest route, but in 1943, Carl Blaurock, Roy Murchison, and Herb Hollister ascended Little Bear via Lake Como Basin and the west ridge, which in Hollister's words, "had plenty of everything wrong with it that any ridge could have." On September 1, 1956, tragedy struck on Little Bear when Banks Caywood fell to his death while descending the west side of the peak. It had become clear that Little Bear had no "easy" route, and the peak remains one of Colorado's most challenging Fourteeners.

One-half mile northwest of Blanca Peak is Ellingwood Peak, which has recently been recognized as a separate Fourteener. Although the status of Ellingwood Peak was once disputed, the achievements of its namesake are not (see page 80). Since Ellingwood was neglected for so many years, no records of a first ascent are available, but it is probable

Ellingwood Peak from the southwest above Lake Como.

that it was climbed before the twentieth century because it is located so near Blanca Peak. In recent years, Ellingwood's northeast face has seen a number of technical climbs.

Some prospecting and mining was done in the Sierra Blanca through the 1930s, but none of the strikes were exceedingly rich. In 1899, free gold was discovered in Big Bear Canyon, in the vicinity of Bear Lake (now Lake Como). The original claim was the Commodore, and a small mining camp known as Commodore Camp was laid out in the canyon. The camp was never more than just that—a mining camp—and was short-lived because ownership disputes over the Commodore halted production before the area boomed. Even false rumors of a fantastic gold strike on the very summit of Blanca Peak in 1932 failed to bring eager prospectors to the area, and today only scattered remains in the basins below Blanca Peak remind the hiker and mountaineer of the prospectors' broken dreams.

In recounting the history of Blanca Peak, it would be an oversight to ignore the exploits of Donald E. Bennett, one-time Alamosa radio announcer. As is understandable, Bennett was quite fond of Blanca Peak, which is highly visible from Alamosa. Perhaps not quite so understandable are the lengths to which Bennett went to have Blanca publicized and calculated as the highest peak in Colorado, if not in all of the forty-eight states. Bennett's promotions began in 1935 with an Easter sunrise service on the summit of the peak. Forty-three people trudged through waist-deep snow to sing "The Old Rugged Cross" and "Rock of Ages" on the summit. The following year Bennett again organized a sunrise service for Easter, but as an added feature, Miss Helen Jacks and D. J. Edgar were to be married on the summit immediately following the service. As things turned out, only about one-half of the thirty who started the climb made the summit, and the couple were actually married in a cabin below timberline.

The semi-failure of the 1936 expedition did not stop Dan Bennett, however. In 1939, Bennett began concentrated efforts to prove that Blanca was the highest point in Colorado. Convinced that modern calculations of the peak's height were too low, Bennett took it upon himself to aid in the measurement of the peak. In August of 1939, he attempted to erect a fifty-foot pole on the summit of the peak that was equipped with a reflector at the top from which surveyors could make accurate measurements and then subtract fifty feet to obtain the height of the peak. In his first attempt, Bennett failed to erect the entire pole on the summit because of the limited space and high winds, but he

Little Bear Peak from the Lake Como Basin; its west ridge runs to the right.

nonetheless personally determined Blanca's elevation as 14,475 feet, by far the highest in Colorado.

When the whole affair was over, the U.S. Geological Survey failed to give Blanca any better than fourth place among Colorado's peaks, and Bennett abandoned his efforts once and for all. Interestingly enough, however, on the latest 7½′ quadrangle of Blanca Peak, published in 1967, Blanca's elevation of 14,345 feet is printed as an unchecked elevation, the only such occurrence for any Colorado Fourteener mapped by the U.S. Geological Survey—just one more confusing detail in the saga of Blanca Peak's much-disputed elevation.

THE ROUTES

Lake Como
Climbers who climb in the Sierra Blanca via the traditional routes usually have one of two basic photos among their records of the climb—either a "this-is-where-we-had-to-walk-from-in-the-middle-of-a-desert" photo or a "this-is-where-the-jeep-broke-down" photo. The Lake Como

Blanca Peak, Ellingwood Peak, Little Bear Peak

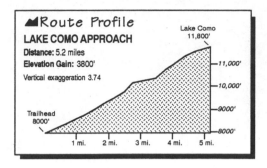

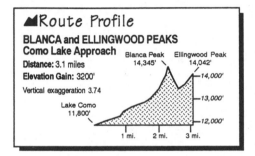

road is undoubtedly one of the roughest in the state. Its large boulders and sharp ledges have claimed the tires, U-joints, and transmissions of countless jeeps and would-be jeeps driven by even those worthy of a C. W. McCall recounting of their exploits. On Colorado 150, either three miles north of U.S. 160 or fourteen miles south of Great Sand Dunes National Monument, turn east on a dirt road running almost directly northeast toward Blanca's summit. After two miles, the decision is usually made as to which type of picture the group will cherish, and the road switchbacks the remaining four and one-half miles up first Chokecherry and then Holbrook canyons to Lake Como (11,740 feet). The lake has some private cabins around it, and camping is best done about a half-mile farther east up the valley amid some pines at timberline beneath the awesome hunk of Little Bear.

For Blanca and Ellingwood, continue northeast on a pack trail past Crater Lake for two miles and then angle east up the imposing but relatively easy west face of Blanca. For the traverse to Ellingwood, those

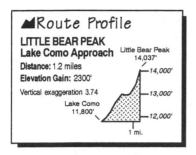

▲Route Profile

LITTLE BEAR PEAK
Lake Como Approach
Distance: 1.2 miles
Elevation Gain: 2300'

Vertical exaggeration 3.74

Little Bear Peak
14,037'

14,000'

13,000'

Lake Como
11,800'

12,000'

1 mi.

who are willing to forgo the scenic ridge route (the north side of the ridge drops sharply off the peaks' north faces) find it easier to descend several hundred feet below the connecting saddle and then scramble up Ellingwood's southeast slopes. Both climbs are relatively easy while affording impressive views, particularly of Little Bear.

▲ *Lake Como to Blanca, Ellingwood traverse, and return: 5 miles, 3,200 feet.*

For Little Bear, from the camp area above Lake Como, climb directly south up the prominent couloir, tricky in late-spring snow, to Little Bear's west ridge. Follow the ridge east until a sharp cut interrupts, dropping a steep couloir north into Como Basin. At the cut, leave the ridge and contour south, maintaining elevation and following a hit-and-miss assortment of cairns about a quarter of a mile to a narrow couloir that climbs directly to Little Bear's summit, six hundred feet above. The couloir is extremely steep, filled with much loose rock, and is almost certain to have snow and ice in it, even late in the season. Use extreme caution. Rockfall is a particular hazard in this couloir. Once on top, the Little Bear–Blanca ridge is one of the classics but should be attempted only by experienced parties when weather permits at least three hours on the tightrope.

▲ *Lake Como to Little Bear: 1.2 miles, 2,300 feet, but tough climbing!*

Mount Lindsey 14,042 feet (42nd highest)

Rising only two miles east of well-known Blanca Peak, Mount Lindsey nonetheless retains an individuality in form and history quite apart from the Blanca massif. While Blanca and its nearer satellites are angular and have some outstanding rock faces, Mount Lindsey is a comparatively smooth massive cone, rising from the high mountain valleys in a single summit with few intervening foothills. In addition, while Blanca, Little Bear, and Ellingwood peaks have histories associated with many great climbers, Mount Lindsey was most familiar to primarily one man who held a deep affection for the peak—that man was Malcolm Lindsey.

Mount Lindsey is highly visible from nearby valleys, and it was therefore natural that the peak would become a landmark for early settlers. Showing a remarkable lack of imagination, some observant pioneer noted the absence of trees on much of the peak and christened it "Old Baldy." When members of the Hayden Survey noted Old Baldy on their June 19, 1875, ascent of Blanca, they made no suggestions for changing the name, nor did they decide that an ascent of Old Baldy was necessary for their purposes. However, the peak was climbed by Wheeler men later in the year—the first official ascent. Missing a golden opportunity, the Wheeler Survey also failed to suggest a substitute name for Old Baldy, and that name remained for seventy-eight more years.

In the years that followed, Old Baldy was one of the least climbed of all Colorado's Fourteeners, and it slumbered in relative obscurity until the arrival of Malcolm Lindsey. He was born in Pennsylvania in 1880 but grew up in Trinidad. There he became acquainted with the slopes of the peak that would one day bear his name, and he developed a genuine love for Old Baldy. In 1906 he was admitted to the Colorado Bar

184

Looking east to Mount Lindsey from the summit ridge of Ellingwood Peak. *(Gary Koontz)*

and subsequently practiced law in a number of the state's communities. He became legal counsel to the city of Denver in 1925 and then served as city attorney from 1937 to 1947. Lindsey took an active part in community affairs, and he was a member of the Sons of The American Revolution and a lay leader in the Episcopal Church for forty-eight years.

Malcolm Lindsey joined the Colorado Mountain Club in 1922 and became a vital force in that organization's junior activities; he led many groups of teenagers to the summit of Old Baldy. Lindsey served very ably on the state board of directors of the Colorado Mountain Club for many years, and was president from 1943-1946. It was with great sadness that members of the Colorado Mountain Club and the citizens of Denver noted his death on November 12, 1951.

In remembrance of Lindsey's years of service to the Colorado Mountain Club, members of that organization submitted a proposal to the United States Board of Geographic Names to change the name of Old Baldy to "Mount Malcolm Lindsey." On July 30, 1953 the name change was approved, and the designation of "Old Baldy" became the superbly appropriate "Mount Lindsey." Formal dedication ceremonies were held on July 4, 1954, when sixty-four climbers reached the summit and forty

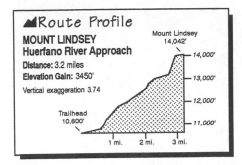

▲Route Profile
MOUNT LINDSEY
Huerfano River Approach
Distance: 3.2 miles
Elevation Gain: 3450'
Vertical exaggeration 3.74

Mount Lindsey
14,042'

14,000'
13,000'
12,000'
11,000'

Trailhead
10,600'

1 mi.   2 mi.   3 mi.

others participated in the ceremonies at a marker on U.S. 160, all in commemoration of a great Fourteener and a great Coloradan.

THE ROUTES

Huerfano River

Because private land surrounds most of Mount Lindsey, only one approach is available, unless one possesses the daring to follow the long and difficult Blanca ridge to the peak. From Gardner, drive southwest on Colorado 69 for eight miles to Redwing. Redwing may also be reached from U.S. 160 atop La Veta Pass via the Pass Creek road. When approaching Redwing, take care to continue on the main road southwest and DO NOT turn left and take the fork that leads directly past the Redwing Post Office. Continue beyond Redwing for nine miles to the Singing River Ranch and the end of the road for most passenger cars driven by sane drivers. Pickups and four-wheel-drives can continue through four miles of the ranch, taking care to close gates and not to camp on private land, to the National Forest boundary and two miles beyond to the end of the road (10,640 feet). A number of fine campsites dot the valley.

From the trailhead, hike south one mile on the trail to just beyond (less than a quarter of a mile) the unmarked Lily Lake turnoff. Here a cairn-marked trail (hard to find on the valley floor) leaves the main trail and climbs southeast (left) along the southern edge of a prominent talus field. The trail climbs up a narrow valley and emerges onto broad flats at the valley's head. Gain the ridge running northeast from the saddle at the valley's head between the saddle and where Mount Lindsey rises behind the ridge. Lindsey is connected to this ridge by a ridge running

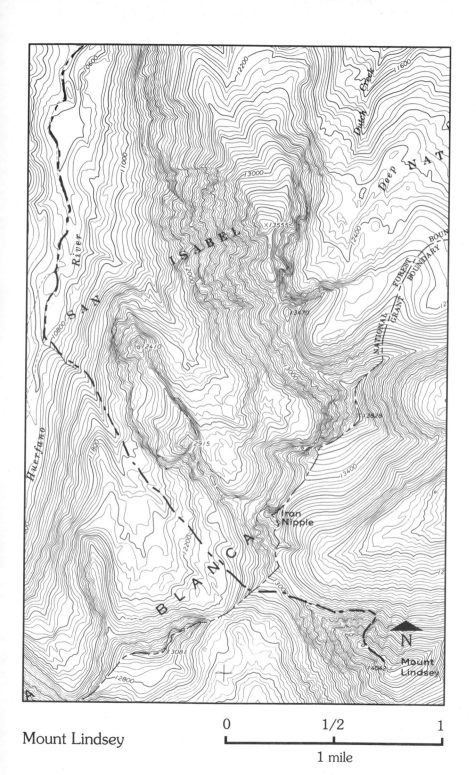

Mount Lindsey

0   1/2   1

1 mile

northwest-southeast. This northwest ridge of Lindsey offers some tricky rock work, but it avoids the loose rock of the route we have always described. That standard cairned route climbs southeast up a scree couloir before turning south up rock slabs to gain the summit ridge just northwest of the summit.

▲ *Trailhead to summit: 3.2 miles, 3,450 feet.*

The Huerfano River Valley also offers access to Blanca's superb north face and to climbs of Ellingwood Peak, Iron Nipple, and California Peak.

Culebra Peak 14,047 feet (41st highest)

The southernmost Fourteener in Colorado, Culebra Peak misses by less than ten miles being the highest peak in New Mexico instead of the forty-first highest in Colorado. Appropriately, Culebra is a peak closely tied with the Spanish heritage of southern Colorado, and while not as heralded as many other Colorado Fourteeners, it retains an individual identity that surpasses many of the state's better-known peaks.

Culebra's Spanish ties begin with its name. *Culebra* means "snake" in Spanish, and the name probably originally applied to Culebra Creek and later to the mountain, for the reptiles are far more plentiful along the lower reaches of streams than on the slopes of Fourteeners. References to the Rio de la Culebra appear as early as 1810, but the stream was probably well known to the Spanish much earlier than that. Culebra as applied to the peak, however, has not been found to be officially documented before 1869.

Due to its geographic location on the Spanish frontier, there is a good possibility that Culebra was first ascended by a Spanish explorer, but no records have been found to support such a hypothesis. There is an even stronger possibility that Culebra was first climbed in the 1840s, for the peak was very near boundaries of the Sangre de Cristo, Vigil and St. Vrain, and Maxwell grants. Culebra Peak was a prominent landmark for the area, and it would not be too unlikely that a Spanish surveyor climbed it in an attempt to define the nebulous boundaries of the three grants. Nonetheless, although Spanish explorers or Spanish land grant surveyors may well have climbed the peak earlier, the first documented ascents of Culebra were made in 1875 by both the Wheeler and Hayden surveys.

As the years passed, the land surrounding Culebra underwent the

Culebra Peak, viewed to the south from the first false summit. *(Gary Koontz)*

typical land-grant selling and subdividing. The huge grants were quickly whittled down, but gradually a sizable chunk surrounding Culebra Peak consolidated into the hands of one man. By buying out all heirs to the land in the vicinity of Culebra Peak, Delfino Salazar eventually gained sole ownership of the mountain and a large portion of the surrounding land. As climbs of Culebra became more popular, those who climbed it also usually met Delfino Salazar, who graciously allowed climbers access to Culebra and, as an added bonus, often gave entertaining campfire talks on the history of the area. When Delfino Salazar died on May 11, 1958, it marked the end of an era in Culebra's history. His vast ranch, totaling some 77,000 acres, was bought by Jack Taylor, a North Carolina lumber and land tycoon. Long a working cattle ranch, the Taylor spread is only just beginning to feel the pressures of those who seek to develop its potential as a high-density recreation area. Jack Taylor died in 1988, but the legal battle that has raged for decades between the Taylor interests and descendants of the area's earliest Hispanic settlers over access and grazing rights continues. There are many who urge that the ranch pass to public ownership or at a minimum be protected by a conservation easement. Culebra has an important role as one of the last private sanctuaries of wilderness in the state—a role poignantly underscored

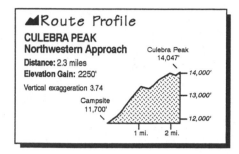

▲Route Profile
CULEBRA PEAK
Northwestern Approach   Culebra Peak
Distance: 2.3 miles   14,047'
Elevation Gain: 2250'   ⌐14,000'
Vertical exaggeration 3.74
          Campsite   ⌐13,000'
          11,700'
                                          ⌐12,000'
               1 mi.   2 mi.

by a reliable sighting during the fall of 1977 of what could have been a grizzly bear, a species long thought to be extinct in Colorado.

THE ROUTES

Taylor Ranch

Culebra Peak is entirely surrounded by private land. Currently, the only approach is from the west via the Taylor Ranch. At present (in 1994), climbing is permitted from mid-May (depending on the year) until mid-August. Reservations are not required, but because access policies have changed frequently, climbers are strongly encouraged to contact the ranch manager at (719) 672-3580 for the latest information before planning a climb.

Currently, ranch policy asks climbers to call from the town of San Luis on the approach so someone can open the ranch gate. From San Luis, drive four miles east to Chama. At the stop sign, turn left and proceed east for three miles to 25.5 Road. Turn right and drive south for a quarter-mile, then turn left at a junction with a No Trespassing sign on a big rock. This road leads to the ranch gate.

Procedures on the ranch itself have varied from year to year. Currently, climbers are permitted to drive above the ranch headquarters after paying a use fee of twenty-five dollars per person. From the headquarters at 9,080 feet, the access road climbs east for three and one-half miles to "Four-way," a junction, and then continues east for another mile to a campsite just above timberline at 11,700 feet. Although this road is passable to many two-wheel-drives, it is steep and uncannily straight. More than one person has missed a gear and had to back down a long

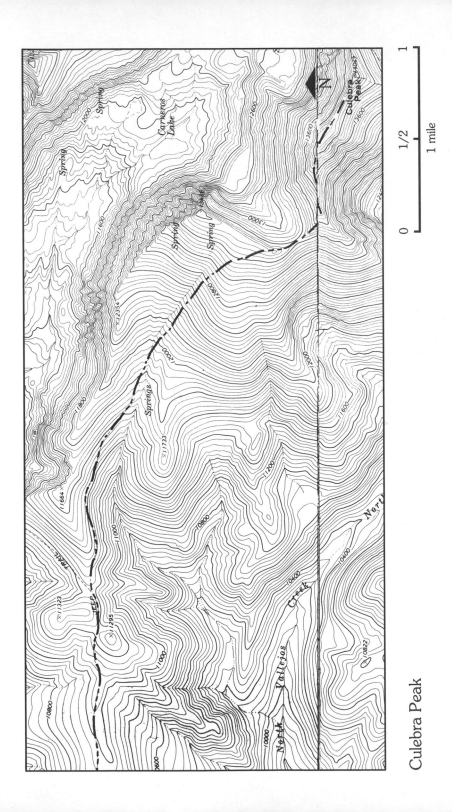

Culebra Peak

section and take another crack at it. Persons driving cars with automatic transmissions should be particularly wary coming down.

Camping is permitted at the end of this road, but please keep camps clean, as most climbers have in the past. From the campsite, a cairn-studded hump rises a half-mile due east. Climb to the saddle immediately south (right) of the prominent cairn and then follow the ridge south for one and one-half miles over two large and discouraging false summits to the true summit.

▲ *Ranch headquarters to summit: 6.5 miles, 5,000 feet.*
▲ *Campsite to summit: 2.3 miles, 2,500 feet.*

A Land of Endless Mountains

The San Juan Range

A land of endless mountains—such has been the impression of many a climber who has stood on a central San Juan summit and marveled at the 360-degree alpine view. No other range in Colorado, and few others in the nation, can equal the territory the San Juans cover—ten thousand square miles of imposing peaks, high lakes, narrow valleys, abandoned mines, and virgin wilderness. The San Juans stand alone in terms of stirring a unique sentiment in the heart of the backpacker or climber who has ventured into them.

One of the range's outstanding features is its overall altitude—no other range in the contiguous United States contains as much land above 10,000 feet as do the San Juan Mountains. Through the heart of this great mass of mountains winds the Continental Divide, which makes a great bend deep within the range; therefore, river drainages in the San Juans run toward every point of the compass. The Rio Grande River heads in the San Juans and drains that portion of the range that is east of the Divide, and the Rio de las Animas, Los Piños, and San Juan rivers flow from the southern peaks of the range. The Lake Fork of the Gunnison and the Uncompahgre are the major rivers to the north, and the Dolores and San Miguel drain to the west.

Passes between drainages in the San Juans are renowned for being high and often inaccessible. Consequently, transportation in the San Juans has been a major problem historically, and today, only Lizard Head, Red Mountain, Spring Creek, and Wolf Creek passes provide year-round paved access across the rugged range. The gold- and silver-hungry miners were a hardy lot, however, and the incredible roads they built

195

across many other high passes have now made the San Juans a mecca for the hardy four-wheeler.

Geologically, the San Juan Range is one of the most complex in the state, but generally its peaks are of extrusive volcanic rock. Near the beginning of the Laramide Orogeny, a huge body of molten rock pushed toward the surface of the earth in the vicinity of today's San Juans and formed a giant blister in the earth's crust. Later, in the Tertiary period, some of the molten rock forced its way to the surface and extensive volcanic activity broke out.

Before the final volcano puffed its last, the San Juan Dome was buried by thousands of feet of extrusive volcanic material. However, erosive forces of water (and eventually huge Quaternary glaciers) wasted no time in stripping off large quantities of volcanic material. Sharp peaks and steep valleys were carved out of the once rolling upland, exposing the Precambrian rock of the Needle Mountains and nearby Grenadiers and making them some of the roughest mountains in the state.

Numerous small mining camps sprang up in the San Juans in the 1870s, but five towns became the principal centers of population in the richest parts of the range—Silverton, Ouray, Telluride, Lake City, and Creede. More isolated than most mining camps, these towns developed unusually rip-roaring histories, almost living up to reputations established by modern Westerns.

As population increased, so did transportation needs. It was in the construction and maintenance of the mountain roads that the San Juan settlers faced perhaps their greatest challenge. Nevertheless, men like Otto Mears succeeded in building many impossible roads to impossible places, and despite the threat of the infamous San Juan avalanches, kept communication and supply links between the towns open one way or another year-round.

Determined miners continued battling the topography and the elements in their quest for silver throughout the 1880s, but their battle lost much of its momentum after the 1893 silver crash. Consequently, the early twentieth century saw little economic prosperity for the San Juans. Ranching, sheepherding, and some lumbering aided the economy of the area, but the rugged terrain remained an awesome limiting factor. Mining is still carried out in several parts of the San Juans, mostly for the base metals of lead, copper, and zinc. The San Juans, however, abound with more than modern mining—they still retain the fascinating remains of the mining era that boomed one hundred years ago.

The end of the twentieth century is seeing the San Juans undergo unprecedented environmental changes. The major ski areas of Purgatory and Telluride have left an indelible mark upon the range, and the disaster of the Summitville Mine near Wolf Creek Pass is a reminder that poor mining practices did not disappear with the mule train. Even those who appreciate the beauty of the land are in danger of overusing the very mountains they love, as attested by the annual blossoming of "tent cities" in Chicago Basin near the Needles and in Blue Lakes Basin below Mount Sneffels.

On the other hand, it is perhaps the San Juans that hold the greatest promise in Colorado for preserving a wilderness legacy for generations to come. Vast tracts of uncrowded and unspoiled country remain preserved in the Weminuche, La Garita, and Uncompahgre wilderness areas, and there is a possibility that a small population of grizzly bears—the very symbols of wilderness—still roams in the southern San Juans. Will the largest range in Colorado, the mighty San Juan, undergo the commercial taming of much of the rest of Colorado? Many an old-timer who knows intimately the toughness of the San Juans would say "No." Nevertheless, history has shown that without vigilant watchfulness, wildness can disappear at an alarming rate, even in the mighty San Juans.

Uncompahgre Peak 14,309 feet (6th highest)
Wetterhorn Peak 14,015 feet (49th highest)

Rising dramatically in an abrupt north face to stand guard over the drainages of the Cimarron River and Big Blue Creek, Uncompahgre Peak is the highest point in the San Juans and certainly one of its most prominent landmarks. While its broad southwest and southeast slopes afford easy access to the summit, the crumbling 1,000-foot north face gives the mountain a striking profile and is a treacherous climbing obstacle.

A. D. Wilson and Franklin Rhoda of the Hayden Survey made the first recorded ascent of Uncompahgre during the summer of 1874, while they were on an extensive study of the San Juans. They found, however, that they had been preceded on the summit by grizzly bears. Indeed, Uncompahgre seems to have been a favorite grizzly haunt, and both Rhoda and Lt. William Marshall, who climbed the peak for the Wheeler Survey later in the summer, reported encountering the noble beasts during their climbs. Grizzlies and their sign were found on a number of San Juan peaks, and eventually their presence prompted Rhoda to write: "When you feel you are treading a path never before trod by a living being . . . if some such vile, worldly thing as a paper collar or a whiskey bottle does not intrude itself on the sight, some beastly quadruped must. . . ."

Undoubtedly, Wilson and Rhoda were also preceded on Uncompahgre's summit by Indians, most likely Utes, who found the place an ideal lookout. The word *Uncompahgre* is a Ute word meaning "hot" (*unca*) "water" (*pah*) "spring" (*gre*). The Hayden Survey gave the peak the name from the Uncompahgre River, which is fed in part by hot springs near present-day Ouray, a favorite Ute camping ground. The peak was described as "Mount Chauvenet" in an 1873 sighting, after a professor of astronomy

The west side of Uncompahgre Peak. *(R. Omar Richardson)*

at Washington University in St. Louis, and was occasionally referred to as "the Leaning Tower" or "Capitol Mountain" by miners in the vicinity.

Marshall's August 29, 1874, climb of Uncompahgre for the Wheeler Survey followed the Hayden men, although Marshall made no reference to their presence, an understandable omission given the competition between the groups. Marshall observed from the summit: "The Wetterhorn, to the south of west a few miles from Uncompahgre Peak, is a shark's nose in form, and its ascent being unnecessary for topographical purposes, was not attempted. It exceeds 14,000 in altitude and appears inaccessible." The name "Wetterhorn" is one of the few Wheeler Survey names that survived. The name was undoubtedly inspired by the Swiss mountain of the same name, although any resemblance to it takes a vivid imagination. The name Wetterhorn prompted the naming of a 13,590-foot peak between Wetterhorn and Uncompahgre "Matterhorn." A rather undistinguished mass, Matterhorn is nonetheless a fine point from which to photograph Wetterhorn and Uncompahgre.

Although no major mining operations were undertaken on the slopes of the peaks, the valley of Henson Creek to the south was a beehive of mining activity. The chief town of upper Henson Creek was Capitol City, laid out in the mid-1870s. Originally called "Galena City," the name

Wetterhorn Peak as seen from Matterhorn Peak. *(R. Omar Richardson)*

was changed at the urgings of George T. Lee. The Lee Mining and Smelting Company was the nucleus of Capitol City's economy, and Lee took it upon himself, as a leading citizen, to dream of the location replacing Denver as the state capital. Lee went so far as to construct a two-story brick house with bricks hauled from Pueblo. The house was referred to as "The Governor's Mansion." The Czar, Czarina, Yellow Jacket, Capitol, Sunshine, and Polar Star were just some of the mining claims near Capitol City. Like George Lee's dreams, the dreams of their owners, too, evaporated with the demonetarization of silver in 1893.

By far the biggest producer of the Henson Creek Valley was the Ute-Ulay Mine, located four miles west of Lake City. The mine was originally discovered on August 27, 1871, by Harry Henson, Joel Mullen, Albert Meade, and Charles Godwin, but the miners were forced to wait for the signing of the 1873 Brunot Treaty, which opened the area, then part of the Ute reservation, to mining. When this was done in 1874, Henson and his partners returned, and within two years they had developed so much promise in the claim that the Crooke Brothers Smelter of Lake City bought them out for $125,000. By 1911, the mine had produced more than ten million dollars in silver and lead. It continues to operate sporadically.

Unlike its neighbor, which attracted outings from Capitol City and Lake City, Wetterhorn remained unclimbed until 1906, when a party of D. Utter, George C. Barnard, C. Smedley, and W. P. Smedley detoured from a planned ascent of Uncompahgre to climb, in Barnard's words, "a peak that was worthy of our metal [sic], both in difficulty and height." The climb was made via the standard south ridge approach. In August of 1920, the competent duo of Albert Ellingwood and Barton Hoag ascended the peak via the east arête. The north face of the Wetterhorn, spectacular from Matterhorn if laced with snow and ice, poses an improbable climbing challenge because of its crumbling volcanic structure.

THE ROUTES

Nellie Creek (usually Uncompahgre only)

From the intersection of Second Street and Colorado 149 in Lake City, at the sign indicating Engineer Pass, drive west up the Henson Creek road for four miles to the Ute-Ulay Mine and 1.4 miles farther to the Nellie Creek road, which branches to the north (right). The road is usually

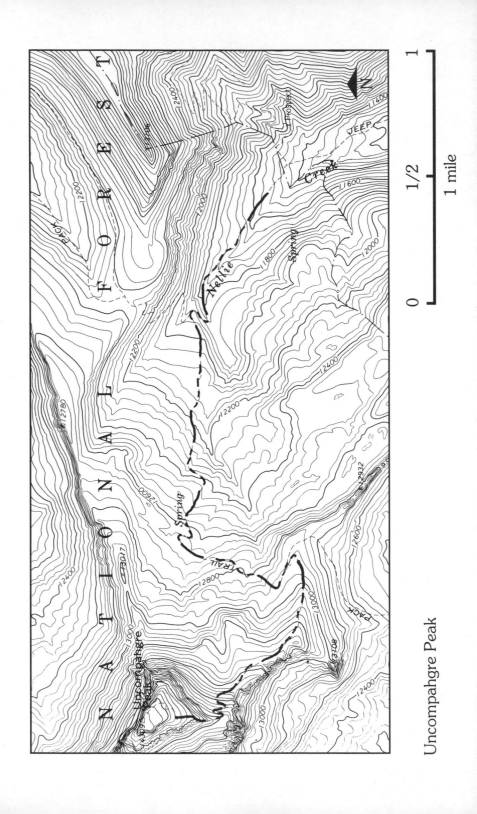

Uncompahgre Peak

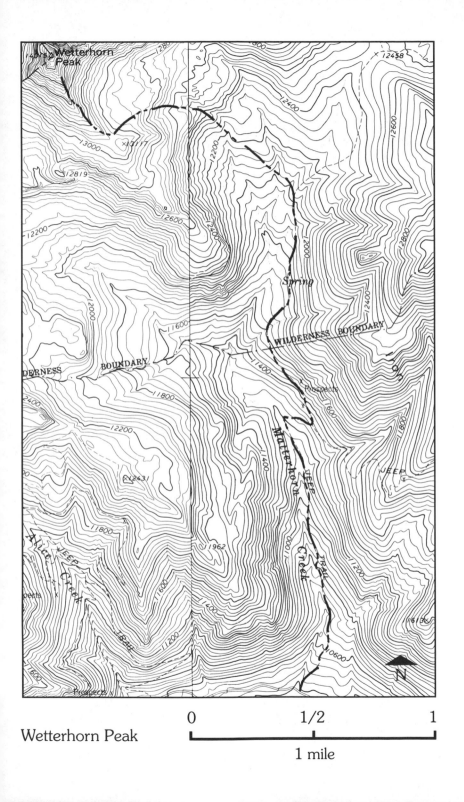

Wetterhorn Peak

| 0 | | 1/2 | | 1 |

1 mile

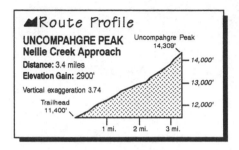

▲Route Profile
UNCOMPAHGRE PEAK Uncompahgre Peak
Nellie Creek Approach   14,309'
Distance: 3.4 miles
Elevation Gain: 2900'
Vertical exaggeration 3.74
Trailhead
11,400'
14,000'
13,000'
12,000'
1 mi.   2 mi.   3 mi.

plowed to the Ute-Ulay in winter. The road up Nellie Creek has been improved considerably in recent years and now is accessible to some high-center two-wheel-drive vehicles, as well as to four-wheel-drives. Don't attempt this road with a two-wheel-drive though, unless you are sure your vehicle can handle some pretty steep grades and one moderate stream crossing.

After the road crosses Nellie Creek and switchbacks up a hill, stay on the main road (left) at a minor road junction through a fine stand of aspen and spruce. A tall horn-shaped peak looms ahead and usually brings a chorus of "There's the Wetterhorn!" from beginners, but it's only a 13,158-foot point south of Uncompahgre's southeast flank, a fact brought poignantly home a mile or so later when timberline is reached and Uncompahgre's unmistakable bulk looms ahead. The Nellie Creek road becomes a foot trail at about 11,400 feet, four miles from Henson Creek at the Uncompahgre (formerly Big Blue) Wilderness boundary. From here, a well-traveled trail winds west to the southeast ridge of Uncompahgre and then north up one short, moderately steep section to the summit. The summit view is spectacular, but have someone hold your feet (make sure your boots are tightly laced!) if you lean too far over the north face to take pictures.

Due to the sensitivity of the alpine environment on Uncompahgre, it is critical that climbers stay on the trail the entire distance to the summit, and on the return. The few seconds saved by cutting a switchback can easily result in damage that will take decades to heal. No other routes on Uncompahgre are recommended; in fact, other routes may be prohibited by forest service order in the near future.

▲ *Wilderness boundary to summit: 3.4 miles, 2,900 feet.*
▲ *Henson Creek road to summit: 7.4 miles, 5,000 feet.*

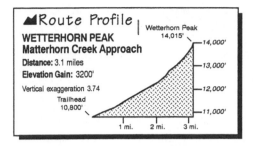

Route Profile
WETTERHORN PEAK
Matterhorn Creek Approach
Distance: 3.1 miles
Elevation Gain: 3200'
Vertical exaggeration 3.74
Trailhead 10,800'
Wetterhorn Peak 14,015'
14,000'
13,000'
12,000'
11,000'
1 mi.   2 mi.   3 mi.

Matterhorn Creek (usually Wetterhorn only)

From Lake City, drive nine miles west on the Henson Creek road (see above) to Capitol City and then northwest for almost two miles up the North Fork of Henson Creek to its confluence with Matterhorn Creek. You may park here, but most high-clearance vehicles can continue another one-half mile up Matterhorn Creek to a parking area at the Uncompahgre Wilderness boundary. Hike north up the Matterhorn Creek Trail, climbing across a broad avalanche run and past the prominent buttress of Wetterhorn's southeast flank.

At about 12,000 feet, where the trail turns away from the Wetterhorn and climbs more steeply, strike out northwest across the rolling basin to its head directly below the peak. At the head of the basin, turn southwest and gain Wetterhorn's southeast ridge at 13,100 feet. The ridge demands the use of hands as it climbs above 13,400 feet. At 13,850 feet, the route passes beneath a prominent shark's tooth and then directly west through a keyhole of sorts between the main peak and the shark's tooth. A series of rock ledges lead the final 150 feet to a small but surprisingly level summit. The ledges are not particularly hard climbing, but a mixture of ice and snow may warrant a rope, because one false step will send a climber plummeting past the keyhole and down the six-hundred-foot southwest face. Be particularly careful of footing when climbing back down these ledges. The view of Wetterhorn's eight-hundred-foot north face makes it plain that every other route on this peak is a technical one!

Uncompahgre is sometimes combined with Wetterhorn via this approach by continuing on the Matterhorn Creek Trail, over a 12,458-foot pass, and continuing to eventually join the Uncompahgre Peak Trail at 12,900 feet. However, this makes for a 5,800-foot, 15-mile round trip! In the past, some have shortcut this route by climbing off-trail up

Uncompahgre's southwest flank, but the particular sensitivity of the alpine environment in this area precludes this as an option. Stay on the trails!
▲ *Matterhorn Creek trailhead to Wetterhorn: 3.1 miles, 3,200 feet.*

Beware of drinking water on any summer climbs in this area, because the threat of giardia is compounded by the presence of large herds of domestic sheep. To avoid the herds of sheep and herds of people on these climbs, consider going in the late spring, when snow gives these peaks a more spectacular character, or in the fall, when aspen leaves illuminate the valleys. An interesting summer climb, however, could be made in conjunction with a backpack trip up any of the three forks of the Cimarron River from National Forest access roads leading south from U.S. 50 between Gunnison and Montrose.

Sunshine Peak 14,001 feet (54th highest)
Redcloud Peak 14,034 feet (46th highest)

Topping the collection of rounded summits that separate the Lake Fork of the Gunnison and Henson Creek are Sunshine and Redcloud peaks, connected to each other by a rolling one-and-one-half-mile ridge. Not as ruggedly impressive as many San Juan summits, the two peaks are often lost in a maze of mountains when viewed from a distance, but at closer range, each possesses distinctive physical characteristics that give it more individuality than merely as a Fourteener. Sunshine's summit rises in a unique symmetrical cone that just barely pierces the 14,000-foot level, while Redcloud Peak displays gently rounded upper slopes of a beautiful dull reddish orange hue found on no other Colorado Fourteener.

Sunshine and Redcloud are easily ascended and therefore may have been climbed by prospectors in the early 1870s, but the first recorded ascents of both peaks were made by members of the Wheeler and Hayden surveys. In 1874, chief topographer A. D. Wilson and assistant topographer Franklin Rhoda of the Hayden Survey made the first recorded ascent of Sunshine, which they had designated as simply "Station 12," one of a series of triangulation stations. They rode donkeys to 13,000 feet and then found the climb itself to be of little difficulty but were confronted with considerable electrical activity once they reached the summit. This storm curtailed their work on Sunshine and also prevented them from continuing north along the ridge to Redcloud. The tickling sensation produced by the electricity in the air and the buzzing of nearby rocks were interesting phenomena indeed, but also warning signals. Wisely, Wilson and Rhoda hightailed down the southeast ridge of Sunshine just as a deadly bolt of lightning struck the summit where they had been standing only moments before.

Redcloud Peak (*left*) and Sunshine (*right*), viewed from the west atop Handies Peak. *(Craig F. Koontz)*

Later in 1874, members of the Wheeler Survey also passed through the valleys above Lake San Cristobal and were impressed by the beautiful color and form of Redcloud. Realizing that the peak was called "Red Mountain" informally but had no official name, topographer J. C. Spiller suggested the beautifully descriptive "Red Cloud," one of the few Wheeler names in the Colorado Rockies that has remained. In addition to naming it, Spiller also made the first recorded ascent of Redcloud and established a triangulation station on its summit. Apparently, Spiller encountered no electrical storms such as the one experienced on neighboring Sunshine by the Hayden Survey and had ample time to complete his surveying work on its summit.

In the late 1870s, silver prospectors flooded the valleys of the San Juans, and the upper Lake Fork of the Gunnison was no exception. In 1877, the town of Sherman was laid out at the foot of the cliffs on Sunshine's south slope, and a number of mines were located near town. An exception among Colorado mining camps, Sherman never really boomed, and it probably never exceeded three hundred in population. The most productive mine in the area was the Black Wonder, which operated into the twentieth century, but Sherman itself was abandoned after the silver crash of 1893, and all mining in the area ceased by the 1920s. If one wonders why Sherman never boomed despite its promising mines, a clue may be found in noting the camp's geographical setting. Sherman was located in the flats at the confluence of the Lake Fork and Cottonwood Creek, and nearly every spring the two streams inundated the town with several feet of runoff water! Undisputedly a victim of very poor land-use planning, Sherman has all but washed away, and only portions of a few cabins remain in defiance of the flood waters.

Although Redcloud has been the official name of the peak since Spiller's christening, "Station 12" was informally known as "Mount Sherman" or "Niagara Peak" by miners until the U.S. Geological Survey of 1904–1905 officially designated it as Sunshine Peak without giving any particular reason for the name choice. Sunshine's most recent claim to fame has been its calculation as the lowest Fourteener in Colorado.

On July 19, 1986, Utah climber David Wilson fell several hundred feet to his death on Sunshine's south cliffs. Wilson was climbing alone and had pushed on to Redcloud despite a severe thunderstorm that had forced other climbers off the peaks. Returning over Sunshine, he missed the descent route and soon faced rain-slickened rocks and 800-foot cliffs. Wilson was ill equipped for bad weather, and hypothermia as well as the lack of a map may have clouded his judgment. His body was located two days later, after a massive search. The lessons are obvious.

THE ROUTES

Silver Creek

From Lake City, drive up the Lake Fork of the Gunnison past Lake San Cristobal and toward Cinnamon Pass for about twenty miles to where the road crosses Silver Creek, which flows from the northeast. Above Sherman, the road is quite steep and narrow, but it should be passable to most cars in good weather. The trailhead is clearly marked at Silver Creek, where camp can also be made near the road or by hiking a couple of hundred yards up the trail into the trees. Please park only in the designated area.

The Silver Creek trail climbs along the left (northwest) side of Silver Creek for about three and one-half miles to a pass at 13,000 feet. Spectacular clumps of columbine are particularly delightful along the trail in the upper portions of Silver Creek. From the pass, Redcloud's summit is three-quarters of a mile and one thousand vertical feet to the southwest

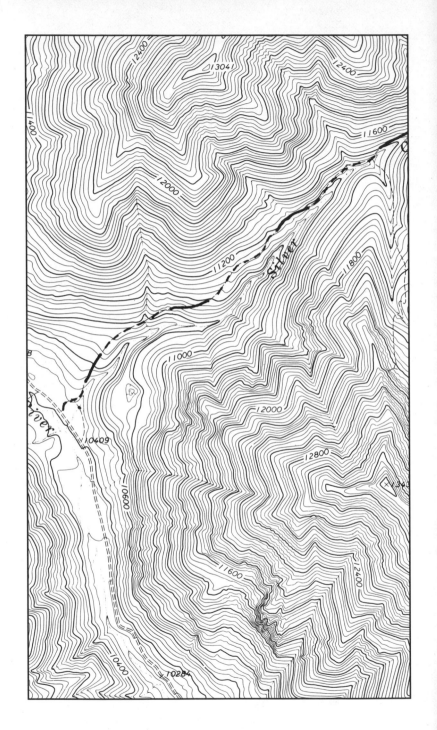

Sunshine Peak, Redcloud Peak

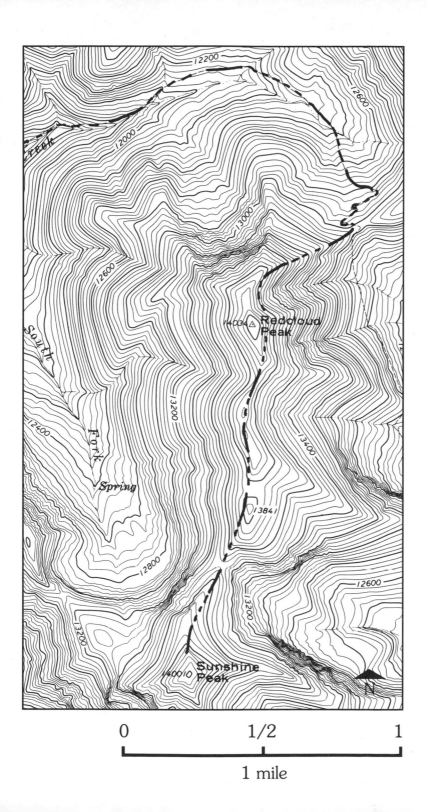

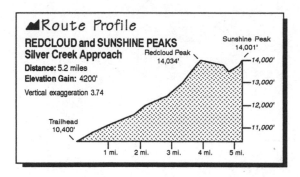

◢Route Profile

REDCLOUD and SUNSHINE PEAKS
Silver Creek Approach
Distance: 5.2 miles
Elevation Gain: 4200'

Vertical exaggeration 3.74

Sunshine Peak
14,001'
Redcloud Peak
14,034'

Trailhead
10,400'

14,000'
13,000'
12,000'
11,000'

1 mi. 2 mi. 3 mi. 4 mi. 5 mi.

along the ridge. For Sunshine, follow the trail south along the ridge for about one and one-half miles, gaining 500 feet above the 13,500-foot connecting saddle. Once on the summit of Sunshine, beware of disturbing rocks, lest you accidentally make it a thirteener! Return to the trailhead via the ascent route; avoid shortcuts down the scree to the South Fork of Silver Creek and the difficult route-finding past the dangerous cliffs on Sunshine's south face.

▲ *Trail to Redcloud: 3.9 miles, 3,650 feet.*
▲ *Trailhead to Redcloud and Sunshine: 5.2 miles, 4,200 feet, with 500 feet on return.*

Handies Peak 14,048 feet (40th highest)

Secluded above the extreme upper reaches of the Lake Fork of the Gunnison River lies Handies Peak, noted for its rich mining history and an unparalleled 360-degree view of the heart of the San Juans.

The exact origin of Handies's name is not known, but by the time the Hayden Survey entered the San Juans in 1874, the name was already in use. George Bancroft has speculated that the peak was named for a San Juan pioneer, but beyond this, no specific details about the man are known. After climbing Sunshine Peak in the summer of 1874, the Hayden party proceeded several miles up the Lake Fork, and Franklin Rhoda and at least one other ascended Handies with the aid of burros to 13,000 feet. Although this was the first recorded ascent of the peak, the men noticed prospect holes as high as 13,500 feet on the peak and undoubtedly correctly surmised that Handies had been scaled by some unknown prospector before them. A short time after this ascent, the Wheeler Survey entered the area, and they too climbed Handies, both teams finding the summit view to be superb for topographic work.

As extensive mining activity was present in the San Juans since the early 1870s, Handies Peak and its environs were well known to prospectors and miners. Formal settlement of the area began in the late 1870s in the valley of the Lake Fork to the northeast of Handies, in the long meadowed area of Burrows Park. By 1880, the small camp of Whitecross had been established at the northern foot of 13,542-foot Whitecross Mountain, so named for the presence of a small white quartz cross high on its side. Whitecross Mountain is located only about one mile northeast of Handies, and most of the mining activity centered around 12,600-foot Cinnamon Pass and in American Basin, just west of Handies.

213

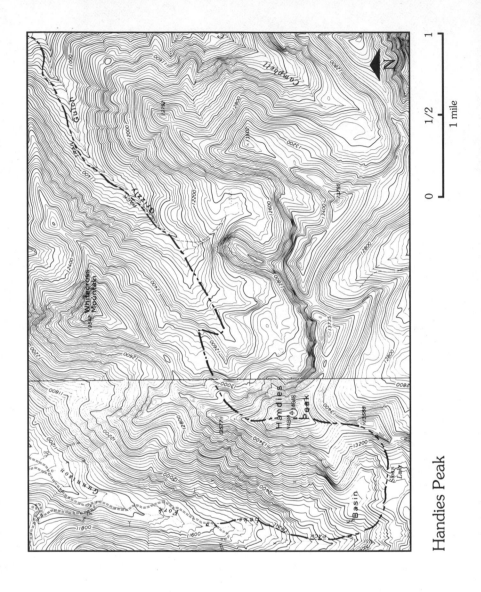

Handies Peak

Handies Peak viewed to the southwest up Grizzly Gulch. *(Lyndon J. Lampert)*

Some of the more prominent silver mines were the Bonhomme, Champion, Cracker Jack, and Tobasco. The latter operation was on the road to Cinnamon Pass and was so named because it was financed largely by the Tabasco Meat Sauce Company. In fact, Handies Peak was sometimes referred to as "Tobasco," but the spicy name did not last as a permanent title for the peak. Whitecross probably never contained more than three hundred people and, crippled by the silver crash of 1893, the area soon lapsed into sporadic production. By the 1920s, production had generally ceased. Today, virtually nothing remains of Whitecross, but in and around American Basin, extensive remains of the once-busy silver operations may still be seen.

THE ROUTES

American Basin
From Lake City, drive approximately twenty-three miles up the Lake Fork of the Gunnison on the road to Cinnamon Pass. The toughest stretch of this road is the "Shelf Road" section above Sherman, and although it is steep and narrow in places, it should be passable by most two-wheel drives.

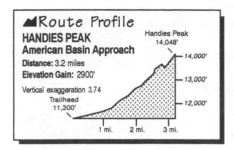

At the upper end of long and narrow Burrows Park, near mile twenty-three, undeveloped campsites become available in the vicinity of Cleveland Gulch (10,700 feet). The road is adequate for most cars for another mile to the first switchback on the Cinnamon Pass Road, where a side road to American Basin joins. Posted private property restricts camping to either the immediate vicinity of Cleveland Gulch or above timberline in American Basin itself.

For the climb, drive or hike to the turnoff to American Basin at the first switchback (11,300 feet). Four-wheel-drive vehicles can continue south into the basin for another three-quarters of a mile to the Old Gnome Mine at 11,600 feet. Directly south at the head of the basin are the imposing American Basin Crags, and bordering on the left (east) side of the basin is the west slope of Handies. From the end of the jeep road, a well-traveled trail climbs south toward the crags. This section of American Basin is a photographer's delight—in the heart of summer it bursts with colors of columbine, larkspur, paintbrush, and dozens of other alpine flowers.

About one mile up the trail, a newly constructed portion climbs more steeply to the shores of idyllic Sloan Lake at 12,900 feet. Sloan Lake is a great spot for pulling a snack out of your pack and watching cutthroat trout cruise by. From the lake, the new trail continues east to gain Handies's south ridge at 13,400 feet. Cross over a minor 13,588-foot hump and finish on the gentle ridge for another half-mile to the summit. Because American Basin receives high use, avoid traveling off the designated trail and return via the ascent route.

▲ *American Basin turnoff to summit: 3.2 miles, 2,900 feet, plus 150 feet on return.*

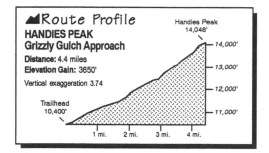

▲Route Profile
HANDIES PEAK
Grizzly Gulch Approach
Distance: 4.4 miles
Elevation Gain: 3650'
Vertical exaggeration 3.74

Handies Peak
14,048'

Trailhead
10,400'

14,000'
13,000'
12,000'
11,000'

1 mi.   2 mi.   3 mi.   4 mi.

Grizzly Gulch

Handies Peak is blessed with two exceptionally scenic routes, and Grizzly Gulch is a fine choice for a weekend that includes climbs of Sunshine and Redcloud peaks as well. The Grizzly Gulch Trail is located directly opposite the Silver Creek Trail for Sunshine and Redcloud. To reach it, drive up the Cinnamon Pass road past Lake San Cristobal to a point about twenty miles from Lake City. Park in the designated area and then strike out to the southwest on the excellent Grizzly Gulch Trail, crossing the Lake Fork of the Gunnison on a log bridge.

Follow the trail up Grizzly Gulch along its north side for about two miles to timberline, at about 12,000 feet. The Grizzly Gulch approach presents a more photogenic side of Handies than the American Basin approach, and there are some fine cliffs to be seen to the east of the peak. From timberline, cross to the south side of the creek at a large cairn and follow the generally obvious trail west and southwest to a broad bench leading to the north ridge of Handies.

▲ *Trailhead to summit: 4.4 miles, 3,650 feet.*

San Luis Peak 14,014 feet (51st highest)

Sometime during the 1600s, Spanish adventurers roamed beyond the mountains north of Santa Fe into a large valley drained by the Rio Grande River and encircled by high peaks. In time, the valley was called "San Luis," after its patron saint, Saint Louis. Although it is doubtful that the peak that took its name from the valley felt the tread of Spanish feet, the valley itself became the cradle of a rich Spanish culture in Colorado.

Although San Luis Peak took its name from the Spanish valley below, its early history was more deeply entwined with that of the Utes and Colorado's most infamous winter picnicker. The Ute treaty of 1868 was concluded between the Utes and the United States in response to growing pressure from miners and farmers to wrest more land for development. Specifically, the treaty gave the Utes all of Colorado west of the 107th meridian, just west of Gunnison, or about the western one-third of the present state. The treaty established two agencies on the reservation, one on the White River near present-day Meeker, and the other on the Los Piños River in southern La Plata County.

As the Tabeguache band of Utes advanced toward the Los Piños site under military escort during the summer of 1868, they halted on a branch of Cochetopa Creek twelve miles northeast of San Luis Peak and refused to go any farther. In an oft-told and hence probably distorted story, the army officer in charge sought to avoid trouble by promptly naming the creek "Los Piños" and establishing the agency on that site even though it was several miles east of the reservation line and a good seventy-five miles from the intended location. The Utes and their most-noted spokesman, Ouray, remained at the Los Piños Agency until 1875, when,

218

San Luis Peak, viewed to the southwest up the drainage of Stewart Creek. *(Lyndon J. Lampert)*

as a result of the Brunot Treaty of 1873, they were moved west to the Uncompahgre Valley.

The winter of 1873-1874 was particularly severe, even by bitter Gunnison standards, and it was with surprise that Los Piños agency officials looked up from their breakfasts of April 16, 1874, to see a bedraggled figure stagger into the compound. Immortalized in story, song, and the University of Colorado's student grill, Alferd Packer was fresh from his grisly deed at the foot of Cannibal Plateau. Packer's route from the plateau, just northeast of Lake City, took him across the upper reaches of Cebolla Creek, below the slopes of San Luis, and on to the agency.

Late in the winter of 1873, just prior to the Packer saga's opening act, a Hayden Survey party climbed San Luis's twin to the north, Stewart Peak (13,938 feet). Long thought to be a Fourteener, Stewart Peak was probably named by the Wheeler Survey for Senator William M. Stewart, a prominent figure in Nevada's Comstock operation and a champion of the free coinage of silver. Neither the Hayden nor Wheeler surveys climbed San Luis Peak, although until Mike Foster's thorough research in *Summits to Reach,* some thought that Hayden Station 2 of 1874 was

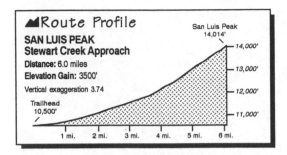

▲**Route Profile**

SAN LUIS PEAK
Stewart Creek Approach
Distance: 6.0 miles
Elevation Gain: 3500'
Vertical exaggeration 3.74

San Luis Peak
14,014'

14,000'
13,000'
12,000'
11,000'

Trailhead
10,500'

1 mi.　2 mi.　3 mi.　4 mi.　5 mi.　6 mi.

San Luis. Station 2 was in fact Peak 13,502, two miles northeast of Baldy Cinco. The first ascent of San Luis was probably by Utes or prospectors.

Activity on the mountain itself has been limited, although the valleys below have seen their share of ranching and mining. To the north, the Cebolla and Powderhorn valleys offer some of the prettiest and best known ranch land in the state. To the south, men with big dreams once roamed the rip-roaring streets of the mining boom town of Creede, causing poet Cy Warman to utter his famous line, "It's day all day in the day-time, and there is no night in Creede."

THE ROUTES

Stewart Creek
From 8 miles east of Gunnison on U.S. 50, drive south 20.6 miles on Colorado 114 and turn right on County Road NN14, the old Cochetopa Pass road. Three and one-half miles farther, at the Los Piños Pass road junction, continue straight ahead for another 3.6 miles past the Dome Lakes. At the south end of Dome Lakes, take the Stewart Creek road (County Road 15GG) to the right for about twenty-one miles to the Stewart Creek trailhead. Keep left at major intersections at miles 8.6 and 16.5 on this road. The Stewart Creek trail climbs from 10,500 feet to timberline, four and one-quarter miles to the southwest. Climb to the 13,107-foot saddle on San Luis's northeast flank, and then west and southwest to the summit, another mile distant.

▲ *Stewart Creek trailhead to summit: 6 miles, 3,500 feet.*

West Willow Creek
San Luis is a simple, though somewhat lengthy, climb from the south.

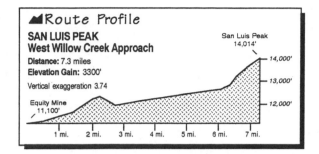

▲◢Route Profile

SAN LUIS PEAK
West Willow Creek Approach

San Luis Peak
14,014'

Distance: 7.3 miles
Elevation Gain: 3300'

Vertical exaggeration 3.74

Equity Mine
11,100'

14,000'

13,000'

12,000'

1 mi. 2 mi. 3 mi. 4 mi. 5 mi. 6 mi. 7 mi.

This route has the attraction of some very pleasant strolling for a few miles along the Continental Divide on the Colorado Trail/Continental Divide Trail.

Starting from the forest service office in Creede, drive south through downtown Creede and into Willow Creek Canyon on Forest Road 503. Bear left at junctions at miles 1 and 3, and continue up West Willow Creek to just below the Equity Mine, at mile 7.5. In good conditions, nearly any car should be able to reach this point. Park on the left (west) side of the creek and hike up the jeep road that begins on the west side of the creek, and on past the private property of the Equity Mine on the other side of the creek. Four-wheel-drives can make it up this road for about one and one-half more miles, to 11,500 feet, where the road climbs out of the valley to the west.

Just past timberline, near where the jeep road turns west, look for a trail angling up-slope to the northeast toward a prominent rocky point on the Continental Divide. Take this trail to the Divide at 12,300 feet, and then drop down the Pacific side a few yards to intersect the excellent Skyline Trail, which is part of the Colorado Trail/Continental Divide Trail system. Continue eastward on the Skyline Trail and drop a few hundred feet into the upper Spring Creek drainage, which shelters the best campsites available on this route. Keep a sharp eye out for bighorn sheep as you climb out of upper Spring Creek and then to a mile of almost flat strolling to reach a 12,600-foot saddle on San Luis's south ridge. San Luis is an easy one-and-one-half-mile hike north from this saddle.

▲ *Equity Mine to summit: 7.3 miles, 3,300 feet, plus 400 feet on return.*

Backpackers may wish to explore an approach to San Luis via Cochetopa Creek. This trailhead begins at the termination of the above-

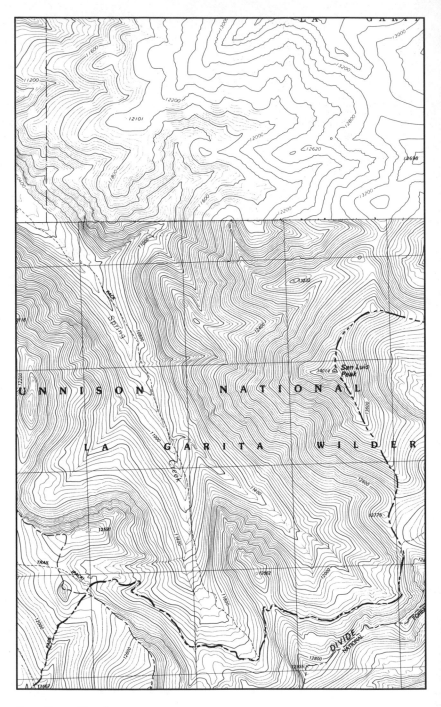

San Luis Peak

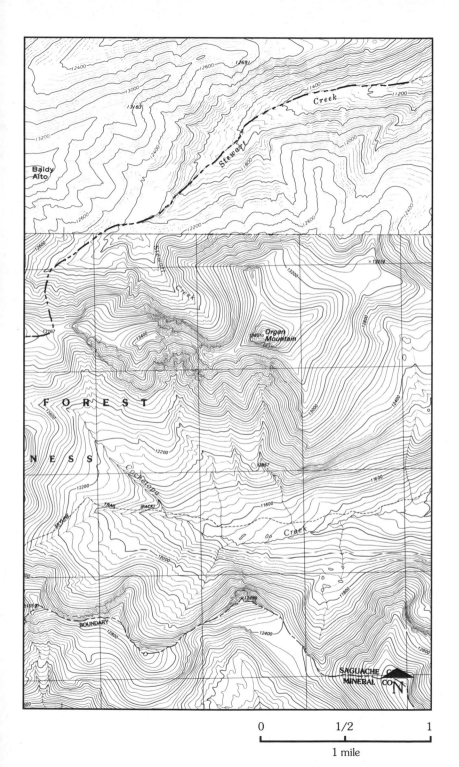

0   1/2   1

1 mile

mentioned Stewart Creek road, one mile beyond the Stewart Creek crossing. This trail (part of the Colorado Trail) climbs gently for six miles in an unspoiled scenic valley before mounting the 12,600-foot saddle on San Luis's south ridge and joining the West Willow Creek route. Cochetopa Creek is a fine approach for those looking for something beyond the shortest and quickest way up.

Mount Sneffels 14,150 feet (28th highest)

Scattered throughout the Rocky Mountains are certain mountain scenes that unfailingly stir the heart anew regardless of how many times they have been viewed. Among these unforgettable vistas is that of the massive wall of alpine grandeur that is topped by the "Queen of the San Juans," Mount Sneffels. Since Franciscan fathers Dominguez and Escalante traveled the region in 1776, and undoubtedly even before their time, the Sneffels Range has been one of those places that leads people to pause momentarily solely to absorb the sheer splendor of the Rockies.

Sneffels's first recorded ascent occurred on September 10, 1874, when A. D. Wilson, Franklin Rhoda, Frederic Endlich, and a packer named Ford of the Hayden Survey reached its summit via the south ridge from Blue Lakes Pass. After the rugged task of negotiating the rock pinnacles on the ridge, Rhoda noted with some consternation that they had been preceded to the summit by grizzly bears.

By most credible accounts, foremost of which are by John L. J. Hart and William Bueler, the naming of Mount Sneffels stems from the Hayden party's view of Sneffels rising above Blue Lakes Basin. One member of the group compared the great basin to the dramatic hole described in Jules Verne's *Journey to the Center of the Earth.* Dr. Endlich excitedly agreed and exclaimed, "There's Snaefell!" pointing to the peak and referring to the Icelandic mountain near the hole that was described in Verne's book.

At nearly the same time as Wilson and company's ascent of Sneffels, Lt. William Marshall's division of the Wheeler Survey passed through the area and christened the peak "Mount Blaine," after James G. Blaine, Maine congressman, Speaker of the House of Representatives, and presidential aspirant. Wheeler's men seemed to be far more ready to please the

Blue Lakes Pass (*left*) and Mount Sneffels (*right*) from upper Yankee Boy Basin. (*R. Omar Richardson*)

men who held the purse strings of the surveys than were Hayden's, but again it is the Hayden name that is remembered. (And indeed how fortunate! How terrible it would be if more of our mountains were named for long-forgotten politicians!)

Close on the heels of the surveys came the first small groups of prospectors who would soon turn the Mount Sneffels region into one of the most heavily mined districts in the San Juans. In doing so, the name "Sneffels" was applied to the entire area west of Ouray, and discoveries were reported as being "on Mount Sneffels" even when they were some miles away.

By far the great mine of the region was and still is the Camp Bird. It grew from several silver claims staked high in Imogene Basin late in the 1870s to a multimillion-dollar asset of mining tycoon Thomas Walsh. Walsh took over the claims in 1895 for twenty thousand dollars after hearing whispers of gold. He named the location "Camp Bird" after the friendly gray jay. He soon controlled a consolidated property that included 103 mining claims, covered some nine hundred acres, and became the second richest mine in Colorado. Tom Walsh's success story allowed his daughter, Evelyn Walsh McLean, to wear the fabled Hope Diamond. She recounted his story in *Father Struck it Rich*.

The town of Sneffels was organized farther up Sneffels Creek in 1877, beneath the slopes of Stony Mountain. The leading mine of the upper valley was the Virginius, located by William Freeland in Governor Basin just south of town. Fifteen miners braved the winter of 1877–1878, operating the claim in an area that was one of the most avalanche-prone of any in the state. Originally the Virginius was a silver mine, but rich gold ore was soon discovered as the shaft was sunk deeper, until it was reported that "gold paid all the expenses of production and treatment, while silver is pure profit." The Virginius found its way into the hands of another San Juan mining tycoon, A. E. Reynolds, who in 1884 financed the famous Revenue Tunnel to the tune of $600,000. The tunnel entered the slopes of Governor Basin twenty-nine hundred feet below the Virginius shaft and squarely tapped the mine's main vein, solving not only ventilation problems but also making access far easier and safer by avoiding high-altitude avalanche danger. Between 1881 and 1919, the Virginius and Revenue Tunnel produced a gross of twenty-seven million dollars. Other famous mines dotting the valley included the Yankee Boy, Ruby Trust, Humboldt, Sweepstakes, and Terrible.

The technical climbing history of Mount Sneffels might well be told in two words—Dwight Lavender. Born in Telluride in 1911, Dwight Lavender, and the San Juan Mountaineers he was instrumental in forming, were pioneers extraordinaire in climbing and chronicling the San Juans, particularly the San Miguel and Sneffels ranges. From 1929 to 1934, Lavender and principal cohorts Mel Griffiths and Carleton Long made ascents on virtually every major peak in the ranges and chronicled their routes, geology, and history in *The San Juan Mountaineers' Climbing Guide to Southwestern Colorado.*

The culmination of those exploits were three ascents of Sneffels's imposing north face, which involved some of the most advanced snow and ice climbing done in the state up to that time. The pioneering July 1931 climb involved Lavender, Griffiths, Charles Kane, and Gordon Williams in an attack that climbed the prominent east couloir of the north face to the northeast arête. In August 1933, Lavender, Griffiths, and several others did the north face direct via the central couloir.

Perhaps the most amazing, and at the same time the most tragic, note of Lavender's career is that he accomplished all of this before he died of infantile paralysis at age twenty-four while studying for his Ph.D. in geology. Most certainly he would have been an asset as highly respected and as competent in his chosen profession as his brother, David, became in his. Perhaps the premier historian of the American West, David Lavender

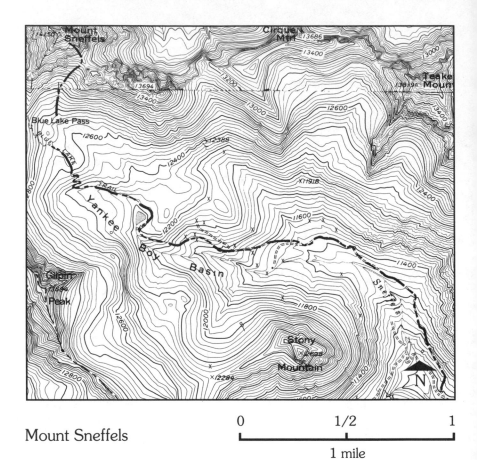

Mount Sneffels

0   1/2   1

1 mile

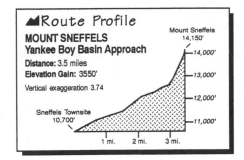

▲Route Profile
MOUNT SNEFFELS
Yankee Boy Basin Approach
Distance: 3.5 miles
Elevation Gain: 3550'
Vertical exaggeration 3.74

Mount Sneffels
14,150'
—14,000'
—13,000'
—12,000'

Sneffels Townsite
10,700'
—11,000'

1 mi.   2 mi.   3 mi.

traveled into the La Platas north of Hesperus Peak in July of 1977 to observe Lavender Peak, named for his brother, truly one of the great mountaineers of his or any day.

THE ROUTES

Yankee Boy Basin

Mount Sneffels is one of those prominent peaks that, seemingly, everyone wants to climb. Although it's not a technical climb, Sneffels is no mere walk-up peak either, and two fatalities due to falls along the standard route occurred in 1992 and 1993. For some reason, people either underestimate the difficulty of Mount Sneffels or overestimate their abilities, or both. Either is a serious mistake on any Fourteener—know the demands of the mountain *and* your abilities.

From just south of Ouray where U.S. 550 begins to switchback up Red Mountain Pass, drive west on Colorado 361 five miles to the Camp Bird Mine (9,800 feet). The road is plowed this far in winter, and once the ice and snow have melted from a spectacularly narrow ledge the road is passable for another two miles to the townsite of Sneffels (10,600 feet). A tough jeep road continues to 12,400 feet, but it is difficult to imagine why climbers would want to bump along this road in a noisy jeep when hiking it offers so much more of the beauties of Yankee Boy Basin. Hike the jeep road from the Sneffels townsite along the main drainage northwest around Stony Mountain and into upper Yankee Boy Basin, which is an unbelievable tapestry of wildflowers in June and July. Where the basin levels near its head and the jeep road finally quits, leave the trail just before the final switchbacks up Blue Lakes Pass, and then climb north up a prominent light-colored couloir to the sharp saddle (13,500 feet) between Mount Sneffels (northwest) and its southeastern 13,694-foot subpeak. This couloir is steep, and footing can be tricky, especially on the descent.

At the 13,500-foot saddle, turn left (northwest) and, depending on snow conditions, climb a much smaller but steeper couloir or its left-hand (south) rock rib to the summit. Both couloirs should be carefully surveyed for avalanche danger early and late in the season, and in the summer the smaller couloir is prone to rolling rocks. The upper portion out of the smaller couloir requires some minor bouldering.

▲ *Sneffels townsite to summit: 3.5 miles, 3,550 feet.*

Backpackers often combine a climb of Sneffels with a trip to the Blue Lakes Basin (access five and one-half miles west of Ridgway) to the west of the peak by climbing east out of the basin to Blue Lakes Pass and to the route described above. However, the extreme popularity of Blue Lakes Basin may diminish the attractiveness of this option, or at least prompt a midweek instead of a weekend trip. For that matter, popular Mount Sneffels is probably better avoided on weekends by any route.

While Sneffels is the key attraction of the area, it is only one point of a ten-mile-long range that includes, from west to east, Mears Peak, Dallas Peak, Mount Sneffels, Cirque Mountain, Teakettle Mountain, and Potosi Peak. Gilpin Peak, Mendota Peak, and Imogene Pass, separating the Sneffels Creek drainage from Telluride, also warrant exploration.

Mount Wilson 14,246 feet (16th highest)
Wilson Peak 14,017 feet (48th highest)
El Diente Peak 14,159 feet (24th highest)

It may seem strange that with only fifty-four peaks over 14,000 feet and a wealth of colorful history, two Colorado Fourteeners should bear the name of A. D. Wilson, topographer extraordinaire with the Hayden Survey. To be sure, Wilson carried an impressive list of credentials, which included topographic work with Clarence King's Fortieth Parallel Survey; the second ascent of Mount Rainier within weeks of the first ascent; and later, the principal organization of the Hayden Atlas. It was largely Wilson's skill as a topographer and surveyor that enabled the Hayden Survey to establish its highly credible reputation, particularly in the San Juans. Despite these feats, it seems unclear if even Wilson himself calculated on his name resting on two 14,000-foot summits.

During the summer of 1874, Wilson led his division of the survey through the San Juans in an extensive campaign of climbing high points and mapping terrain. (See individual San Juan chapters.) As the season neared an end, Franklin Rhoda, Wilson's half-brother and highly competent assistant, wrote in the division report that "only one peak of which we had any dread remained yet to be ascended, and that was Mount Wilson." Rhoda's reference suggests that the mountain, a dominant landmark on the western horizon when viewed from the Uncompahgre-Sneffels region, was named for their chief at some time during the summer.

On September 13, 1874, a party that included Wilson and Rhoda reached the summit of Mount Wilson via its jagged southern ridge. *Roof of the Rockies* recaps Rhoda's report of the ascent, which Rhoda asserted was the most dangerous of the summer. The south ridge of Mount Wilson with its series of sharp needles over 14,000 feet remains a formidable

231

The summit of Mount Wilson and the infamous Mount Wilson-El Diente ridge, as viewed to the east from El Diente Peak.

Mount Wilson (*left*) and El Diente Peak (*right*) with the connecting ridge, as viewed to the southwest from the slopes of Wilson Peak. *(Gary Koontz)*

route. The Wilson-Rhoda climb was a first ascent, although J. C. Spiller of the Wheeler Survey tried without success to obtain the summit earlier in the summer. In 1908, William S. Cooper and John Hubbard found a rusty tin can that bore Spiller's name in a particularly difficult spot on the south ridge, presumably left to mark his farthest advance.

As the silver boom of the early 1880s hit the San Juans, Mount Wilson felt the tread of prospectors' feet. Claims were staked all around the mountain, but by far the reigning sovereign of the vicinity was the Silver Pick Mine, located by L. D. Ratliff and others on July 17, 1882, high in what became called Silver Pick Basin. Contrary to its name, the Silver Pick was chiefly a gold mine. Its greatest period of productivity was from 1882 to 1900, although it operated sporadically after the turn of the century, including during the 1930s and from 1959-1961. Production from 1882 to 1961 totaled $682,751 in gold and $124,310 in silver.

The Silver Pick included thirteen claims and eight thousand feet of tunnel work on eight levels, all between 12,120 and 13,200 feet. From the mine, a mile-long aerial tram carried ore to a mill located at 11,000 feet. A large stone building that served as living quarters for the miners

Wilson Peak (*left*), as viewed to the east from the saddle above the Silver Pick Mine. *(Gary Koontz)*

still stands near the upper tram terminus. Once a haven for climbers, the building suffered the collapse of its roof several years ago.

After the Silver Pick, the mountain's leading mines were the Morning Star, Rock of Ages, and Synopsis. The Morning Star, located in Magpie Gulch at the end of Wilson Peak's east ridge, was a combination lead, gold, and silver producer. Although located in 1880, it was most productive just prior to World War I. The Rock of Ages Mine was discovered about 1886 high in Navajo Basin between Mount Wilson and Wilson Peak. Although it contained seven hundred feet of cross-cuts and drifts, its production figures were never anything to write home about. Climbers know the Rock of Ages as the small, adequately ventilated cabin that serves as a welcome port in the region's frequent storms. The Synopsis Mine was patented in 1914 at the 12,800-foot level of Wilson Peak and boasted a 300-foot tunnel.

In addition, the Homerhart, Coxey, and Cleveland claims were located in 1905 between 13,000 and 13,500 feet on the north slope of what was then considered Mount Wilson's western subpeak. Some mining continues in the Mount Wilson area today, with the most recent interest centering on copper deposits in Navajo Basin.

With all of the mining activity, miners probably were the first to reach the summit of Wilson Peak. As mentioned, it does not appear that Wilson consciously named two peaks after himself, but rather that subsequent mapmakers, after Wilson's own 1877 edition of the Hayden Atlas that listed only Mount Wilson, added the name "Wilson Peak." Conspicuously absent from Henry Gannett's Gazetteer, Wilson Peak appears to have been first listed on the 1904 version of the Silverton 15M U.S. Geological Survey quadrangle map.

Despite the high level of mining activity and relative ease of a Wilson Peak ascent, Mount Wilson and its western subpeak continued to be mountaineers' mountains. In the summer of 1930, after some investigative work by John Hart and others, Dwight Lavender (see page 227), Forrest Greenfield, and Chester Price ascended the west ridge of Mount Wilson's western subpeak. They were confident that the peak's distance from Mount Wilson and the intervening drop warranted its placement on the Fourteener list.

When the party reached the summit, they found no evidence of prior ascent. Lavender duly reported a first ascent, and in an admirable show of originality named the peak "El Diente," Spanish for "The Tooth," for its sharp appearance from the Dunton Meadows area. As if to further assert El Diente's qualifications as a separate Fourteener, Lavender wrote in May of 1931, "I actually believe it would be impossible to ascend both Mount Wilson and El Diente between sunrise and sunset even under the most favorable conditions."

A few months later, in an extraordinary case of the keen inspection for which Dwight Lavender was known, he went into painstaking detail to refute his own claim of a first ascent. "Prowling," in his words, through the pages of the *Alpine Journal* (vol. XV, August, 1891) Lavender discovered a Percy Thomas account of a visit to the San Juans entitled, "Mountaineering in Southern Colorado." By comparing the route description to landscape, Lavender concluded that Thomas's description of an ascent of Mount Wilson in August of 1890 with N. G. Douglass was in fact a first ascent of El Diente. Both Lavender's account of his investigations in *Trail and Timberline* (September 1931) and Bueler's subsequent recounting in *Roof of the Rockies* make for interesting reading.

While Mount Massive came under fire from name changers three times, the twin Wilsons were seriously assaulted only once. The 1937 Colorado General Assembly asked the U.S. Board of Geographic Names to change the name of Mount Wilson to Franklin Roosevelt Peak. The Board's response that the name of a living person could not be given postponed

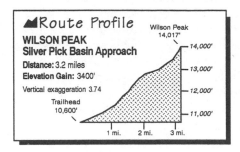

▲Route Profile

WILSON PEAK
Silver Pick Basin Approach

Distance: 3.2 miles
Elevation Gain: 3400'

Vertical exaggeration 3.74

Wilson Peak
14,017'

Trailhead
10,600'

14,000'
13,000'
12,000'
11,000'

1 mi.   2 mi.   3 mi.

the matter until April of 1945, when Governor John C. Vivian sought to carry out the edict. In following Vivian's efforts, the *Denver Post* reported that the General Assembly had selected Mount Wilson to honor F.D.R. because of "its presidential magnificence and because Wilson Peak in San Miguel County already commemorates the name of the 1918 wartime president." Poor A. D. Wilson! With one swoop he was almost conveniently lost to history. The change, however, never occurred.

THE ROUTES

When talk invariably turns to a list of Colorado's toughest Fourteeners, El Diente and Mount Wilson must be placed in anyone's top ten. And too, while far less difficult than its two neighbors, Wilson Peak can be equally unforgiving to the novice who strays off the standard route.

Silver Pick Basin

From Placerville, at the junction of Colorado 62 and 145, drive southeast for four miles to Sawpit and then two and one-half miles farther, to the remnants of Vanadium and a dirt road leading south across the San Miguel River and up Bear Creek. (This junction is six miles west of the Telluride turnoff on Colorado 145.) Drive south across the bridge and at mile 3.3 stay left where an unmarked road turns right; take the middle fork of a three-pronged intersection at mile 4.1; then, bear left at mile 6.4 when a road marked "Big Bear Creek" turns right. Another mile will bring you to a gate and the Forest Service trailhead for Silver Pick Basin. Most sturdy two-wheel-drive vehicles can make it to this trailhead.

From the trailhead at about 10,600 feet, hike for a mile along the road into Silver Pick Basin proper, passing the site of the Silver Pick Mill

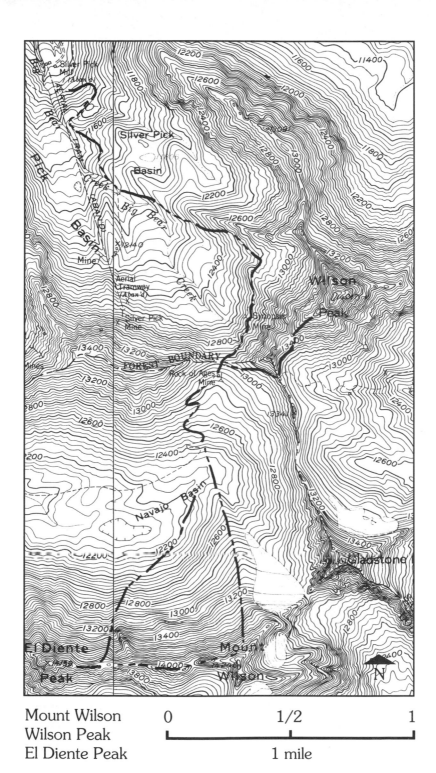

Mount Wilson
Wilson Peak
El Diente Peak

0   1/2   1

1 mile

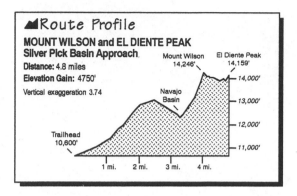

▲Route Profile

MOUNT WILSON and EL DIENTE PEAK
Silver Pick Basin Approach
Distance: 4.8 miles
Elevation Gain: 4750'
Vertical exaggeration 3.74

Mount Wilson 14,246'
El Diente Peak 14,159'
Navajo Basin
Trailhead 10,600'

14,000'
13,000'
12,000'
11,000'

1 mi. 2 mi. 3 mi. 4 mi.

en route. For Wilson Peak, hike from the millsite at 11,000 feet along the trail leading to the 13,000-foot pass separating Silver Pick Basin from Navajo Basin. An increasingly used trail leads from the saddle east and northeast a half-mile to Wilson's summit ridge, staying below and to the south of the southwest ridge. The summit ridge involves some minor hand-over-hand climbing. Return to the trailhead via the same route.
   ▲ *Trailhead to summit: 3.2 miles, 3,400 feet.*

Mount Wilson and El Diente via the connecting ridge is a long day. Begin by crossing the Silver Pick–Navajo pass and contour south past the Rock of Ages Mine at the head of Navajo Basin, under Gladstone Peak's impressive 13,913-foot bulk. Snow conditions may dictate a choice or combination of two couloirs and an intervening rock rib that climbs directly to the summit. Snow exists year-round along the northern face of Wilson and El Diente; ice axes are highly recommended. Indeed, snow conditions are such that Dwight Lavender named the Wilson–El Diente snowfield "Navajo Glacier." A 1975 climbing team reported a bergschrund northeast of El Diente that in spots measured eight feet wide by some twenty feet deep.
   Near the top of the rock rib, several hundred feet of extensive bouldering brings one to Mount Wilson's summit and a feeling of awe as he surveys the distance and obstacles to El Diente. The ridge is long and precarious but of reasonably good rock. Allow at least three hours. Its absolute top affords the best avenue, with pinnacle obstacles usually best skirted on the south (left). About two-thirds of the way across, a thirty-foot cut is a place where a rope comes in handy for a rappel, but it may be skirted and down-climbed to the south by agile souls. A series of

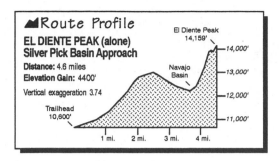

◢Route Profile

EL DIENTE PEAK (alone)
Silver Pick Basin Approach

Distance: 4.6 miles
Elevation Gain: 4400'

Vertical exaggeration 3.74

Trailhead
10,600'

El Diente Peak
14,159'

Navajo
Basin

14,000'
13,000'
12,000'
11,000'

1 mi.   2 mi.   3 mi.   4 mi.

needles, called the Organ Pipes by some, are then skirted to the south before the final summit pull. For the descent, return to a cut just below the Organ Pipes and descend into the couloir running off the northeast face. Then it is a seven-hundred-foot climb back to the Rock of Ages saddle. El Diente can be climbed alone from Navajo Basin via the descent route.

Campfires are prohibited in the entire Navajo Basin–Navajo Lake area. If you must stay overnight in Navajo Basin, please use existing sites and strict minimum-impact standards.

▲ *Trailhead to Mount Wilson alone: 4.4 miles, 4,400 feet, plus 700 feet on return.*

▲ *Trailhead-Mount Wilson-El Diente ridge round trip: 10.5 miles, 5,600 feet.*

▲ *Trailhead to El Diente alone: 5.3 miles, 4,250 feet, plus 700 feet on return.*

Windom Peak 14,082 feet (34th highest)
Sunlight Peak 14,059 feet (39th highest)
Mount Eolus 14,083 feet (33rd highest)

Isolated deep in the heart of the San Juans, the Needle Mountains are true to their name, their peaks rising in a spectacular mass of spiny ridges, broken slopes, and craggy summits. The culmination of the Needles are three Fourteeners that cluster around the upper Chicago Basin in majestic ruggedness. Windom, Sunlight, and Eolus are seldom viewed by the casual tourist, and being accessible only by long trails remain three of Colorado's vanishing breed of classic wilderness peaks for the mountaineer.

Isolated as they are, the Needle Mountains were long unexplored, and although the Hayden Survey saw them from a distance, their descriptions were shrouded in awe and mystery. On his ascent of Uncompahgre in 1874, Franklin Rhoda received a distant view of the Needles and Grenadiers far to the south and wrote, "in the distance appeared a group of very scraggy mountains, about which the clouds were continuously circling, as if it was their home." Later, from Mount Sneffels, Rhoda again penned, "we have never yet seen the group from any station (and we have viewed it from all sides) without feeling both deep respect and awe for their terrible ruggedness. The fact already stated, that the storm clouds seemed to hover about them before starting their meandering way, only served to add to our other feelings one of uneasiness."

Although Rhoda's descriptions may sound as if they came from the pages of *Wuthering Heights,* his awe of the view of the craggy Needles rising behind the precipitous Grenadiers and encircled with threatening clouds is indeed understandable. Although neither the Hayden nor the Wheeler surveys entered the Needle Range, Rhoda's assessment that the range was a "regular 'manufactory of storms'" gave rise to naming

240

Sunlight Peak (*left*) and Windom Peak (*right*) as viewed to the east from Mount Eolus, across the Twin Lakes Basin. *(Lyndon J. Lampert)*

the highest peak in the range "Aeolus," for the Greek god of the winds. Sunlight and Windom, however, were not named until about 1902, when the area was mapped by the U.S. Geological Survey. Sunlight was apparently named for rays of sunlight shimmering through its summit needles. Windom was named for William Windom, senator from Minnesota and secretary of the treasury during James Garfield's abbreviated administration, in 1881.

Despite Franklin Rhoda's ominous descriptions of the character of the Needles, the area was soon entered by prospectors. In the summer of 1877, Frank Trimble and other prospectors worked their way to the very headwaters of Needle Creek and into Chicago Basin, where they found promising amounts of silver ore. The following year the Needle Mountains Mining District was formed, and a number of claims were staked in Chicago Basin, nearly all of them above timberline. In all likelihood, Windom, Sunlight, and Eolus were scaled by miners in the late 1870s or early 1880s, for despite the rugged appearance of the range as a whole, the three Fourteeners require only moderate bouldering for ascent.

The Needle Mountains Mining District was without question one of the most isolated mining districts in the state until the Denver and Rio

Mount Eolus and North Eolus from the slopes to the south of Sunlight Peak. The Twin Lakes are on the basin floor. *(Lyndon J. Lampert)*

Grande came to its aid in 1882 by completing its spectacular line from Durango to Silverton via the Animas River Canyon. At Needleton, the line passed the confluence of Needle Creek and the Animas, only six miles below Chicago Basin. A crude wagon road was soon constructed from Needleton into the basin, and more miners came in. The district never boomed, however, for its ore was not exceptionally rich, and it was still quite isolated, being accessible only in the summer months.

While many claims were staked in Chicago Basin, only a few were actually developed. One of the largest groups of claims was the Mastadon Group, which was comprised of claims on the southwest and southeast slopes of Mount Eolus as well as some about one mile up Needle Creek from Needleton. The Sheridan and Anaconda claims were located on the north side of Chicago Basin and yielded about twelve ounces of silver per ton. In the Twin Lakes Basin, or the Upper Chicago Basin, was the Lake Lode, not exceptionally rich and therefore never tunneled but nevertheless responsible for the construction of a small cabin near the lakes that still stands in weatherbeaten condition.

The isolation of the Needle Mountains district doomed it to very little gold and silver production after 1900, and the last gold shipment of any consequence was in 1934. The collapse of silver and gold mining turned the area into the domain of the backpacker and mountaineer rather than the miner, but lately, mineral exploration in the Needles has intensified, now with the aid of noisy helicopters instead of braying burros.

Since the 1920s, the Needles and neighboring Grenadiers have been a favorite haunt of mountaineers because the area contains some of the most challenging peaks in the state. If any peak in Colorado is yet unclimbed, it could well lie within the wilds of the Grenadiers or Needles. Most new routes have been pioneered on nearby thirteeners, but the three Fourteeners in the range have also seen some new rock routes. The west face of Eolus was first climbed by Joe Merhar, Chris Schoredos, and H. L. and Frank McClintock in 1940. The north face of Sunlight was first conquered in 1934 by William House and Elizabeth Woolsey. Also in 1934, the impressive Needle Ridge, which runs west of Sunlight and dominates the skyline above the Twin Lakes, was first traversed by Robert Ormes and T. M. Griffiths.

Although summer climbs of the Needles became increasingly popular throughout the mid-1900s, Sunlight and Windom were not climbed in the winter until 1966. On December 18, 1966, Don Monk, Kermith Ross, and Phil Schmuck began hiking along the narrow-gauge right-of-way from Rockwood, and with the aid of food caches placed in August, reached the cabin at the Twin Lakes in three days. On December 22, 1966, the trio reached the summit of Windom, and on the following day they climbed Sunlight. On December 24, they reached the 13,500-foot level on Eolus but were turned back by threatening weather and a precarious-looking snow-covered north ridge. Eolus remained unconquered in the winter until January 26, 1971, when Barry Nash, Steve Lewis, Floyd Frank, and Rick Nolting reached the summit via the north ridge and northeast face after snowshoeing in from the Purgatory Ski Area. This ascent made Mount Eolus one of the last of Colorado's Fourteeners to be climbed in the winter, an indication of the rugged isolation of the Needle Mountains.

THE ROUTES

Chicago Basin

"All Ab-o-o-o-ard!" This is how most climbers begin their approach to climb in the Needles or Grenadiers—the Durango to Silverton narrow-gauge train! This is definitely recommended, for being dropped off deep in the Animas River Canyon by an 1880 steam-locomotive-drawn train at

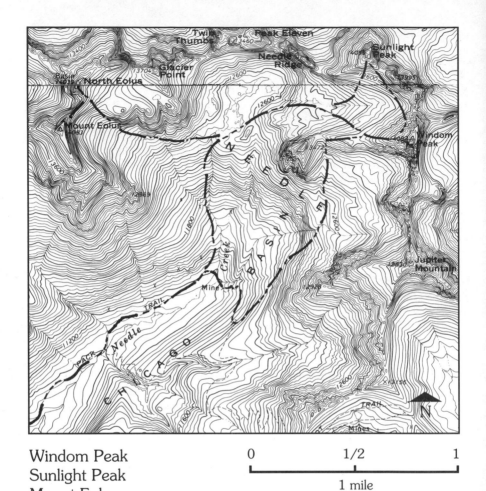

Windom Peak
Sunlight Peak
Mount Eolus

0	1/2	1

1 mile

Needleton is an experience not to be forgotten, and it avoids a long, long backpack from trailheads reached by roads. The Durango & Silverton Railroad operates from about May 1 through October 30. During the peak summer season, four trains run on the line daily. Because of the numerous schedules, it is very important to make reservations well in advance and then confirm boarding and departure times with the depot in Durango. Policies for backpackers will vary depending on the time of year. The depot is located at 479 Main Avenue and the reservation number is (303) 247-2733. Tickets must be picked up by 6:00 P.M. the evening before the trip. Firearms, pets, and alcoholic beverages are not permitted on the train.

Get off the train at Needleton and cross the suspension bridge east over the Animas River. The Chicago Basin–Columbine Pass trail leads gently south along the Animas for about a mile, then climbs east and then northeast up Needle Creek to Chicago Basin for a total of six and one-half miles and three thousand vertical feet. Camping in Chicago Basin is generally not an experience in solitude. Backpackers should take special care to camp trace-free and should be aware that no wood fires are allowed anywhere in the Needle Creek drainage.

In the past, camping has been popular at the Twin Lakes, 1,300 feet above Chicago Basin to the north, but heavy use of this alpine area should cause most environmentally sensitive climbers to seriously consider camping in the trees in the lower basin instead. If you must camp at Twin Lakes, please stay on the steep trail into the basin, in which the Forest Service has placed large rocks to help prevent erosion, and do not cut your own trail. Once at the lakes, keep your campsite away from the shoreline proper, and locate it on rock instead of fragile tundra. The Twin Lakes trail climbs out of Chicago Basin from about 11,200 feet just before the main trail swings south to cross Needle Creek and climbs out of the basin toward Columbine Pass.

Windom, West Ridge

From your camp near tree line in Chicago Basin, locate the Twin Lakes trail (see above) and climb steeply to the Twin Lakes. From the Twin Lakes, proceed east up the talus slope to the right of the waterfall and into the small basin above the waterfall at 13,000 feet. The relatively rounded summit of Windom appears directly ahead to the east. Keep to the right and gain the 13,400-foot saddle on Windom's west ridge, between it and Peak 18. From the saddle, it is a simple scramble east up the ridge to the summit, a half-mile. While climbing Windom, you

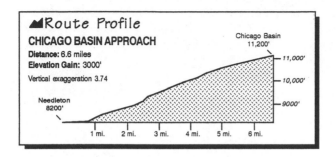

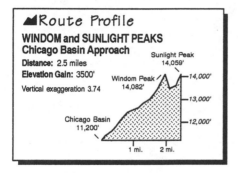

may find yourself saying, "Holy smokes! What is that?!" in reference to a high and spectacular spire on the ridge to the north of Windom. Don't panic—it's not the summit of Sunlight Peak, but rather the Sunlight Spire, calculated to be 13,995 feet high and first climbed with direct aid in 1961.

▲ *Upper Chicago Basin to summit: 2 miles, 2,900 feet.*

Sunlight, South Couloir

From Windom, a prominent reddish couloir is visible that leads to the saddle between Sunlight Peak and the Sunlight Spire. This couloir provides the easiest route on Sunlight. Pick your way down Windom's north face and stay fairly high in the basin, dropping to about 13,600 feet, and then traverse below the cliffs to enter the red couloir. Climb up this couloir to near its top, then angle left and upward along the south face toward the top of the ridge. Easy bouldering will bring you to within sight of a window on the ridge above. Continue contouring below this window to the left of the ridge and go around the corner of a large outcropping, then climb upward to a keyhole that you climb through, and then you are within sight of the summit, only a short distance ahead.

Upon closer inspection, it will be evident that the summit register is not found on the true summit at all but several feet below the crest of the huge summit blocks. It is not a difficult friction climb to the true summit, but the exposure on the north side makes gaining the true summit at least a psychological triumph. Standing on the true summit has become traditional, although airy, and believe it or not, on a 1920 CMC outing, Carl Blaurock stood on his head on the summit rock!

While on the summit of Sunlight, you can enjoy the view of Arrow and Vestal peaks in the Grenadiers to the north (13,803 and 13,864 feet, respectively). These peaks are two of the most challenging mountains in Colorado, and as is evident from Sunlight, two of the most spectacular. You may also wish to contemplate whether or not the summit of the Sunlight Spire *really* is sixty-four feet below you!

The descent from Sunlight can be made via the ascent route down the red couloir, or by picking your way through the slabs and talus on the south face.

▲ *Upper Chicago Basin to Sunlight alone: 2 miles, 2,900 feet.*
▲ *Upper Chicago Basin to Windom and Sunlight: 3.5 miles, 3,500 feet.*

Eolus, East Basin-Northeast Ridge

From Twin Lakes, contour southwest around the hillside and enter the small sloping basin to the east of Eolus's summit. Continue west up the grassy basin to the headwall. At this point a large granite-slab bowl is seen directly to the right with a narrow ledge traversing the top of it. Pass this ledge and reach the next, much broader, one above, which has a cairn-marked trail and passes below the slab cliffs on Eolus's east face. Follow this route as it angles up to the northeast and come out above a flat area and small lakelet about a quarter-mile to the east. Turn to the west up the slope and scramble up the rocks or up a shallow greenish crack that is easily negotiated to gain the 13,840-foot saddle between Eolus and North Eolus.

Immediately to the southwest side of the saddle, stroll along the "Sidewalk in the Sky," a solid catwalk two feet wide at its narrowest, and examine the two possible routes ahead to the summit of Eolus. A good bouldering route with some exposure lies almost directly along the top of the northeast ridge to the summit. An easier but more complicated route may be negotiated by picking your way up the series of grassy ledges on the east face and will put you within twenty feet of the summit.

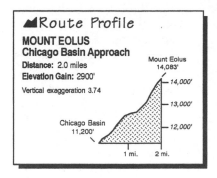

▲Route Profile
MOUNT EOLUS
Chicago Basin Approach
Distance: 2.0 miles
Elevation Gain: 2900'
Vertical exaggeration 3.74

Dominating the view to the west-northwest are 13,835-foot Turret Peak and 13,972-foot Pigeon Peak; the latter is one of Colorado's most striking Matterhornlike peaks; it rises nearly 6,000 feet from the depths of the Animas River Canyon, seen far below to the left of Pigeon. Descend Eolus the same way it was climbed. You may want to make the easy two-hundred-foot scramble from the northeast saddle, a quarter-mile to the summit of North Eolus (14,039), which is probably not distinct enough to warrant separate status as a Fourteener, but you never know. . . .

▲ *Upper Chicago Basin to Eolus alone: 2 miles, 2,900 feet. With North Eolus, an additional .25-mile and 200 feet.*

▲ *Upper Chicago Basin to Windom, Sunlight, and Eolus: 7.5 miles round-trip, 5,100 feet.*

Windom, Sunlight, and Eolus in a single day is a strenuous trip, but not an unreasonable one if the weather is good. Most parties will prefer more leisurely climbing of Windom and Sunlight on one day and Eolus on another.

Appendix

The 53 or 54 Issue Resolved:
But Still, Just What is a Fourteener?

What is a Fourteener? When we posed this question in the first edition in 1978, the debate of how many *separate* Colorado Fourteeners there were centered around Ellingwood Peak. One-half mile west of Blanca Peak and rising 342 feet (plus or minus 20 feet) above the connecting saddle, Ellingwood was or was not a separate mountain depending on the criteria applied and the authority consulted. Since then, both the U.S. Geological Survey and the Colorado Mountain Club have included Ellingwood in Fourteener ranks.

Ellingwood's presence in the Fourteener club and the current answer that there are fifty-four Fourteeners in Colorado to the contrary, there will always be an ongoing debate on what constitutes a *separate* summit. Quantitative standards may be laudable goals, but when one considers that a three-hundred-foot elevation-drop standard would demote North Maroon Peak and El Diente Peak from the Fourteener list, the debate becomes emotionally charged.

One of the most recent and thorough discussions of peak criteria is found in Mike Garratt and Bob Martin's *Colorado's High Thirteeners: A Climbing and Hiking Guide.* Garratt and Martin apply a strict three-hundred-foot saddle drop, which has the effect of boosting newly named Challenger Point on Kit Carson Peak into the Fourteener ranks—if one is to believe the accuracy of a survey showing the vertical drop of the saddle to be 301 feet *and* ignore any requirement of horizontal distance. Challenger's .2-mile distance from Kit Carson's main summit and the very name Challenger *Point* should be enough to quell any talk of fifty-five Fourteeners!

249

The following list of Colorado Fourteeners includes their most recent elevations from the named USGS maps. The maps reproduced in the guide include some county maps and are not necessarily these maps. Following the list of Fourteeners is a list of subsidiary points that rise above 14,000 feet. The saddle drops and distances from the main peak are listed and compared with the statistics for some of the peaks already accepted as separate Fourteeners. While perhaps interesting, the numbers themselves should never overshadow the peaks.

Rank	Peak	Elevation in Feet	Elevation in Meters	Quadrangle
1.	Mount Elbert	14,433	(4,399)	Mt. Elbert 7½'
2.	Mount Massive	14,421	(4,395)	Mt. Massive 7½'
3.	Mount Harvard	14,420	(4,395)	Mt. Harvard 7½'
4.	Blanca Peak	14,345	(4,372)	Blanka Pk. 7½'
5.	La Plata Peak	14,336	(4,369)	Mt. Elbert 7½'
6.	Uncompahgre Peak	14,309	(4,361)	Uncompahgre Pk. 7½'
7.	Crestone Peak	14,294	(4,357)	Crestone Pk. 7½'
8.	Mount Lincoln	14,286	(4,354)	Alma 7½'
9.	Grays Peak	14,270	(4,349)	Grays Pk. 7½'
10.	Mount Antero	14,269	(4,349)	Mt. Antero 7½'
11.	Torreys Peak	14,267	(4,348)	Grays Pk. 7½'
12.	Castle Peak	14,265	(4,348)	Hayden Pk. 7½'
13.	Quandary Peak	14,265	(4,348)	Breckenridge 7½'
14.	Mount Evans	14,264	(4,347)	Mt. Evans 7½'
15.	Longs Peak	14,255	(4,345)	Longs Pk. 7½'
16.	Mount Wilson	14,246	(4,342)	Mt. Wilson 7½'
17.	Mount Shavano	14,229	(4,337)	Maysville 7½'
18.	Mount Princeton	14,197	(4,327)	Mt. Antero 7½'
19.	Mount Belford	14,197	(4,327)	Mt. Harvard 7½'
20.	Crestone Needle	14,197	(4,327)	Crestone Pk. 7½'
21.	Mount Yale	14,196	(4,327)	Mt. Yale 7½'
22.	Mount Bross	14,172	(4,319)	Alma 7½'
23.	Kit Carson Peak	14,165	(4,317)	Crestone Pk. 7½'
24.	El Diente Peak	14,159	(4,315)	Dolores Pk. 7½'
25.	Maroon Peak	14,156	(4,315)	Maroon Bells 7½'
26.	Tabeguache Mountain	14,155	(4,314)	St. Elmo 7½'
27.	Mount Oxford	14,153	(4,314)	Mt. Harvard 7½'
28.	Mount Sneffels	14,150	(4,313)	Mt. Sneffels 7½'
29.	Mount Democrat	14,148	(4,312)	Climax 7½'
30.	Capitol Peak	14,130	(4,307)	Capitol Pk. 7½'
31.	Pikes Peak	14,109	(4,300)	Pikes Peak 7½'
32.	Snowmass Mountain	14,092	(4,295)	Snowmass Mtn. 7½'
33.	Mount Eolus	14,083	(4,292)	Columbine Pass 7½'
34.	Windom Peak	14,082	(4,292)	Columbine Pass 7½'

35.	Mount Columbia	14,073	(4,289)	Mt. Harvard 7½'
36.	Missouri Mountain	14,067	(4,287)	Winfield 7½'
37.	Humboldt Peak	14,064	(4,286)	Crestone Pk. 7½'
38.	Mount Bierstadt	14,060	(4,285)	Mt. Evans 7½'
39.	Sunlight Peak	14,059	(4,285)	Storm King Pk. 7½'
40.	Handies Peak	14,048	(4,282)	Handies Pk. 7½'
41.	Culebra Peak	14,047	(4,281)	Culebra Pk. 7½'
42.	Mount Lindsey	14,042	(4,280)	Blanca Pk. 7½'
43.	Ellingwood Peak	14,042	(4,280)	Blanca Pk. 7½'
44.	Little Bear Peak	14,037	(4,278)	Blanca Pk. 7½'
45.	Mount Sherman	14,036	(4,278)	Mt. Sherman 7½'
46.	Redcloud Peak	14,034	(4,277)	Redcloud Pk. 7½'
47.	Pyramid Peak	14,018	(4,272)	Maroon Bells 7½'
48.	Wilson Peak	14,017	(4,272)	Mt. Wilson 7½'
49.	Wetterhorn Peak	14,015	(4,272)	Wetterhorn Pk. 7½'
50.	North Maroon Peak	14,014	(4,271)	Maroon Bells 7½'
51.	San Luis Peak	14,014	(4,271)	San Luis Pk. 7½'
52.	Mount of the Holy Cross	14,005	(4,269)	Mt. of the Holy Cross 7½'
53.	Huron Peak	14,003	(4,268)	Winfield 7½'
54.	Sunshine Peak	14,001	(4,267)	Redcloud Pk. 7½'

Subsidiary Peak	Elevation in Feet	Main Peak	Miles Separation	Drop to Saddle from Lower Peak (±20 Feet)
Tabeguache*	14,155	Shavano	.8	435
Little Bear*	14,037	Blanca	1.0	377
Ellingwood*	14,042	Blanca	.5	342
Bross*	14,172	Lincoln	1.1	312
Challenger Point	14,081	Kit Carson	.2	301
North Massive	14,320	Massive	.8	260
El Diente*	14,159	Mount Wilson	.7	259
Conundrum	14,060	Castle	.4	240
South Elbert	14,134	Elbert	1.0	234
North Maroon*	14,014	Maroon	.4	234
South Massive	14,132	Massive	.7	232
North Eolus	14,039	Eolus	.25	179
Cameron	14,238	Lincoln	.5	138

*Considered a separate Fourteener by both the U.S. Geological Survey and the Colorado Mountain Club.

Index